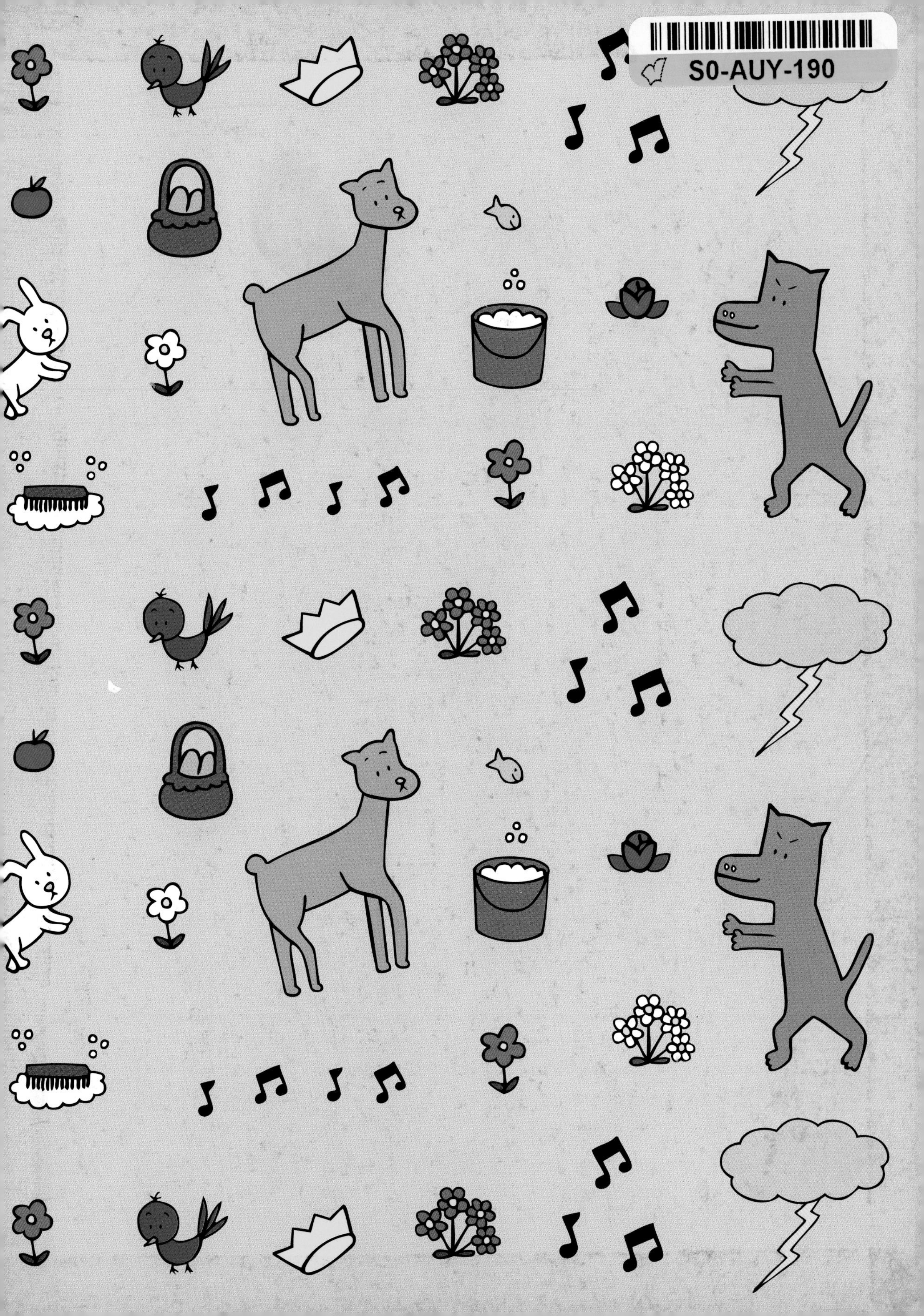

~ for ~
ANGRY
LITTLE GIRLS

by Lela Lee

Abrams ComicArts
New York

Editor: Tamar Brazis
Designer: Vivian Kimball
Production Manager: Jacquie Poirier

Library of Congress Control Number:
2010934624

ISBN 978-0-8109-9593-2

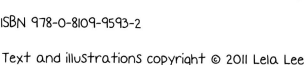

Printed and bound in China
10 9 8 7 6 5 4 3 2 1

Abrams ComicArts books are available at special discounts when purchased in
quantity for premiums and promotions as well as fundraising or educational
use. Special editions can also be created to specification. For details, contact
specialmarkets@abramsbooks.com or the address below.

ABRAMS
THE ART OF BOOKS SINCE 1949
115 West 18th Street
New York, NY 10011
www.abramsbooks.com

For Lucas

an ANGRY LITTLE GIRL'S FAIRY TALE

Snow Yellow and the Seven Short Men

Starring

?!

Kim the "Angry Little Asian Girl"

Once upon a time, a little girl was born to a beautiful queen.

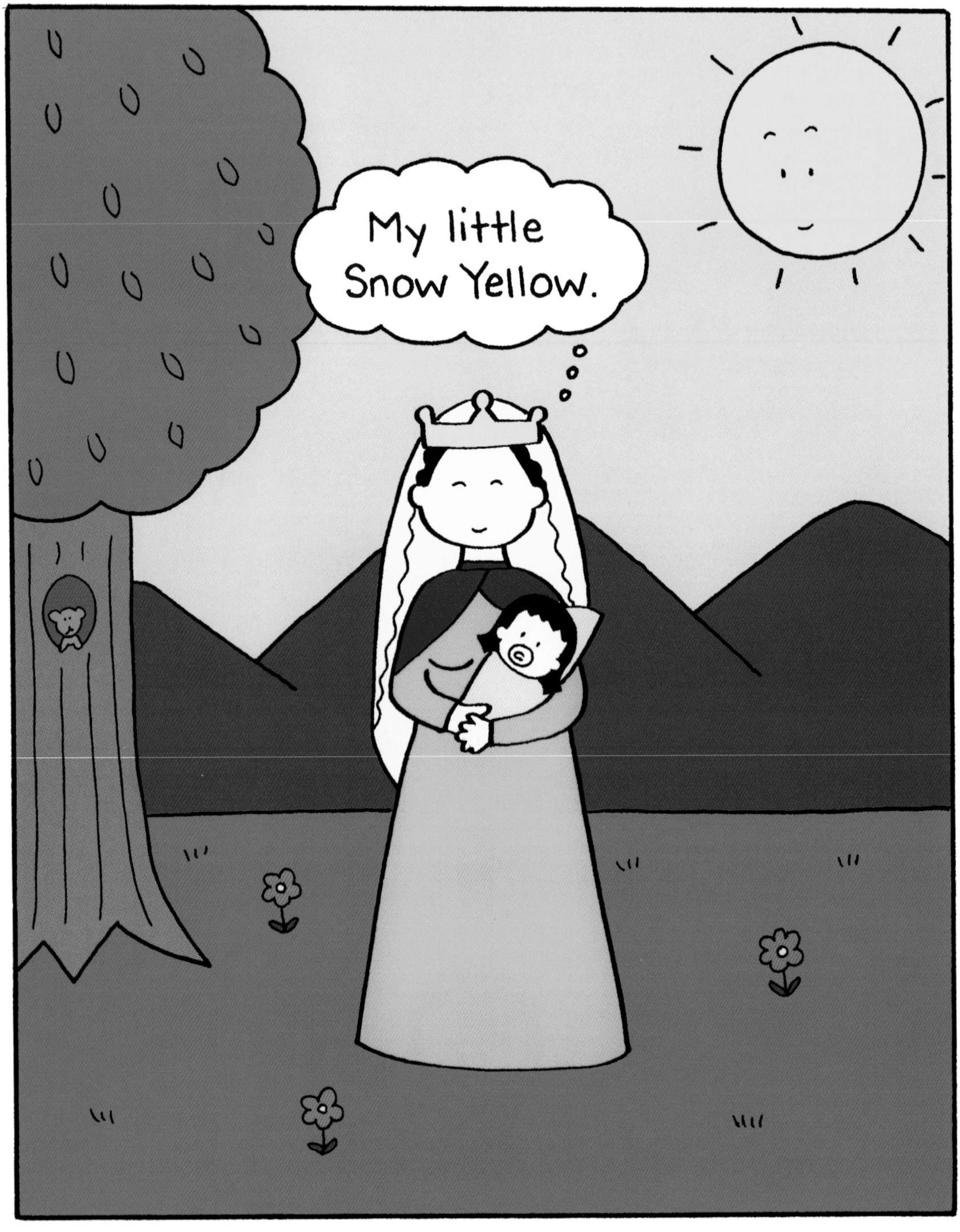
My little Snow Yellow.

But alas, the beautiful queen died soon after her daughter's birth.

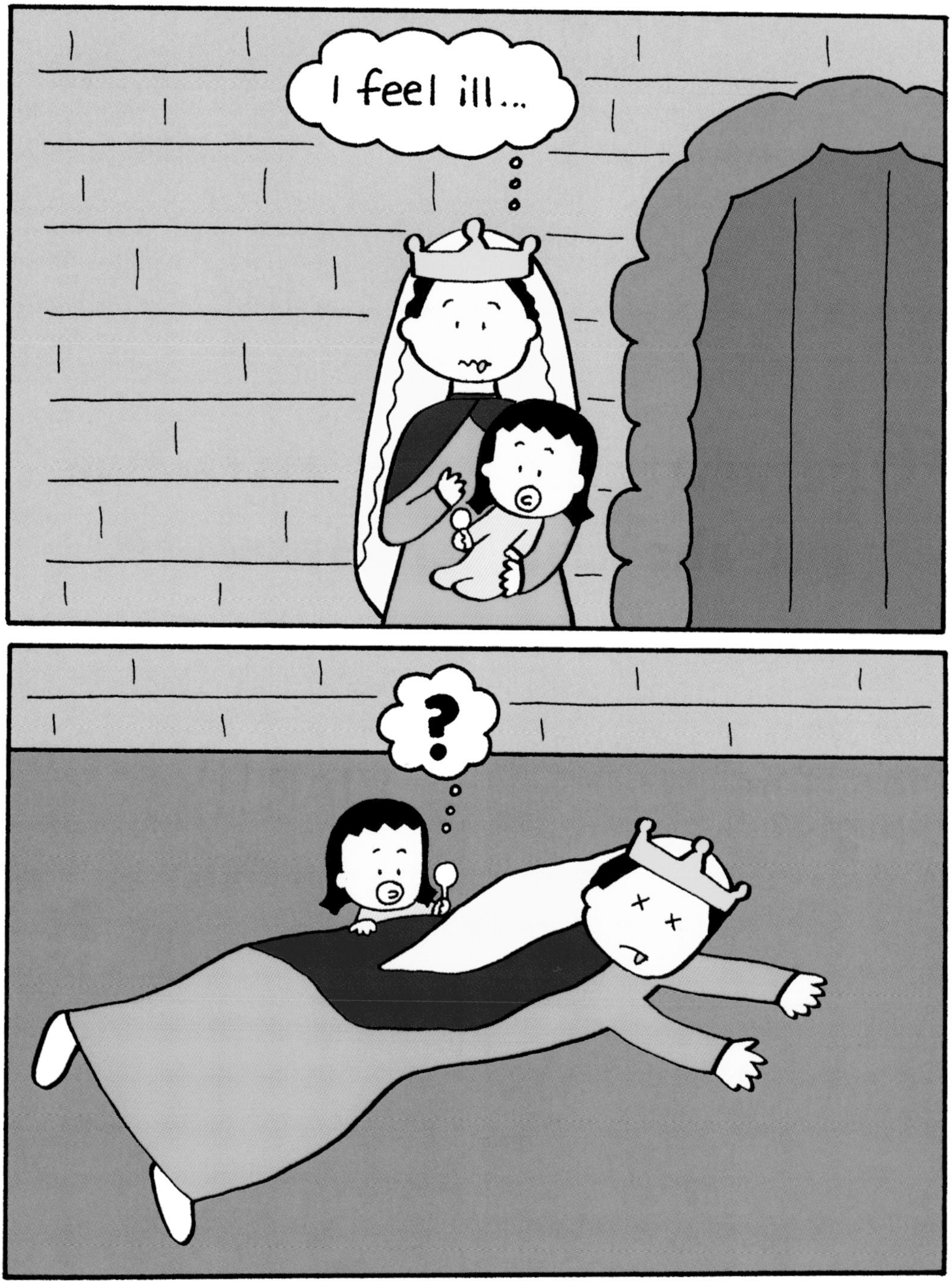
I feel ill...
?

The girl's father married again.

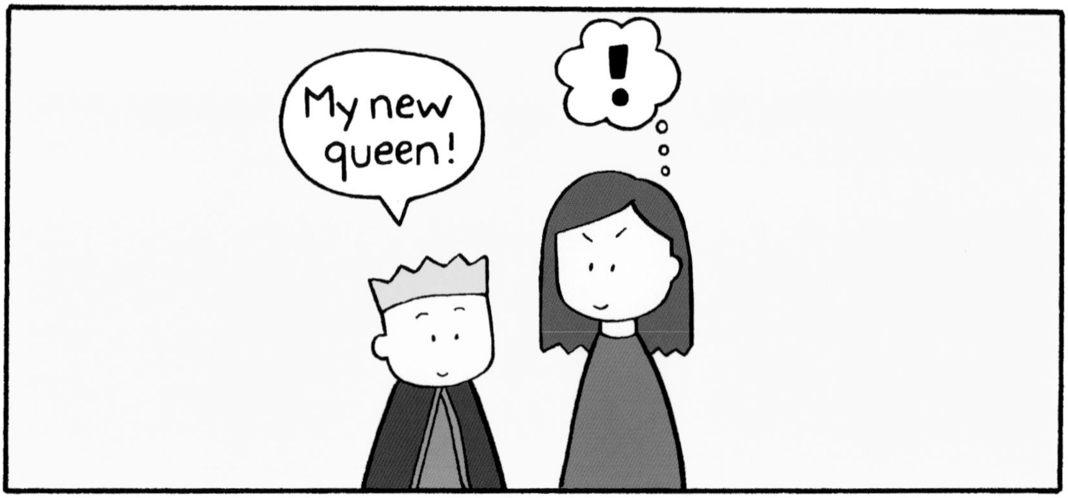
My new queen!
!

The new queen was attractive, but she was very insecure.

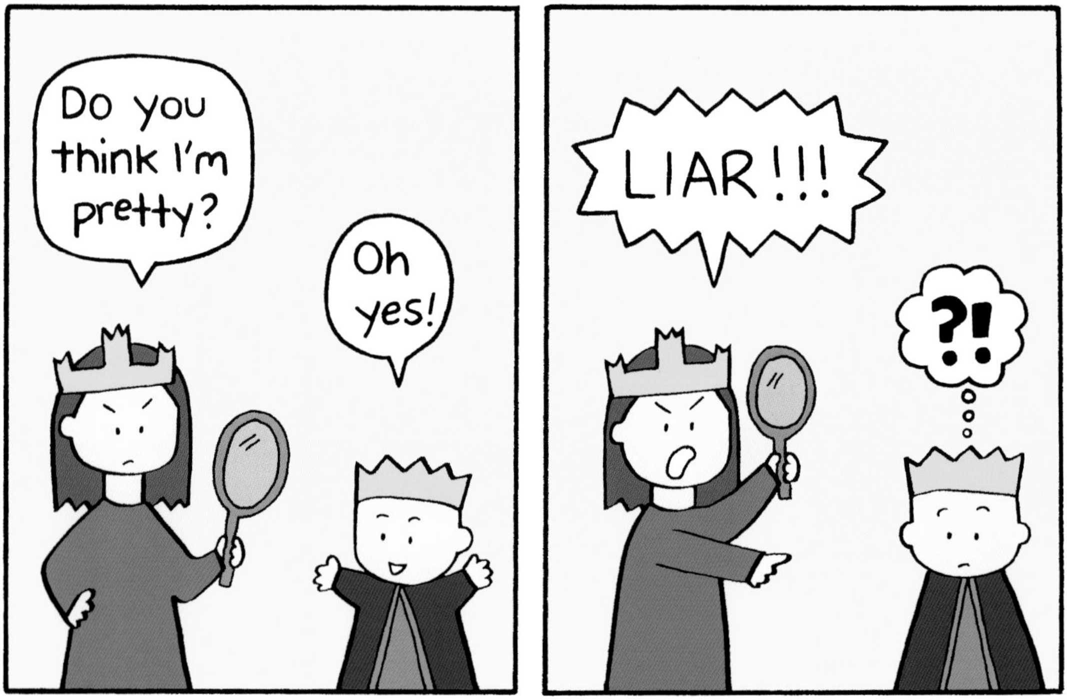
Do you think I'm pretty?
Oh yes!
LIAR!!!
?!

She was also not of sound mind.

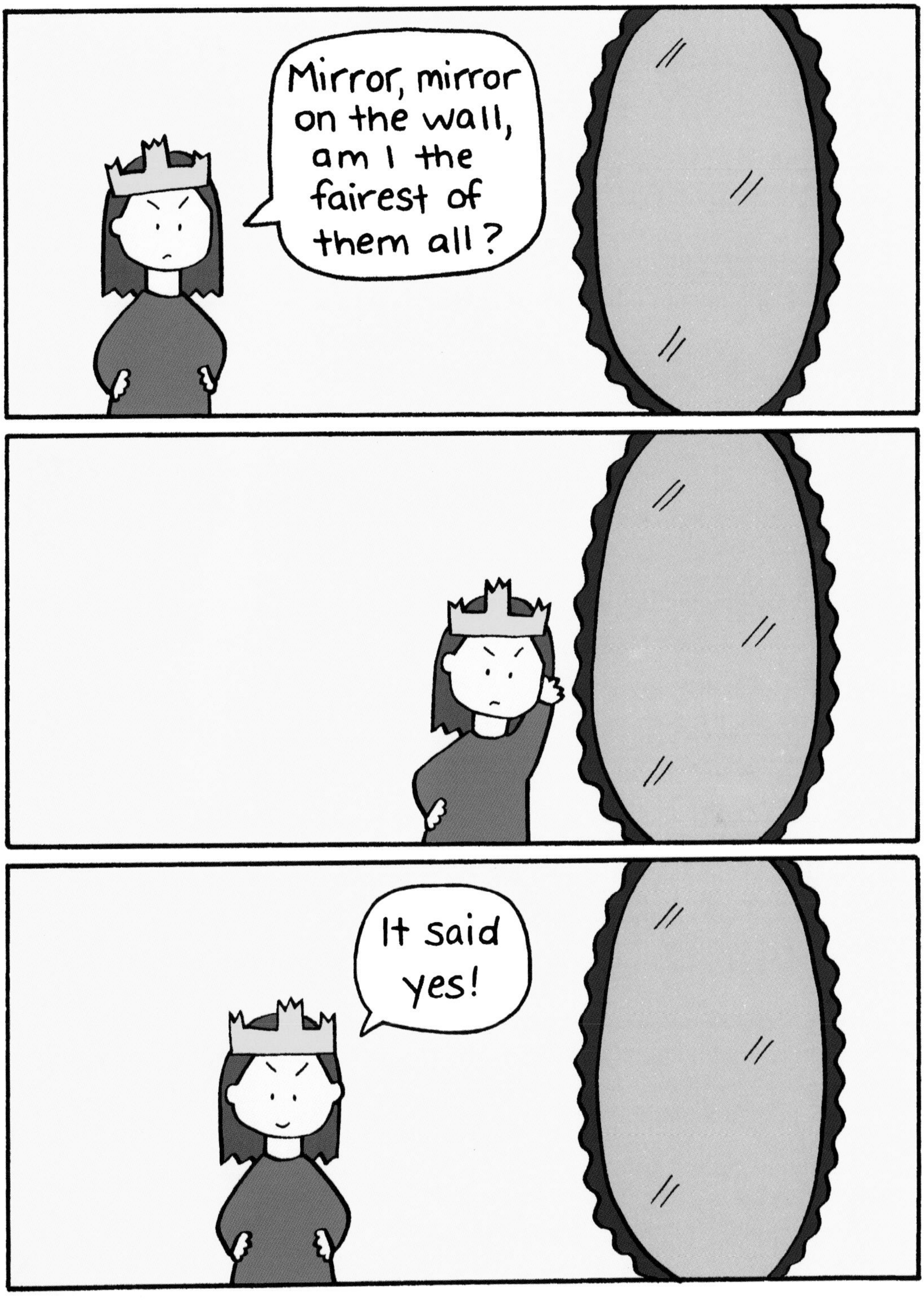
Mirror, mirror on the wall, am I the fairest of them all?
It said yes!

As the years passed, Snow Yellow grew more and more beautiful.

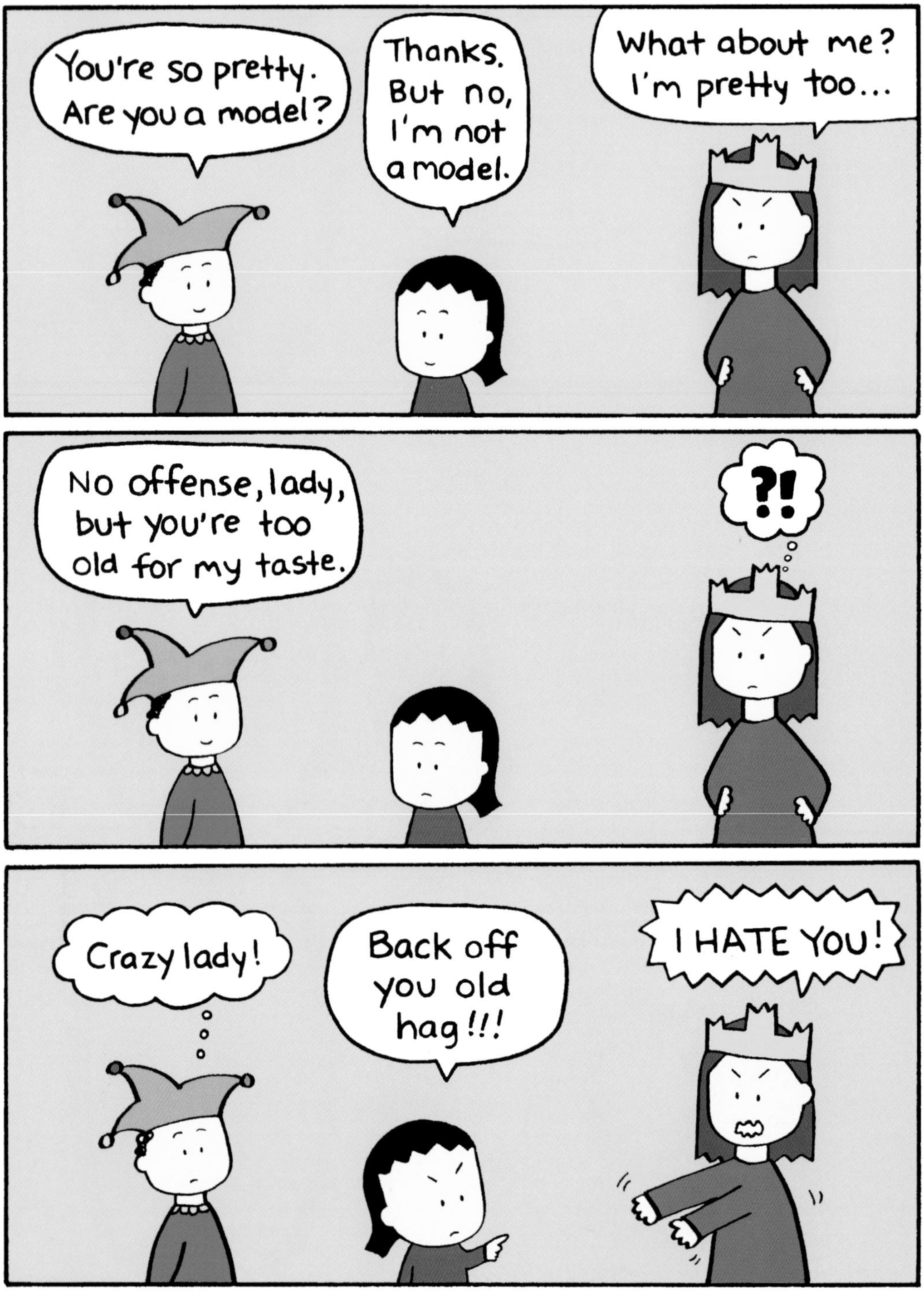

You're so pretty. Are you a model?
Thanks. But no, I'm not a model.
What about me? I'm pretty too...
No offense, lady, but you're too old for my taste.
?!
Crazy lady!
Back off you old hag!!!
I HATE YOU!

The new queen was jealous, and treated Snow Yellow with cruelty.

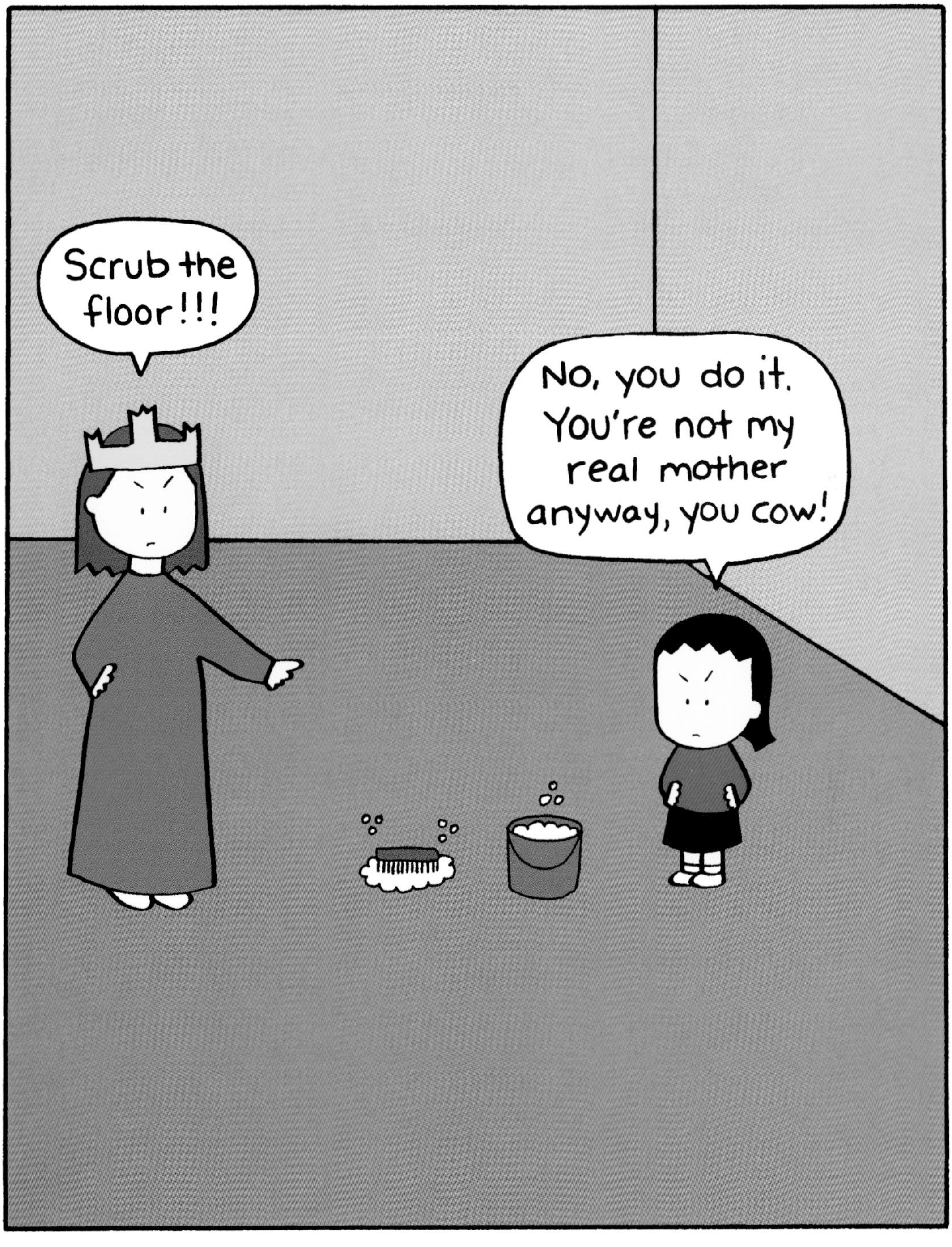
Scrub the floor!!!
No, you do it. You're not my real mother anyway, you cow!

At last, the day the queen had been dreading finally came...

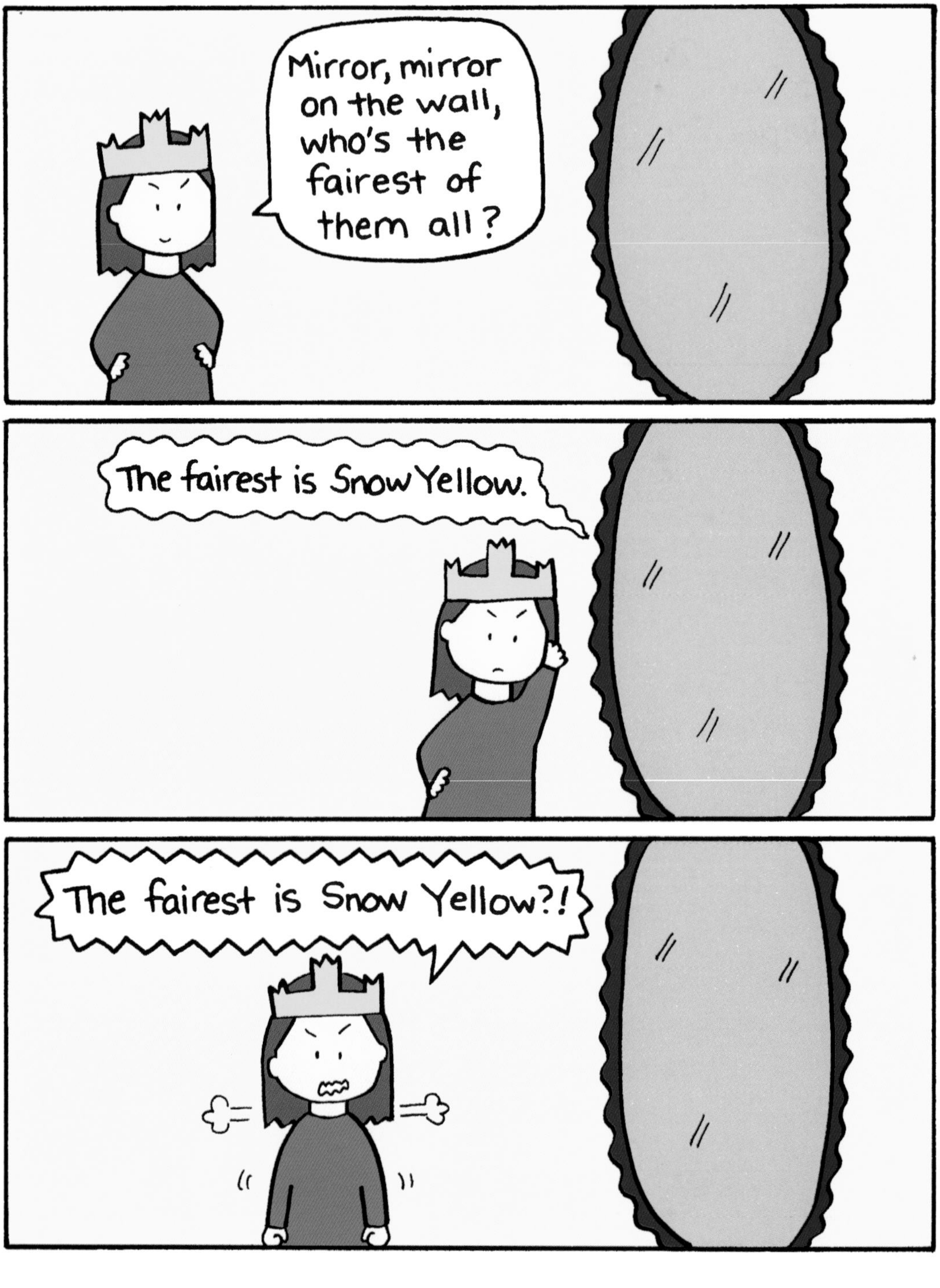
Mirror, mirror on the wall, who's the fairest of them all?
The fairest is Snow Yellow.
The fairest is Snow Yellow?!

The queen called her huntsman.

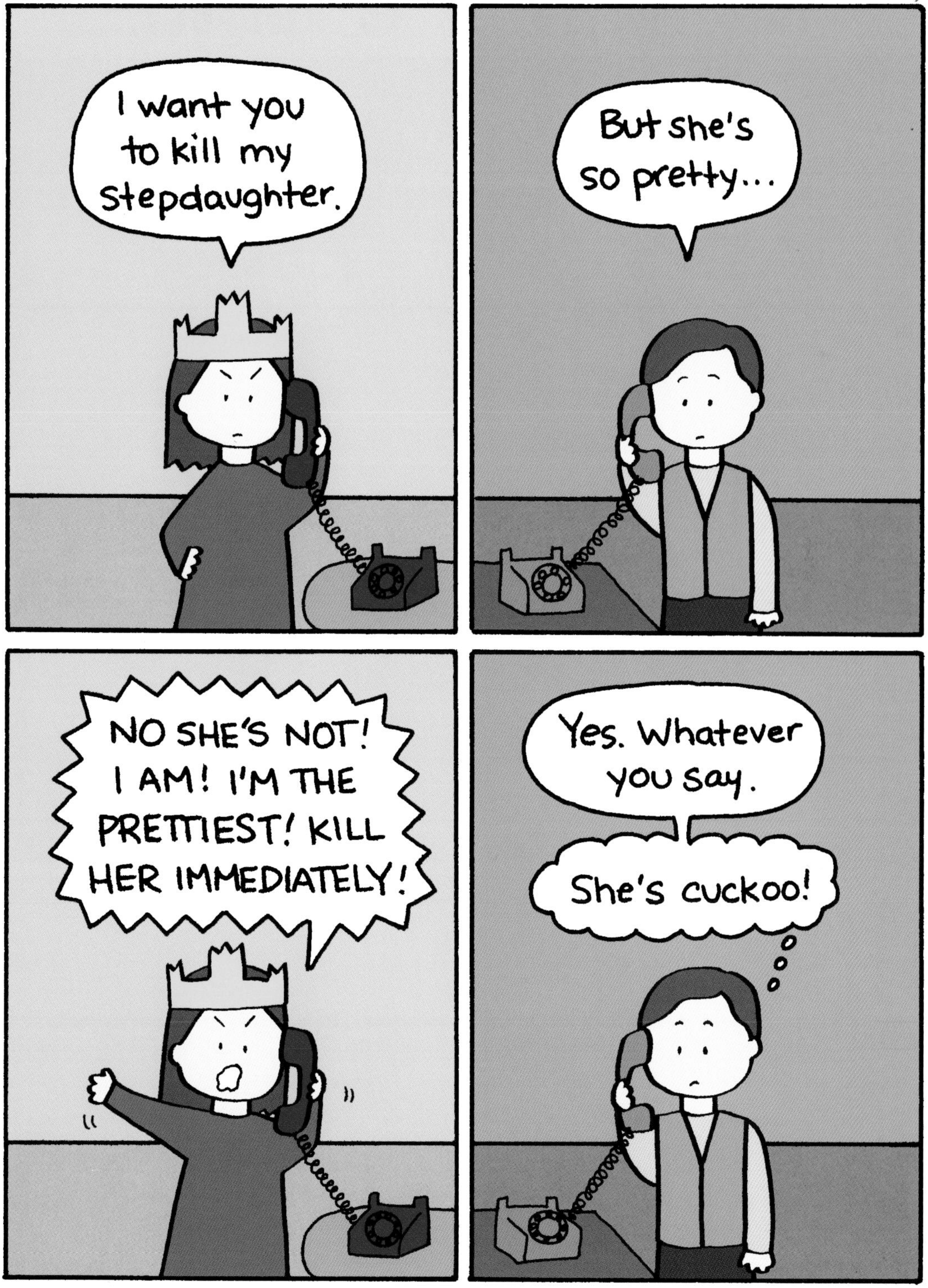
I want you to kill my stepdaughter.
But she's so pretty...
NO SHE'S NOT! I AM! I'M THE PRETTIEST! KILL HER IMMEDIATELY!
Yes. Whatever you say.
She's cuckoo!

The huntsman took Snow Yellow into the forest to kill her...

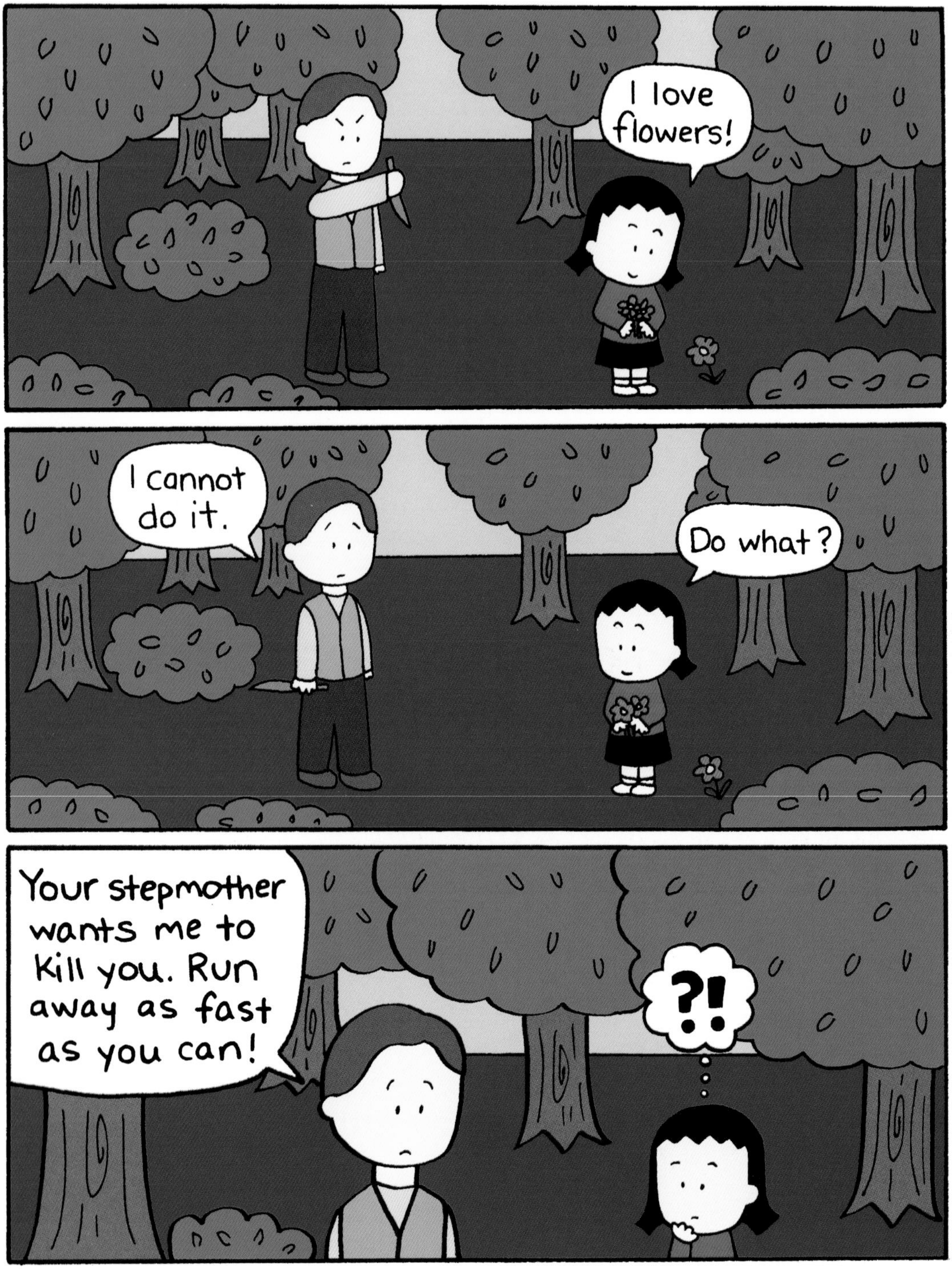
I love flowers!
I cannot do it.
Do what?
Your stepmother wants me to kill you. Run away as fast as you can!
?!

Snow Yellow ran as far as she could.

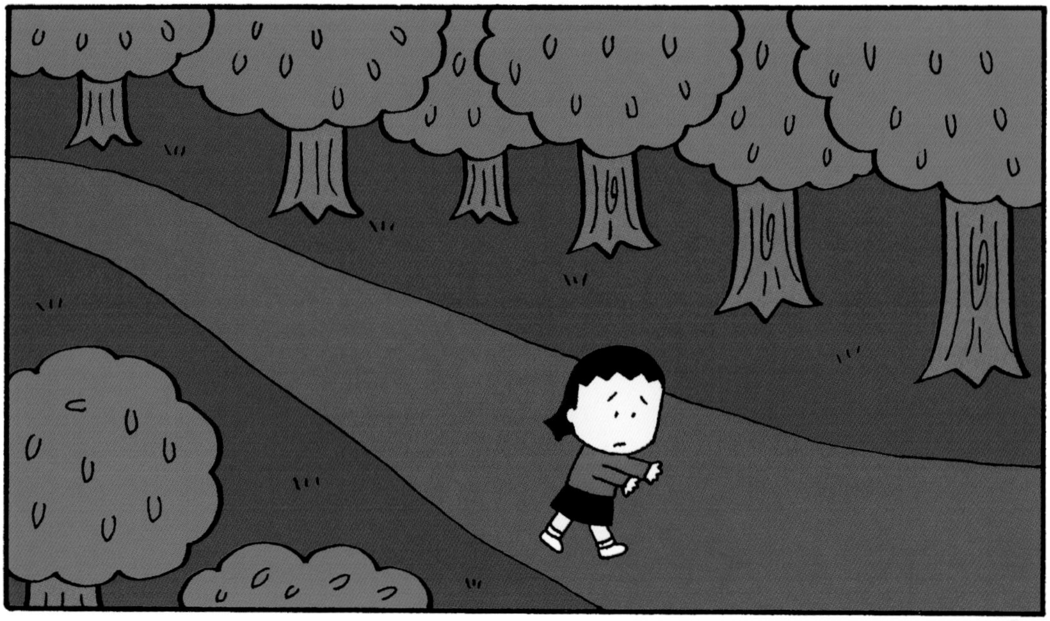

She finally collapsed from exhaustion.

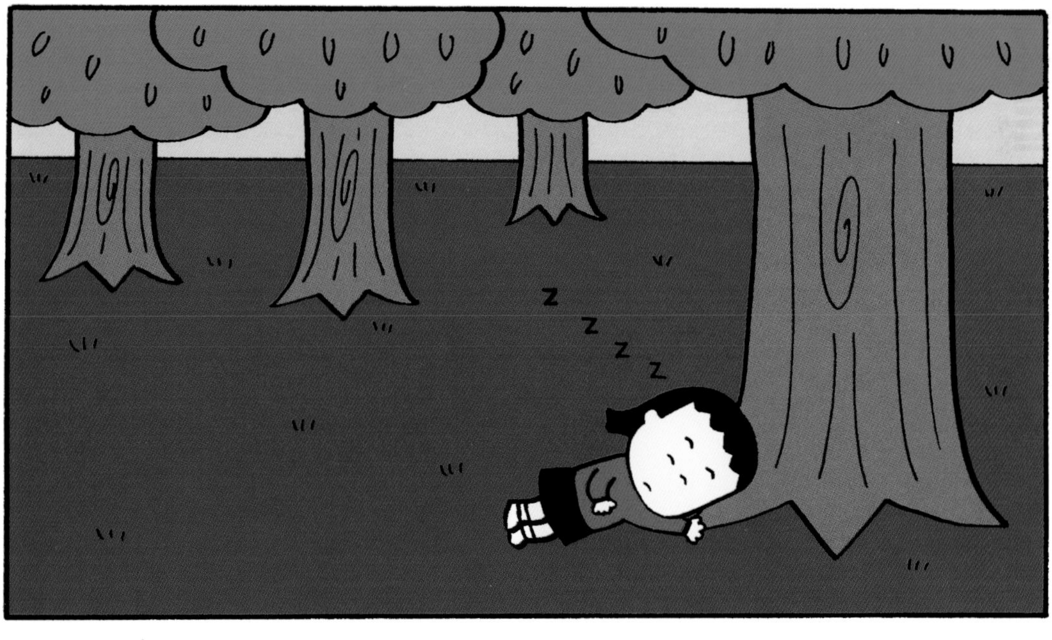
Z
Z
Z
Z

She was awoken by friendly animals.

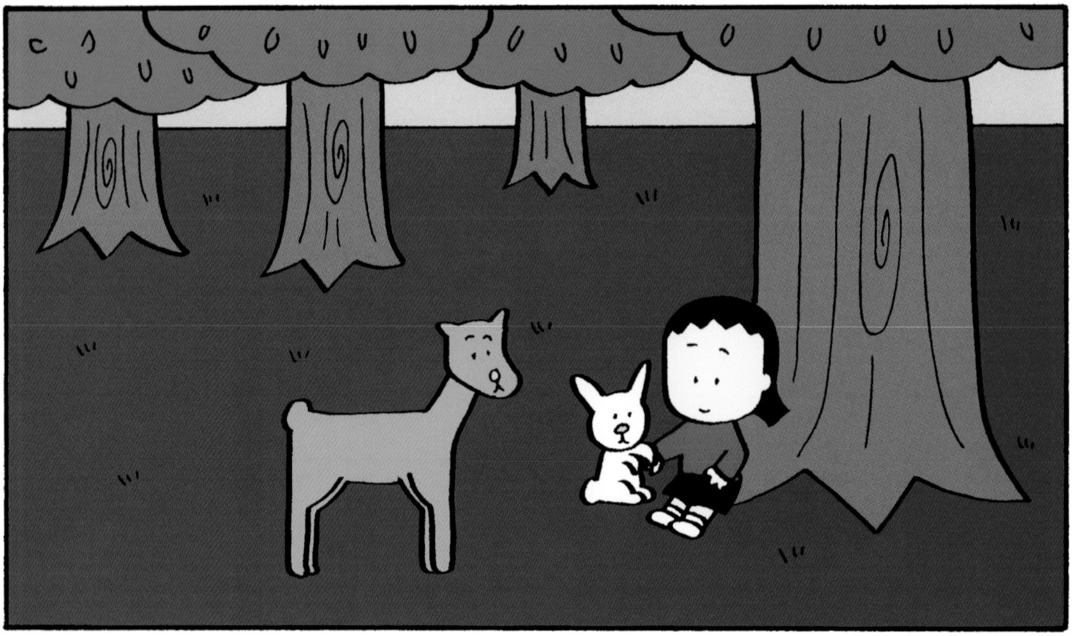

They took her to a little cottage.

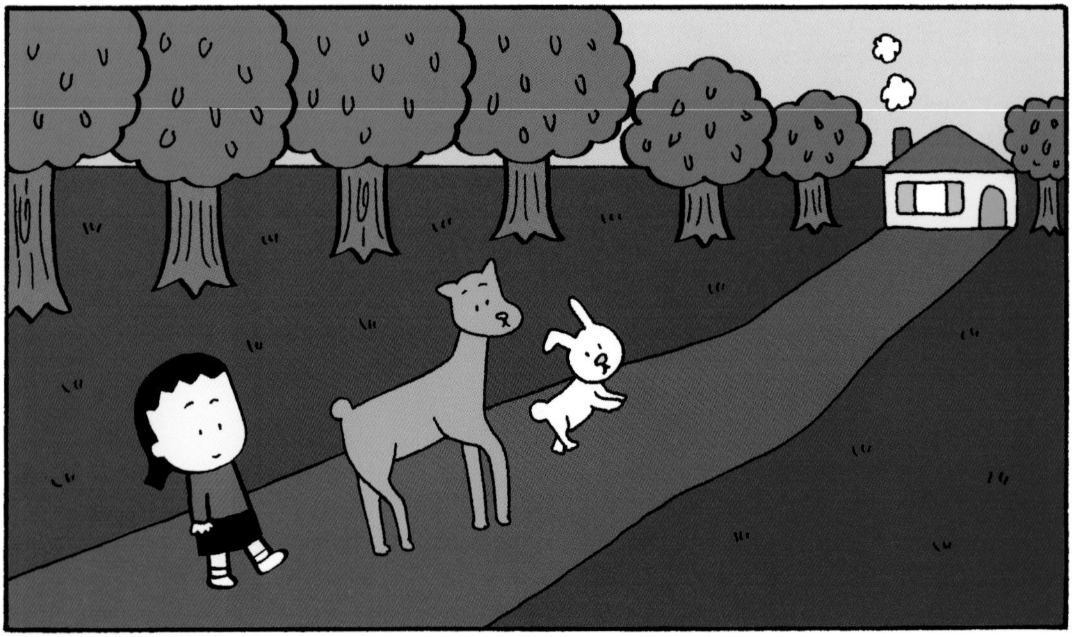

No one answered her knock, so she opened the door and went inside.

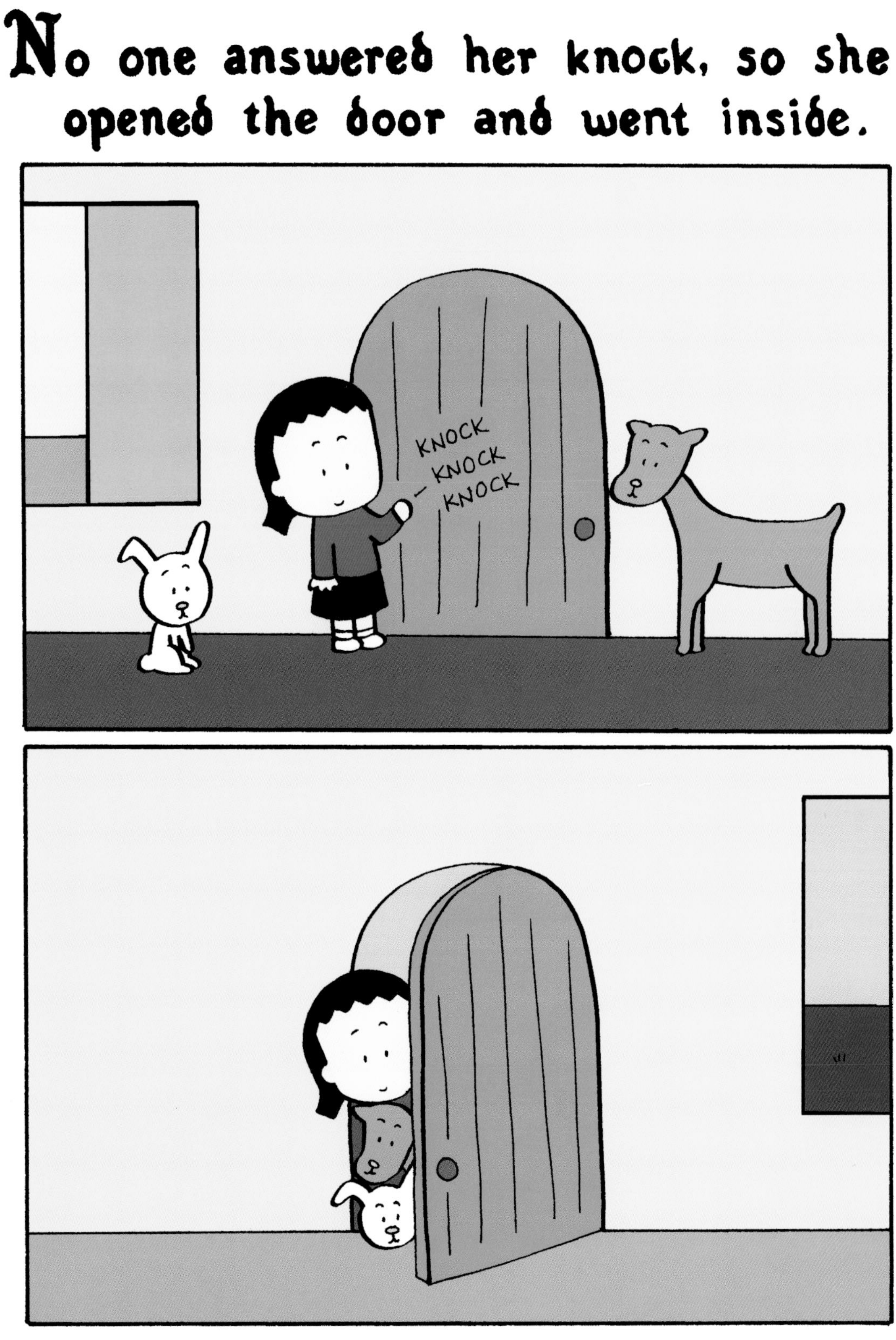
KNOCK
KNOCK
KNOCK

She noticed the cottage was dirty,
so she decided to clean up.

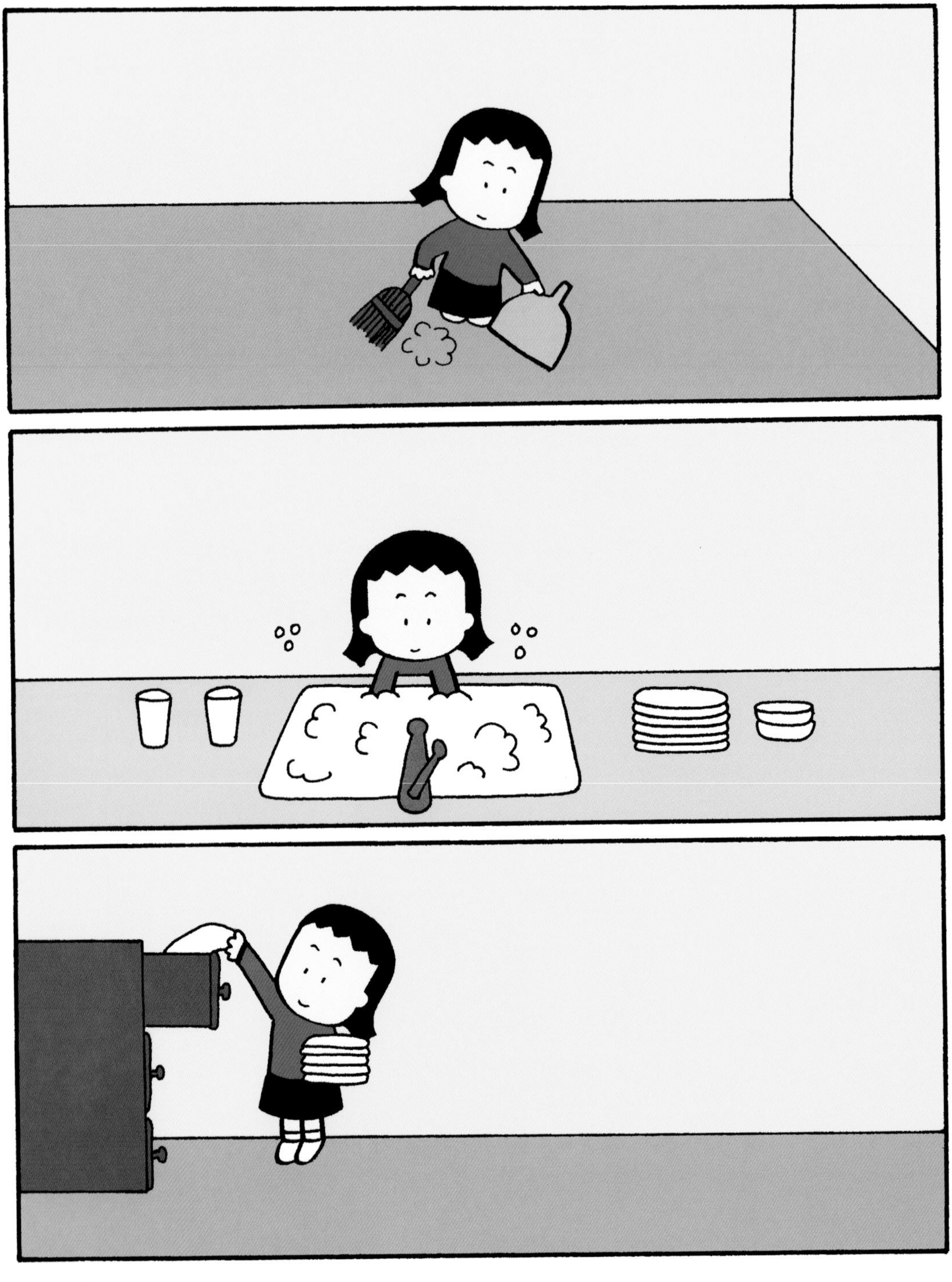

Upstairs, she found seven beds.

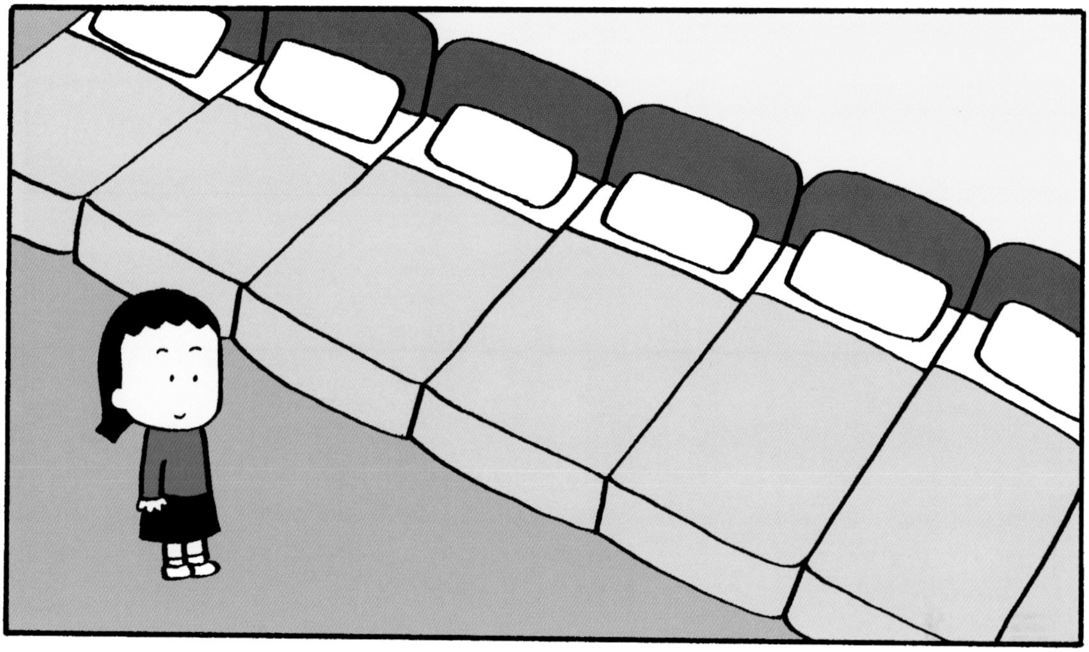

Snow Yellow slept peacefully.

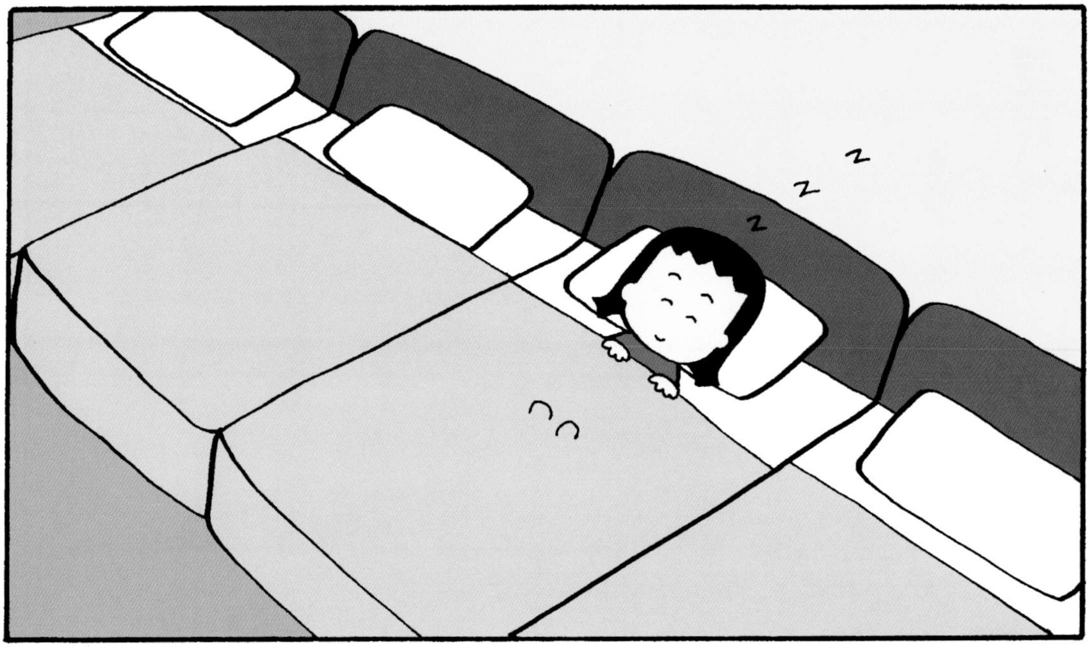
z
z
z

Meanwhile, the seven little men who lived there came home.

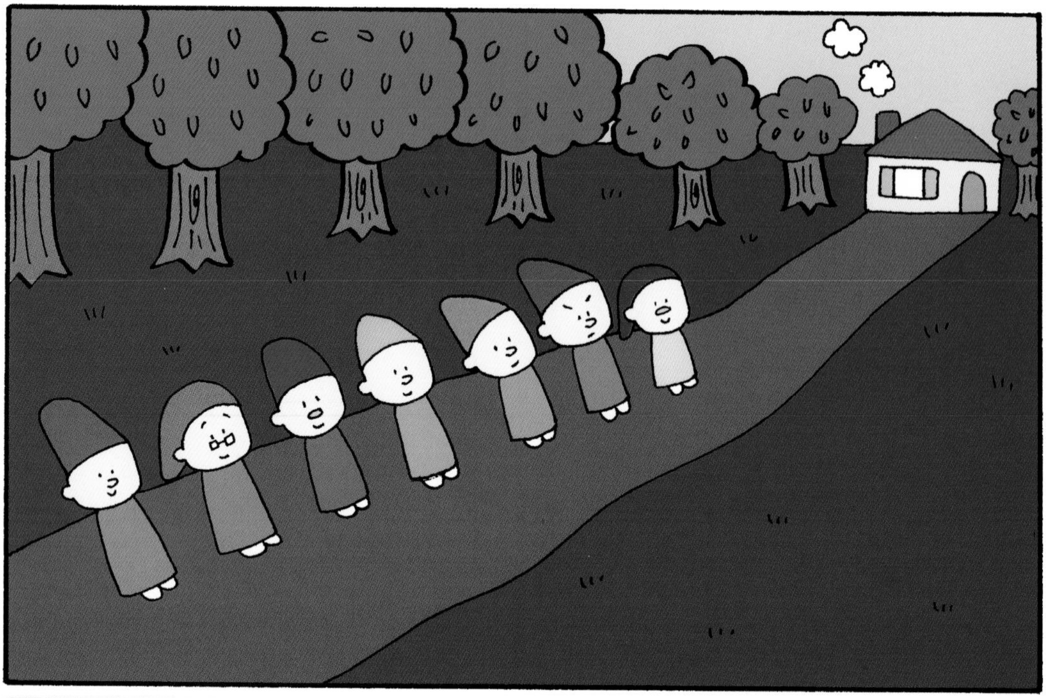

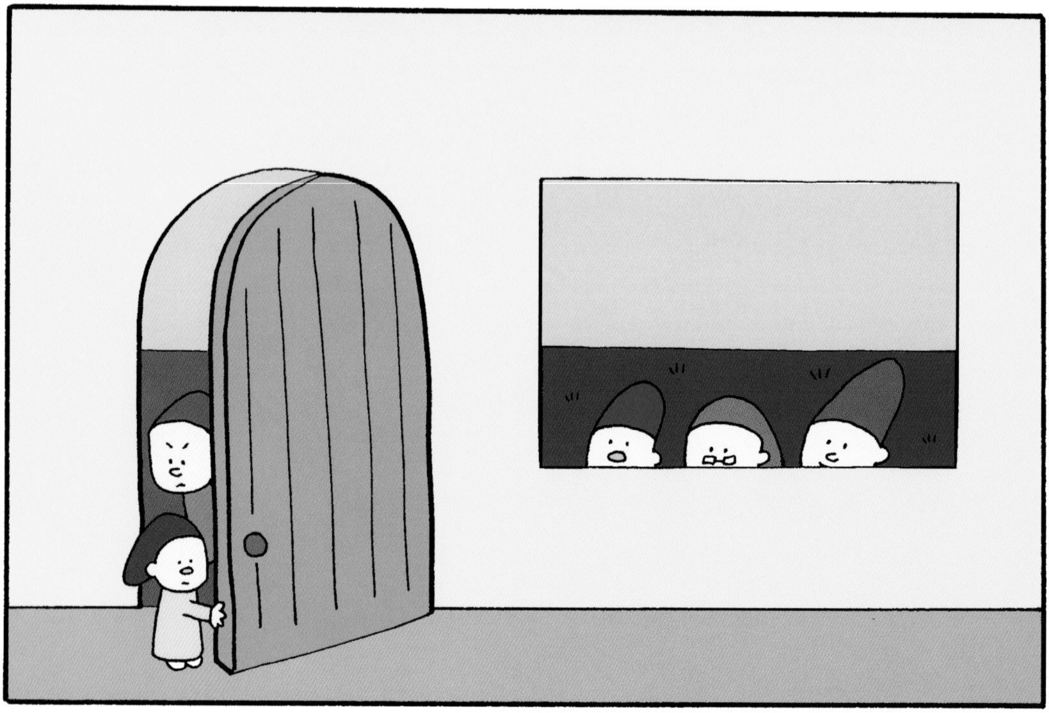

Snow Yellow was startled awake!

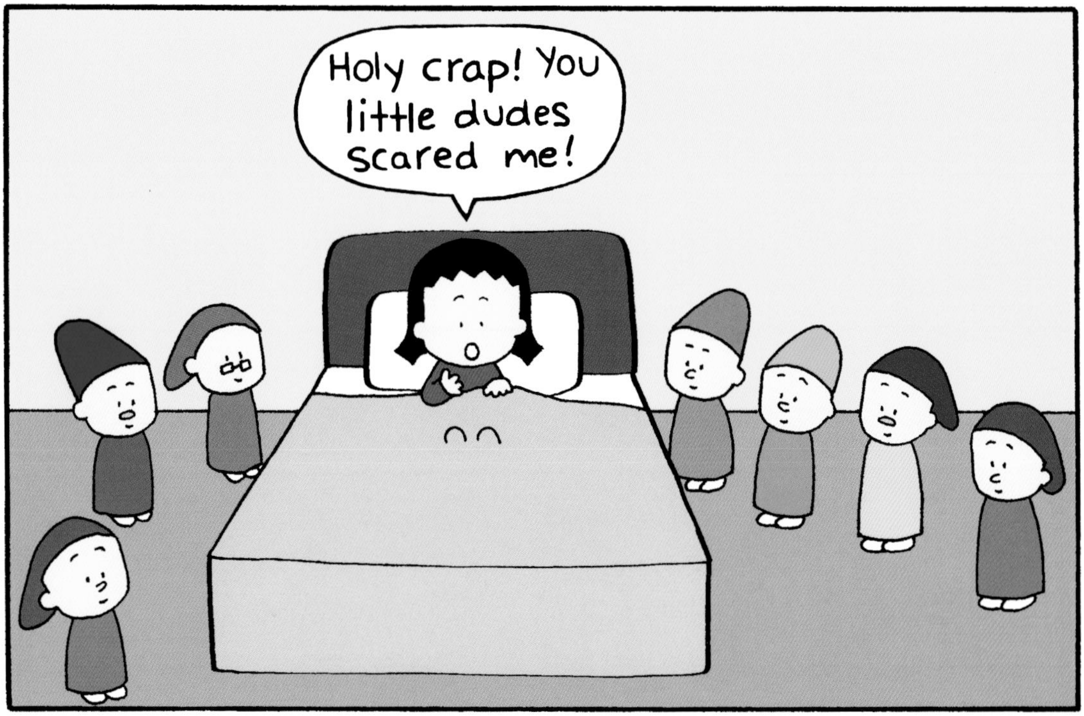
Holy crap! You little dudes scared me!

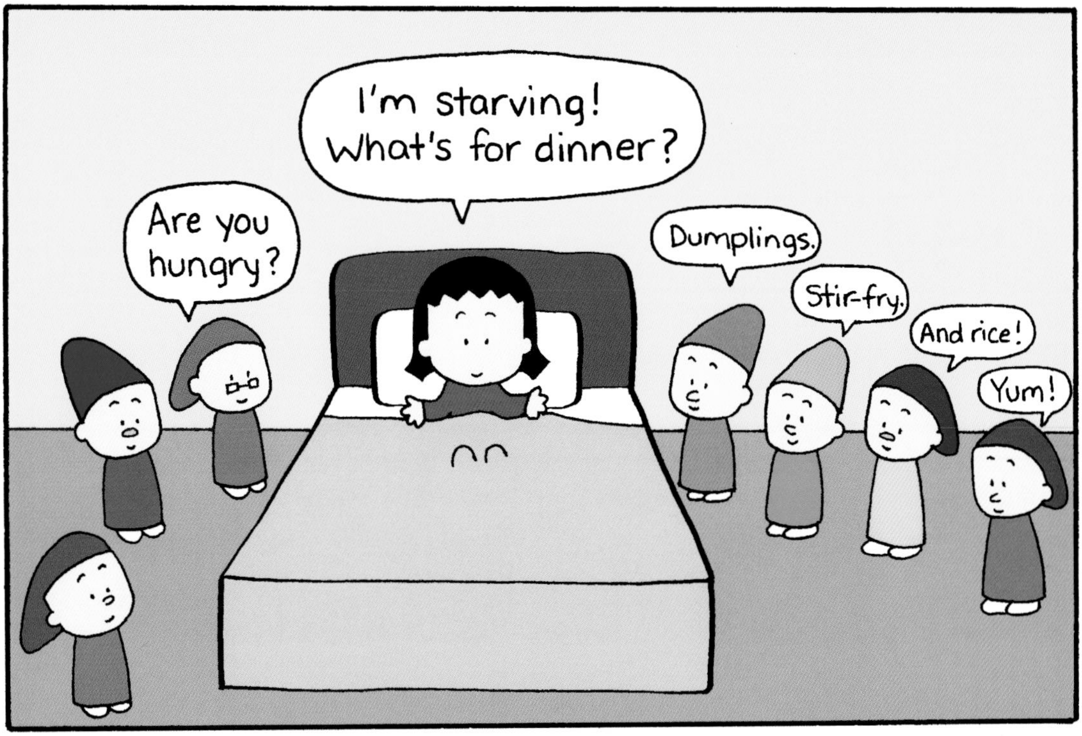
I'm starving! What's for dinner?
Are you hungry?
Dumplings.
Stir-fry.
And rice!
Yum!

They ate. They sang. They danced.

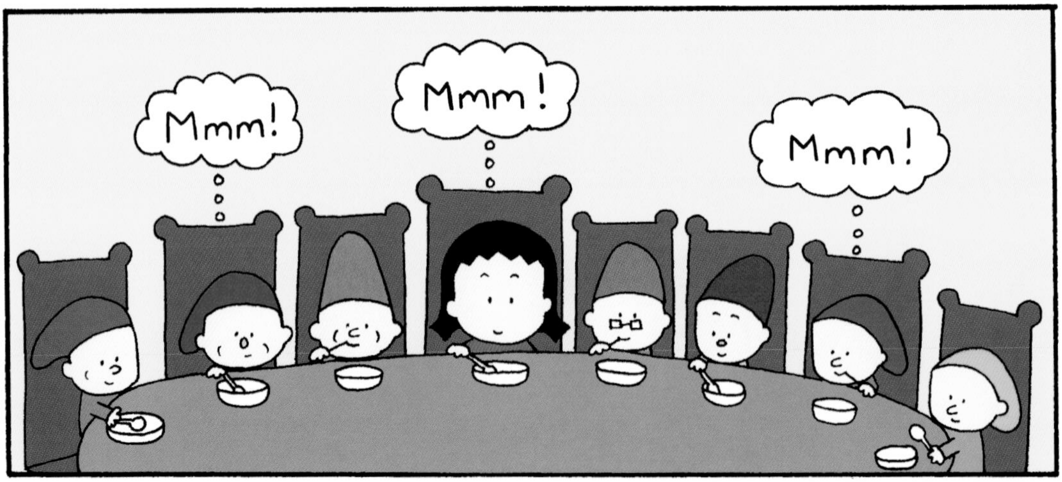
Mmm!
Mmm!
Mmm!

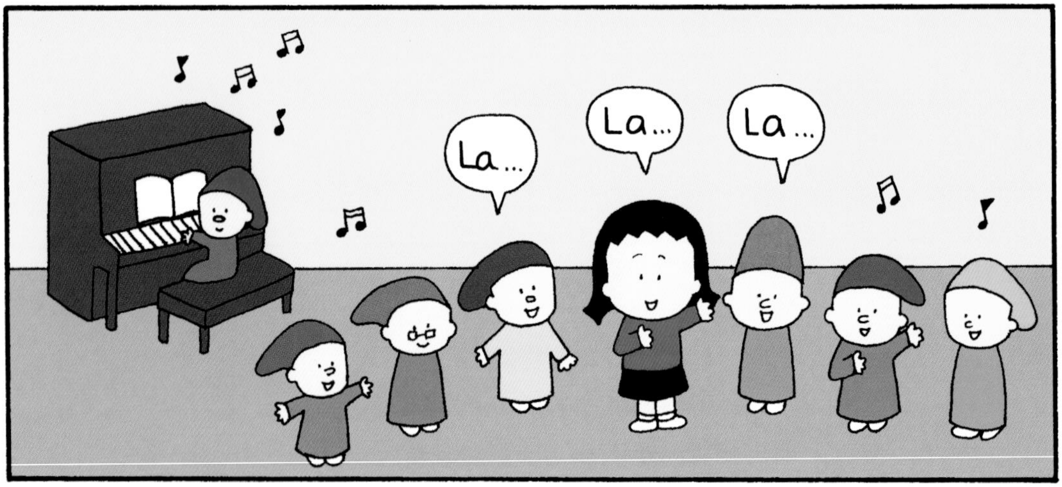
La...
La...
La...

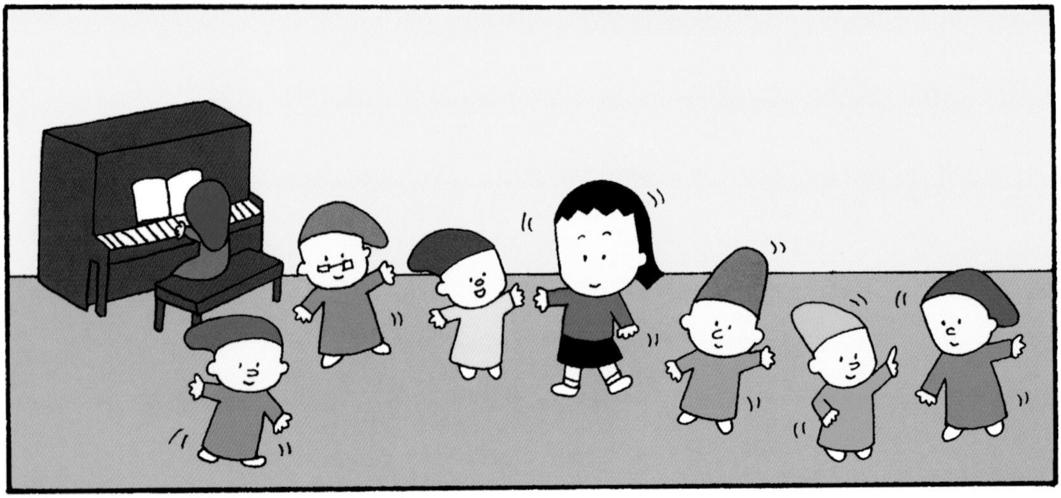

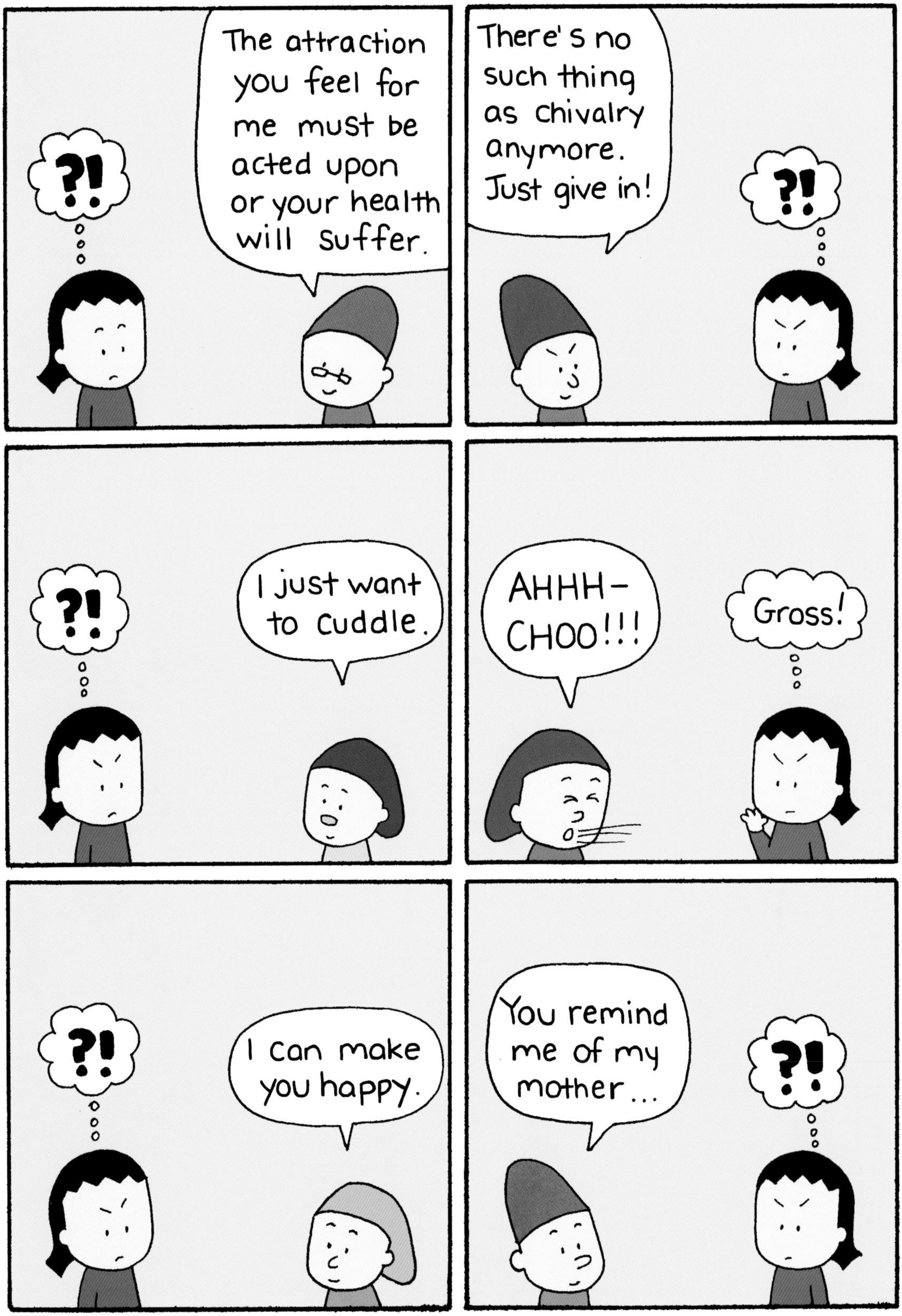
?!
The attraction you feel for me must be acted upon or your health will suffer.
There's no such thing as chivalry anymore. Just give in!
?!
?!
I just want to cuddle.
AHHH-CHOO!!!
Gross!
?!
I can make you happy.
You remind me of my mother...
?!

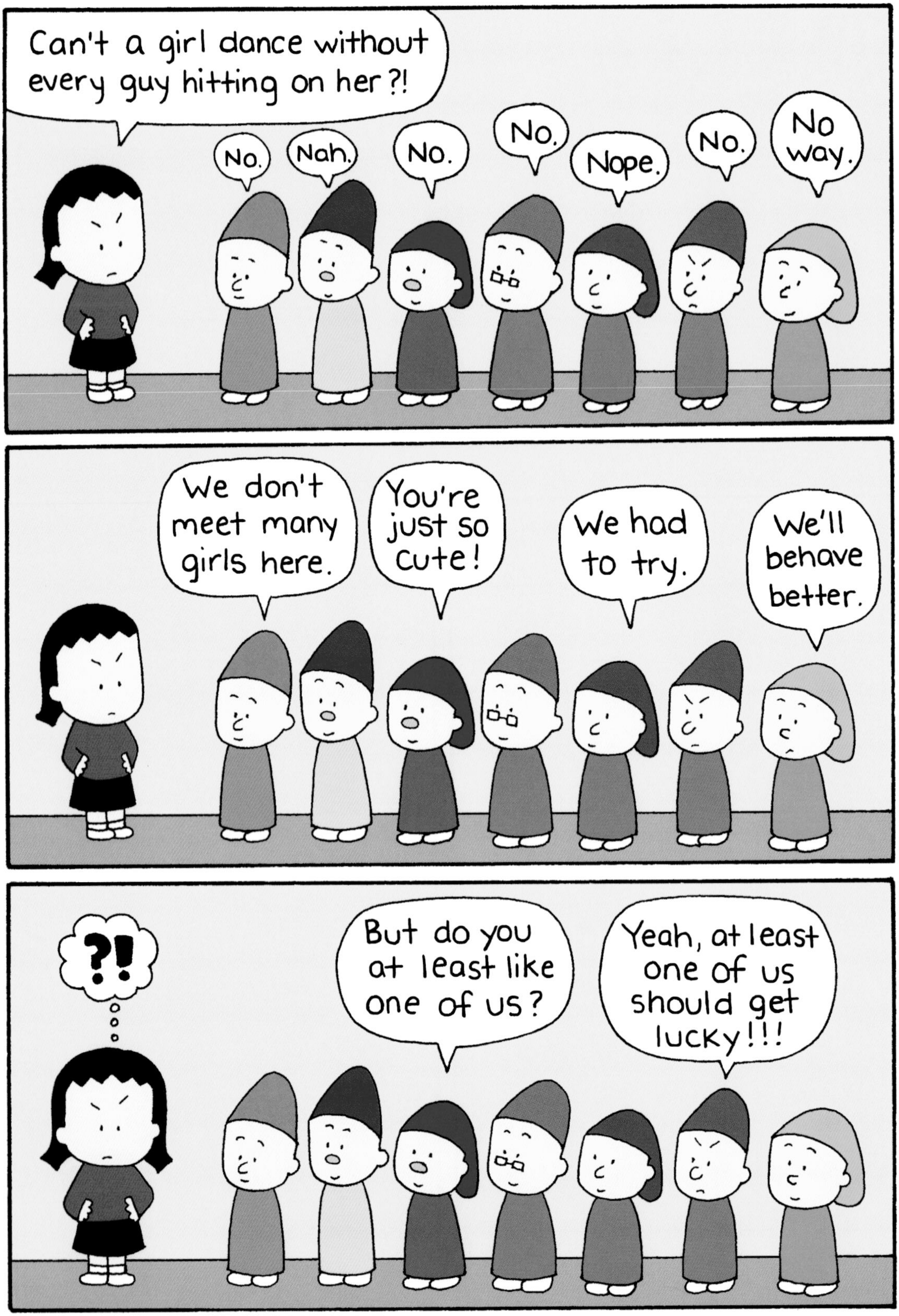
Can't a girl dance without every guy hitting on her?!
No.
Nah.
No.
No.
Nope.
No.
No way.
We don't meet many girls here.
You're just so cute!
We had to try.
We'll behave better.
?!
But do you at least like one of us?
Yeah, at least one of us should get lucky!!!

Meanwhile, back at the castle...

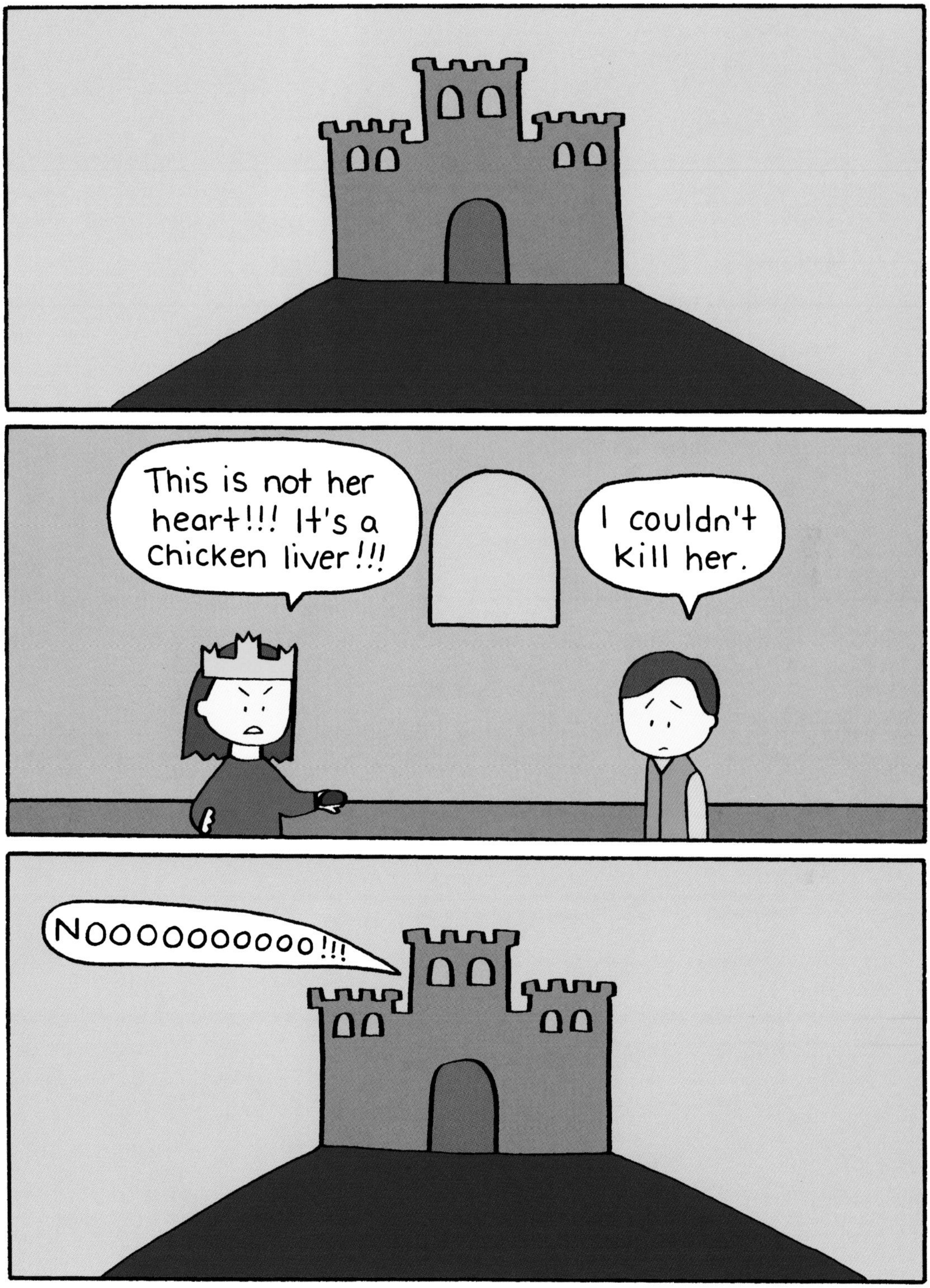
This is not her heart!!! It's a chicken liver!!!
I couldn't kill her.
NOOOOOOOOOOO!!!

The queen hatched an evil plan...

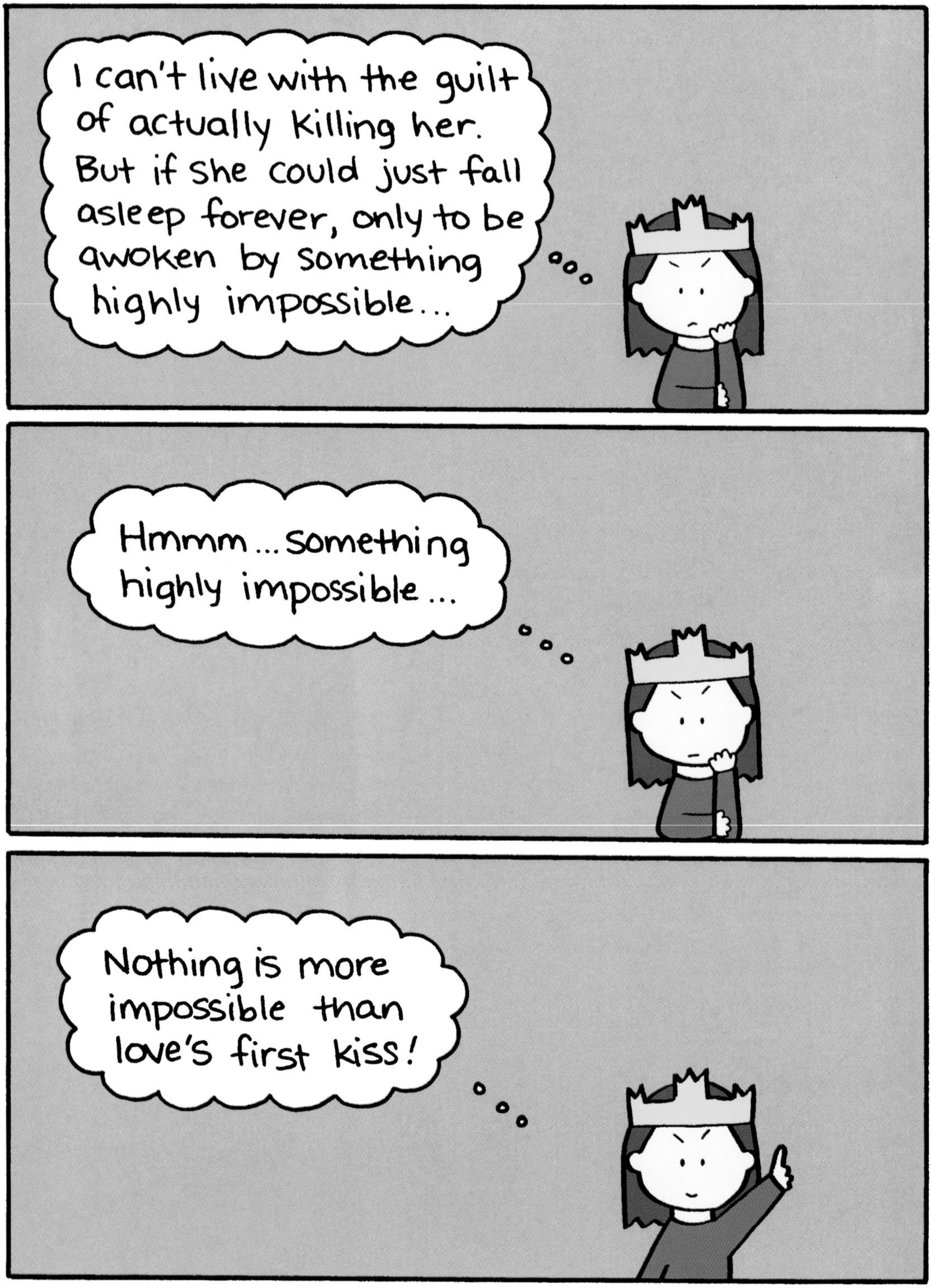
I can't live with the guilt of actually Killing her. But if she could just fall asleep forever, only to be awoken by something highly impossible...
Hmmm...something highly impossible...
Nothing is more impossible than love's first kiss!

The queen disguised herself and set out to find Snow Yellow.

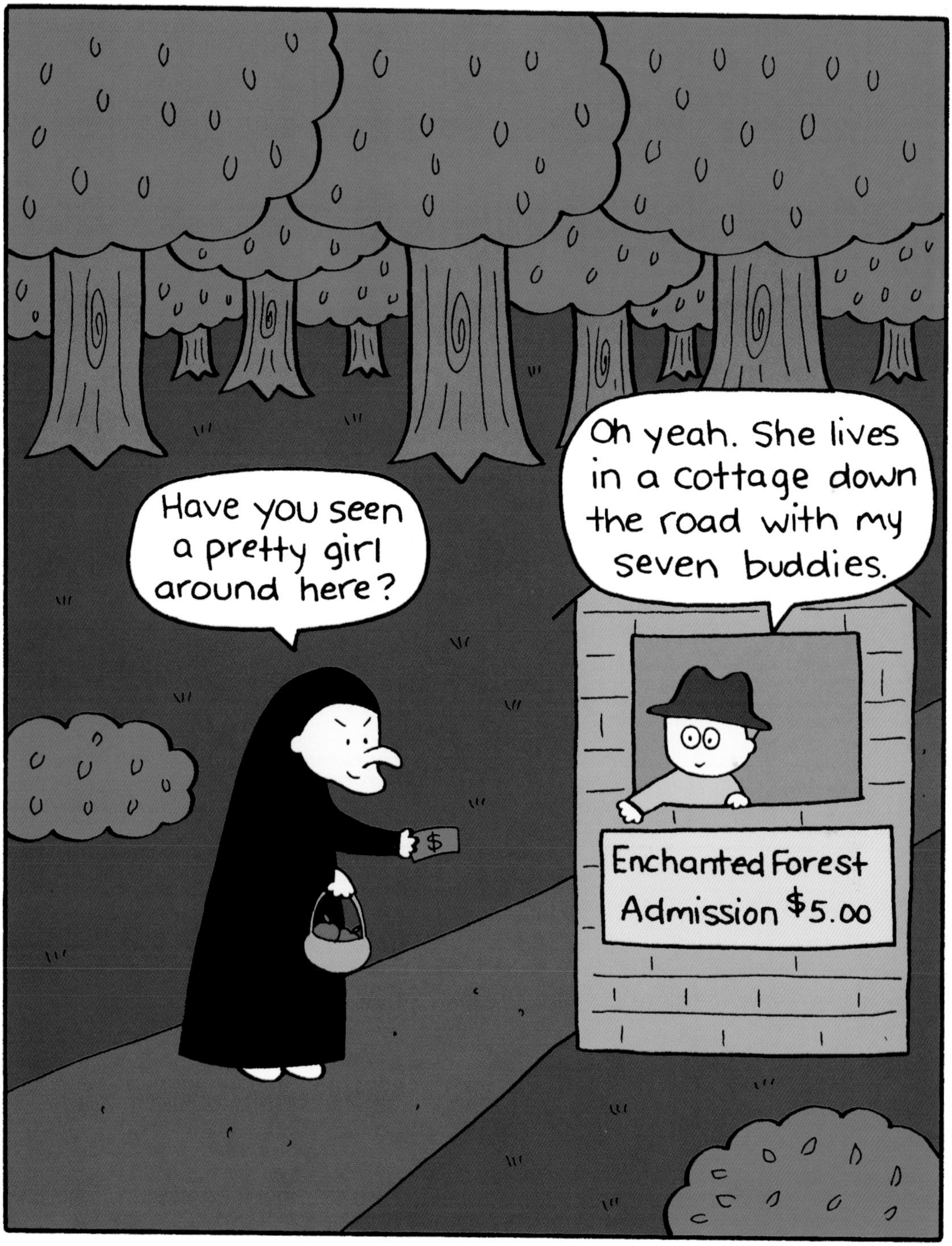
Have you seen a pretty girl around here?
Oh yeah. She lives in a cottage down the road with my seven buddies.
Enchanted Forest Admission $5.00

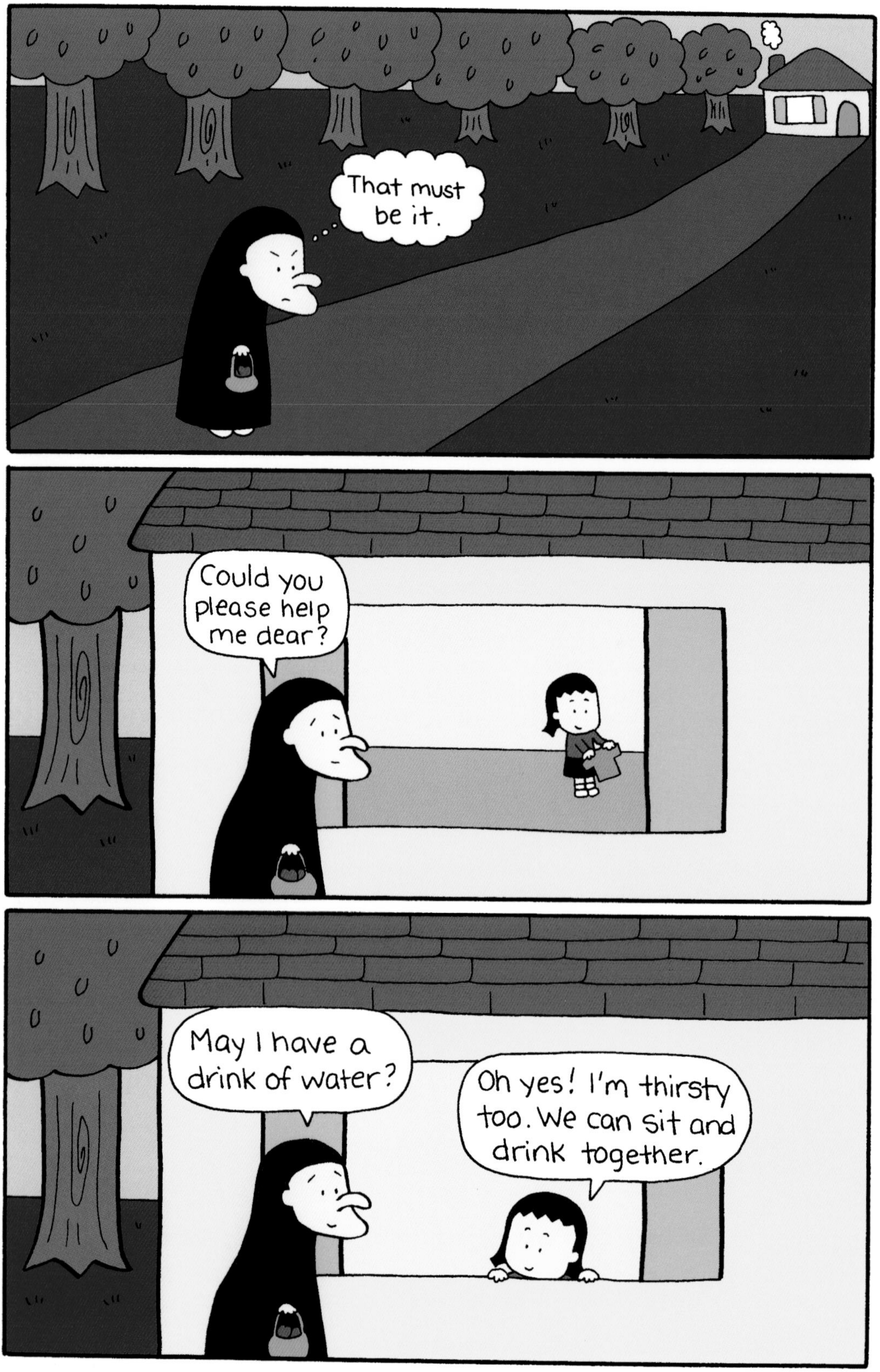
That must be it.
Could you please help me dear?
May I have a drink of water?
Oh yes! I'm thirsty too. We can sit and drink together.

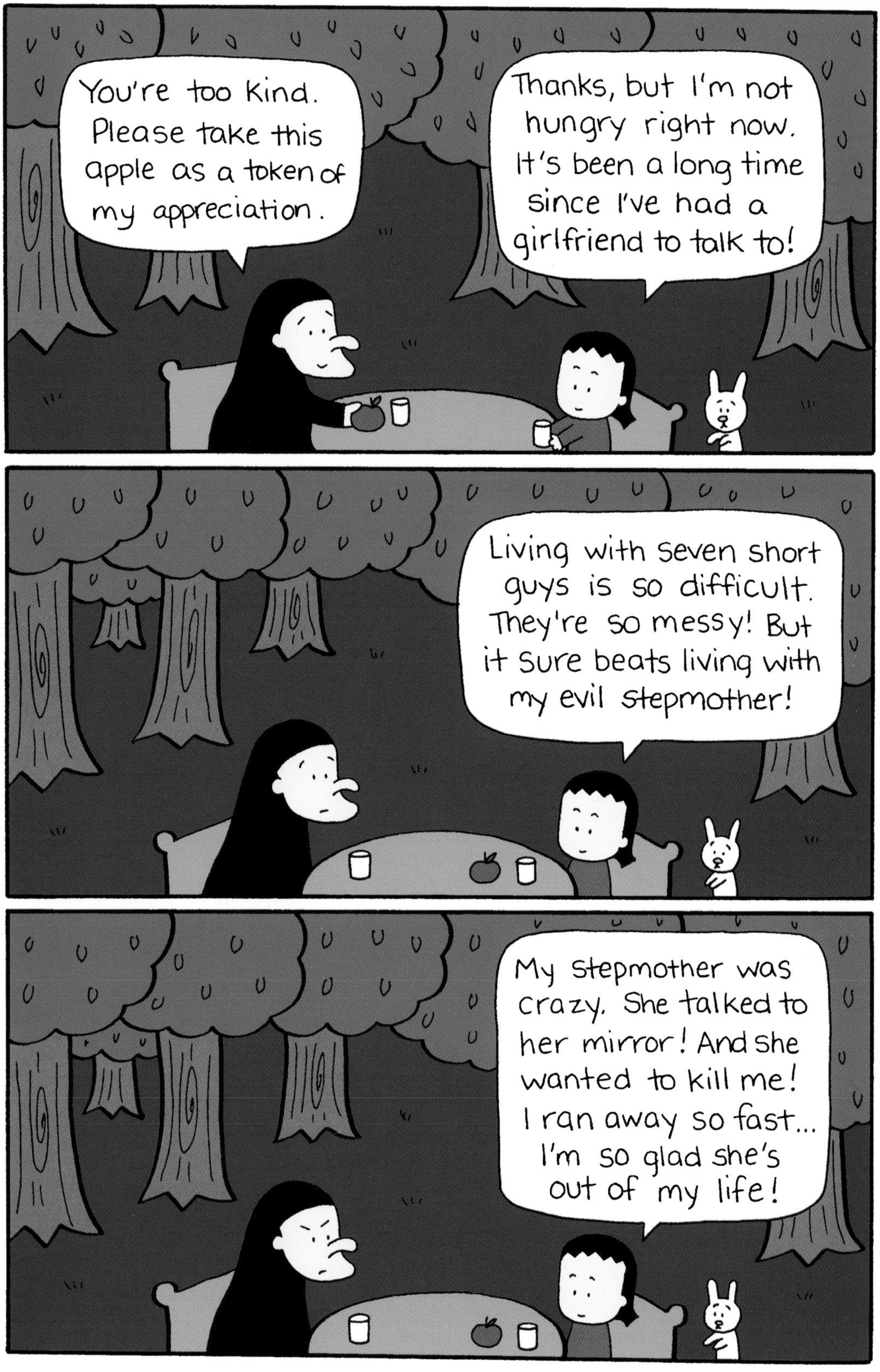
You're too kind. Please take this apple as a token of my appreciation.
Thanks, but I'm not hungry right now. It's been a long time since I've had a girlfriend to talk to!
Living with seven short guys is so difficult. They're so messy! But it sure beats living with my evil stepmother!
My stepmother was crazy. She talked to her mirror! And she wanted to kill me! I ran away so fast... I'm so glad she's out of my life!

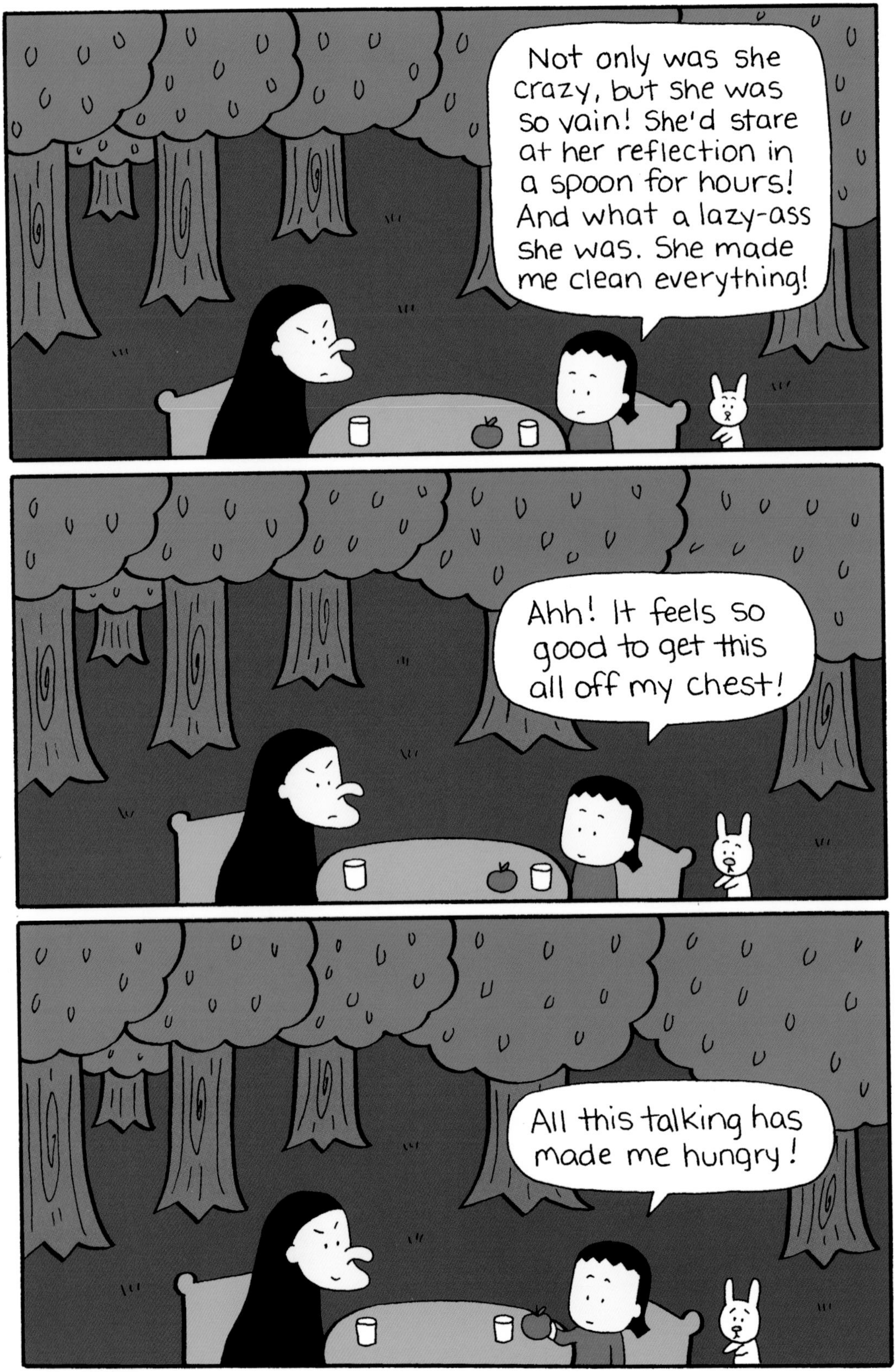
Not only was she crazy, but she was so vain! She'd stare at her reflection in a spoon for hours! And what a lazy-ass she was. She made me clean everything!
Ahh! It feels so good to get this all off my chest!
All this talking has made me hungry!

Snow Yellow ate the poisoned apple.

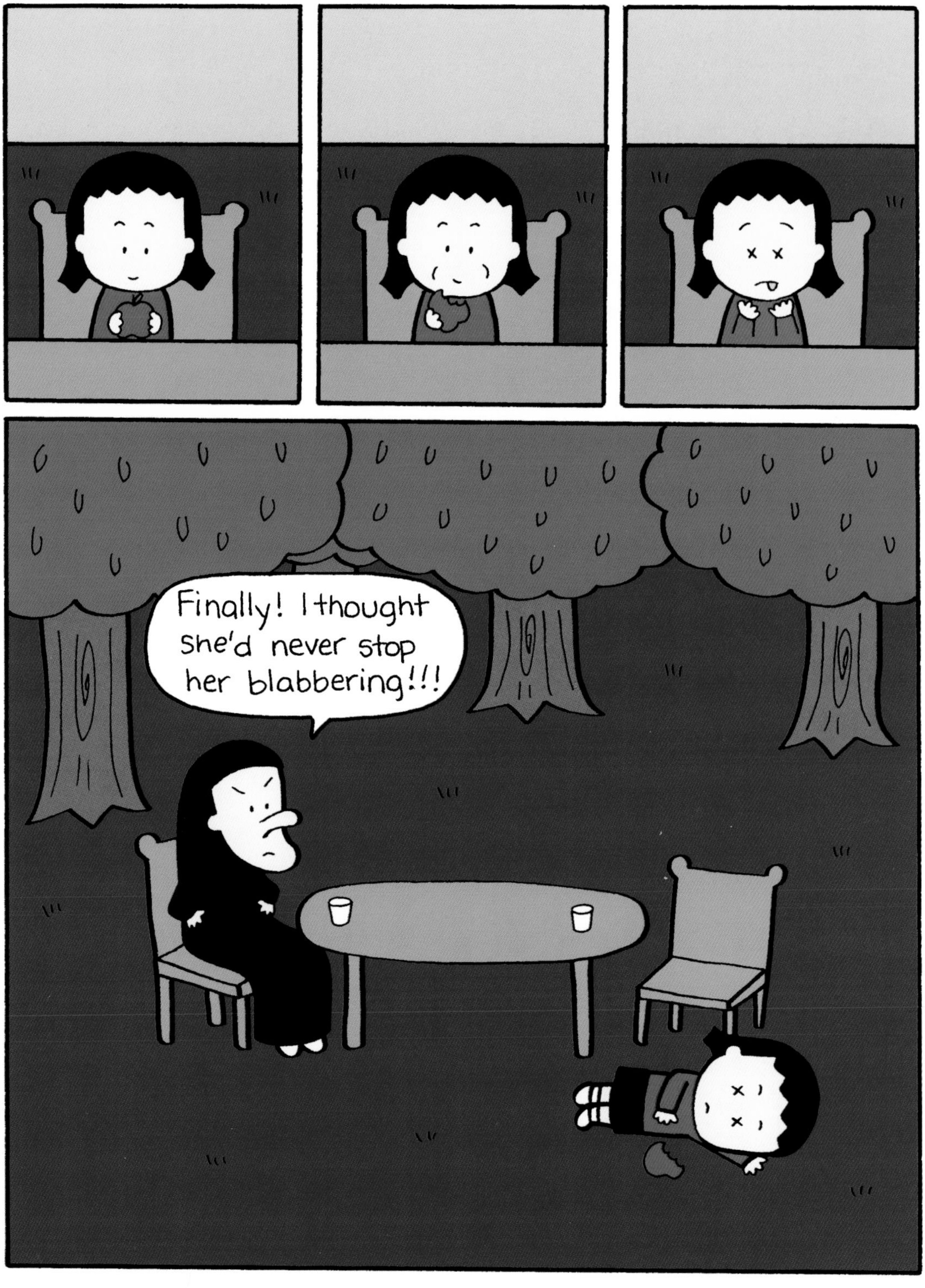
Finally! I thought she'd never stop her blabbering!!!

Snow Yellow fell into a deep sleep.

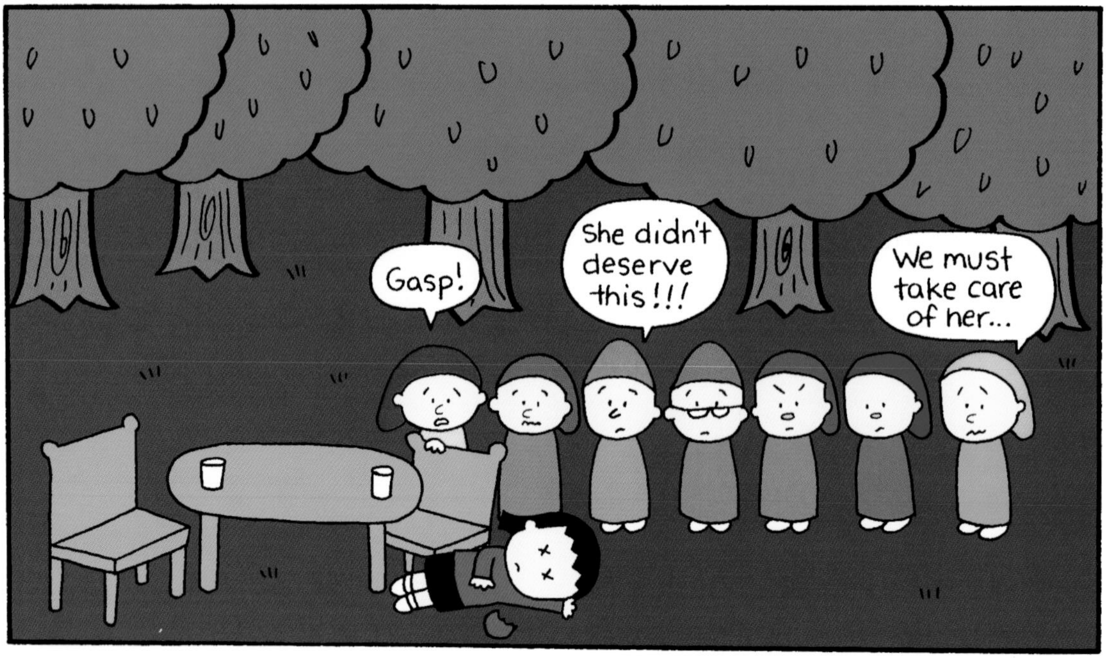

Gasp!
She didn't deserve this!!!
We must take care of her...

The seven short men kept watch over the sleeping Snow Yellow.

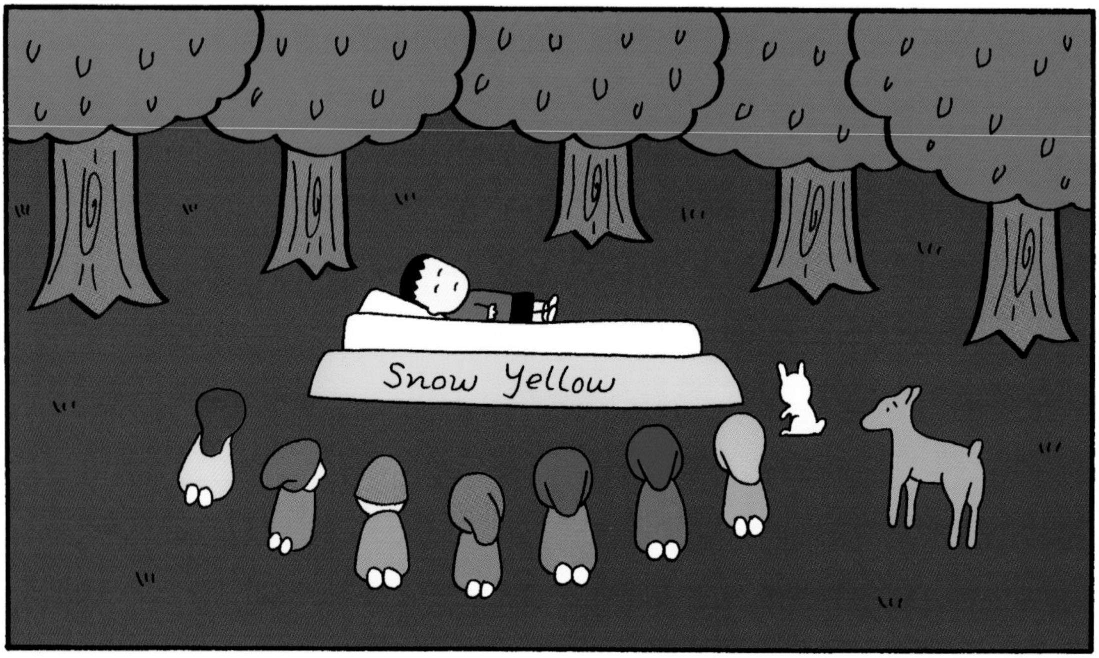

Snow Yellow

They kept watch day and night.

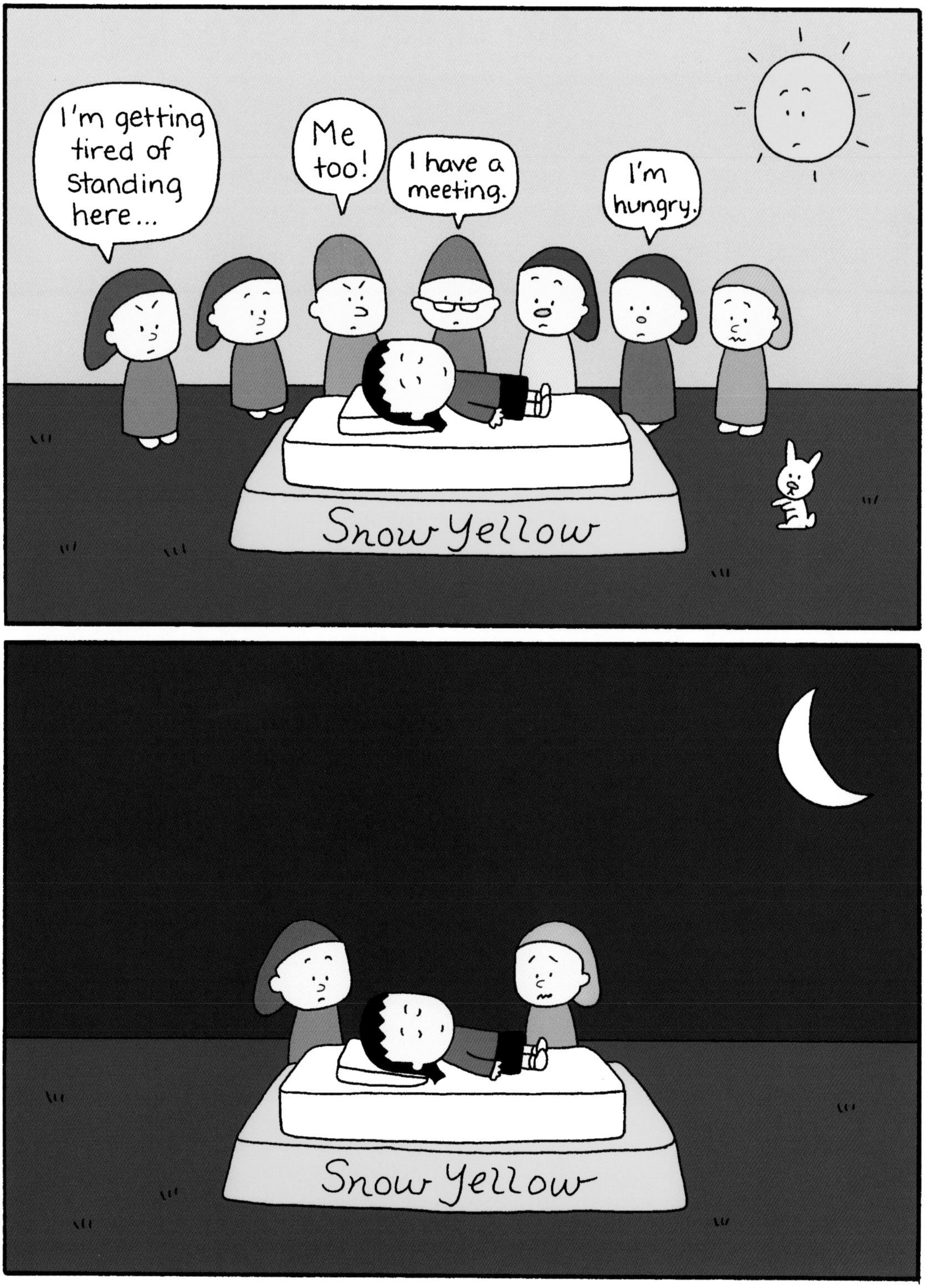
I'm getting tired of standing here...
Me too!
I have a meeting.
I'm hungry.
Snow Yellow
Snow Yellow

A handsome prince heard about Snow Yellow and rode out to see her.

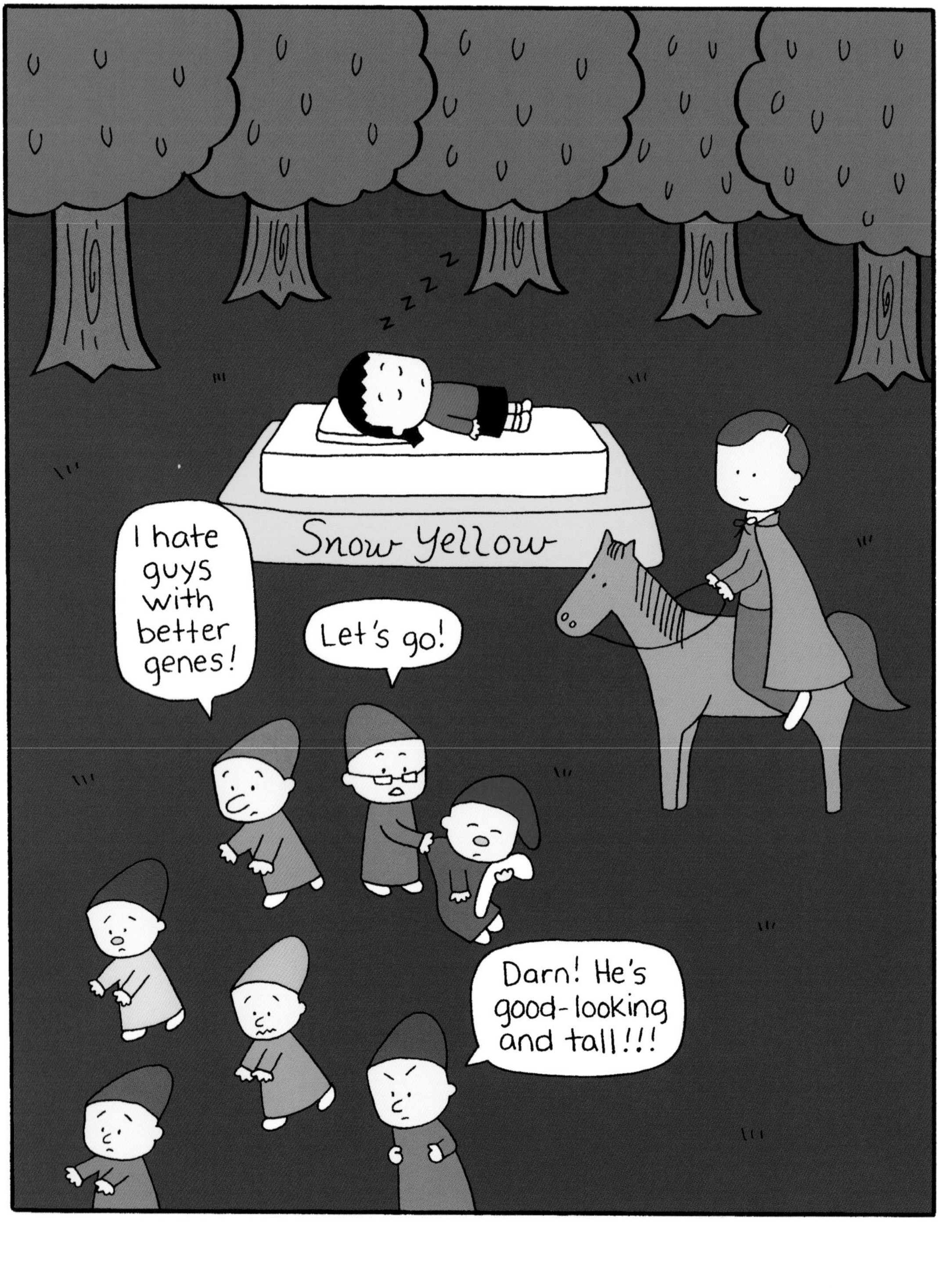
Z Z Z Z
Snow Yellow
I hate guys with better genes!
Let's go!
Darn! He's good-looking and tall!!!

The prince kissed Snow Yellow.

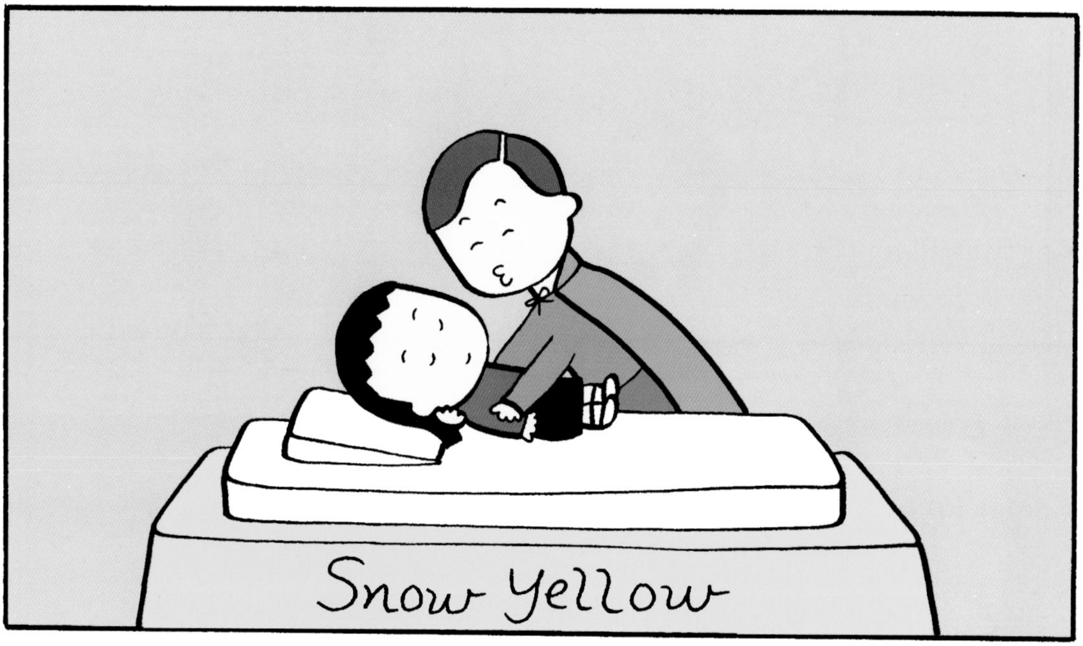
Snow Yellow

She finally awoke to love's first kiss.

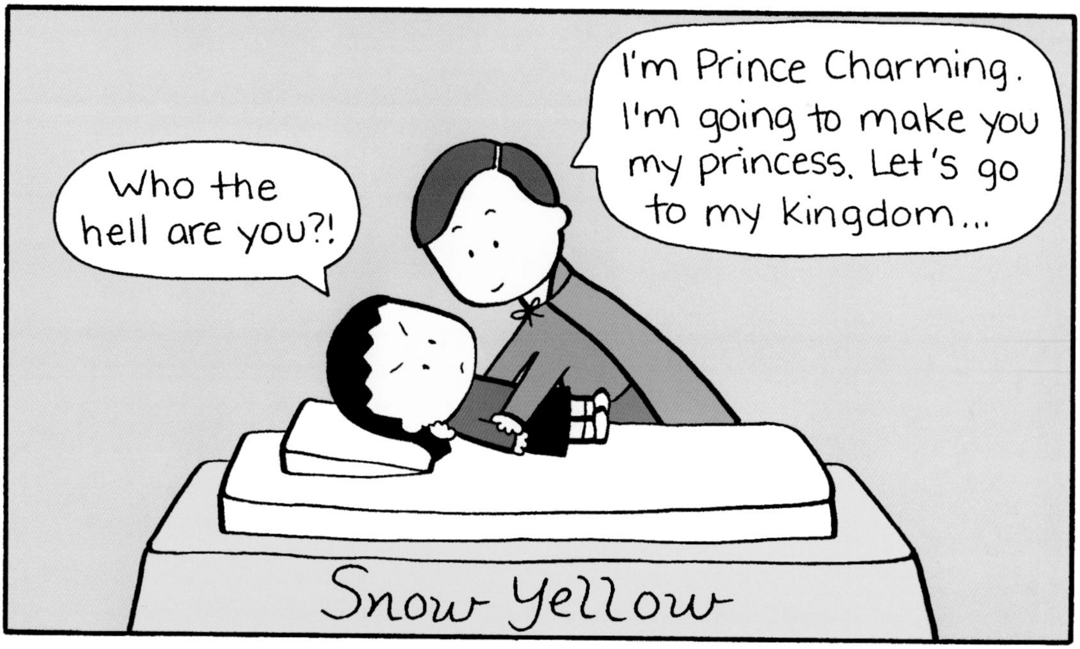
Who the hell are you?!
I'm Prince Charming. I'm going to make you my princess. Let's go to my kingdom...
Snow Yellow

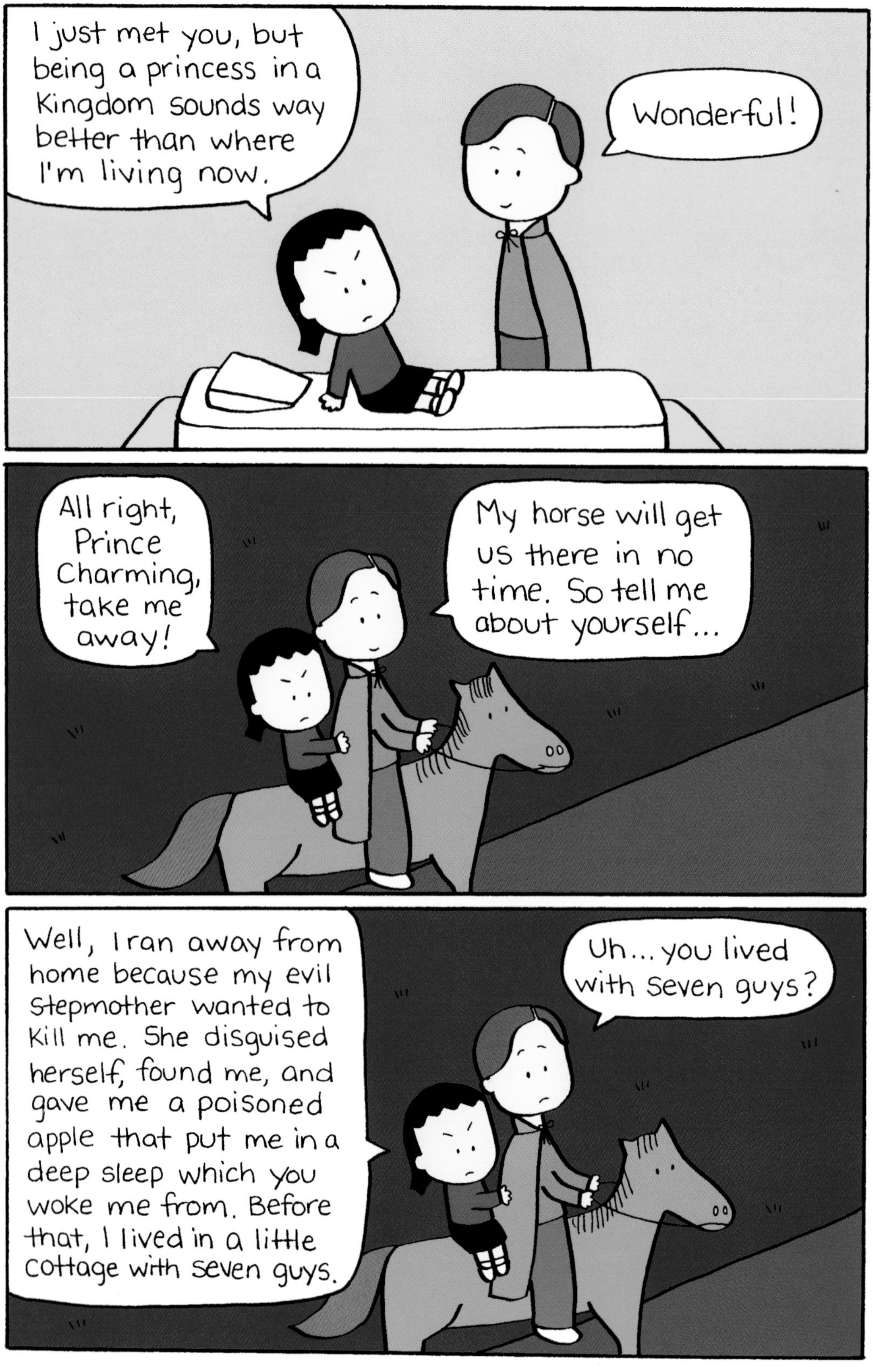
I just met you, but being a princess in a Kingdom sounds way better than where I'm living now.
Wonderful!
All right, Prince Charming, take me away!
My horse will get us there in no time. So tell me about yourself...
Well, I ran away from home because my evil stepmother wanted to Kill me. She disguised herself, found me, and gave me a poisoned apple that put me in a deep sleep which you woke me from. Before that, I lived in a little cottage with seven guys.
Uh... you lived with seven guys?

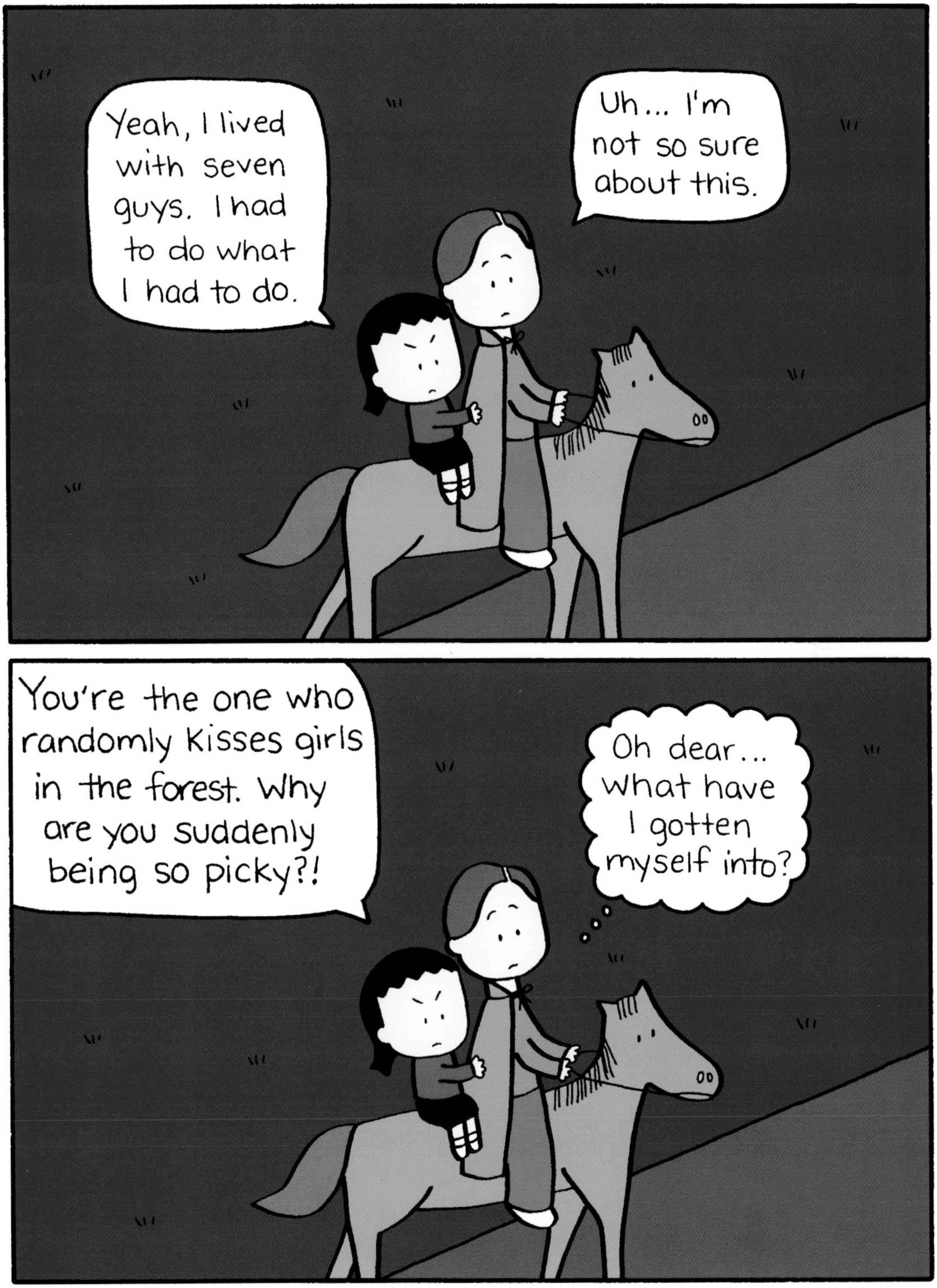
Yeah, I lived with seven guys. I had to do what I had to do.
Uh... I'm not so sure about this.
You're the one who randomly kisses girls in the forest. Why are you suddenly being so picky?!
Oh dear... What have I gotten myself into?

And they lived happily ever after...

an ANGRY LITTLE GIRL'S
FAIRY TALE

The Princess Got the Third Degree

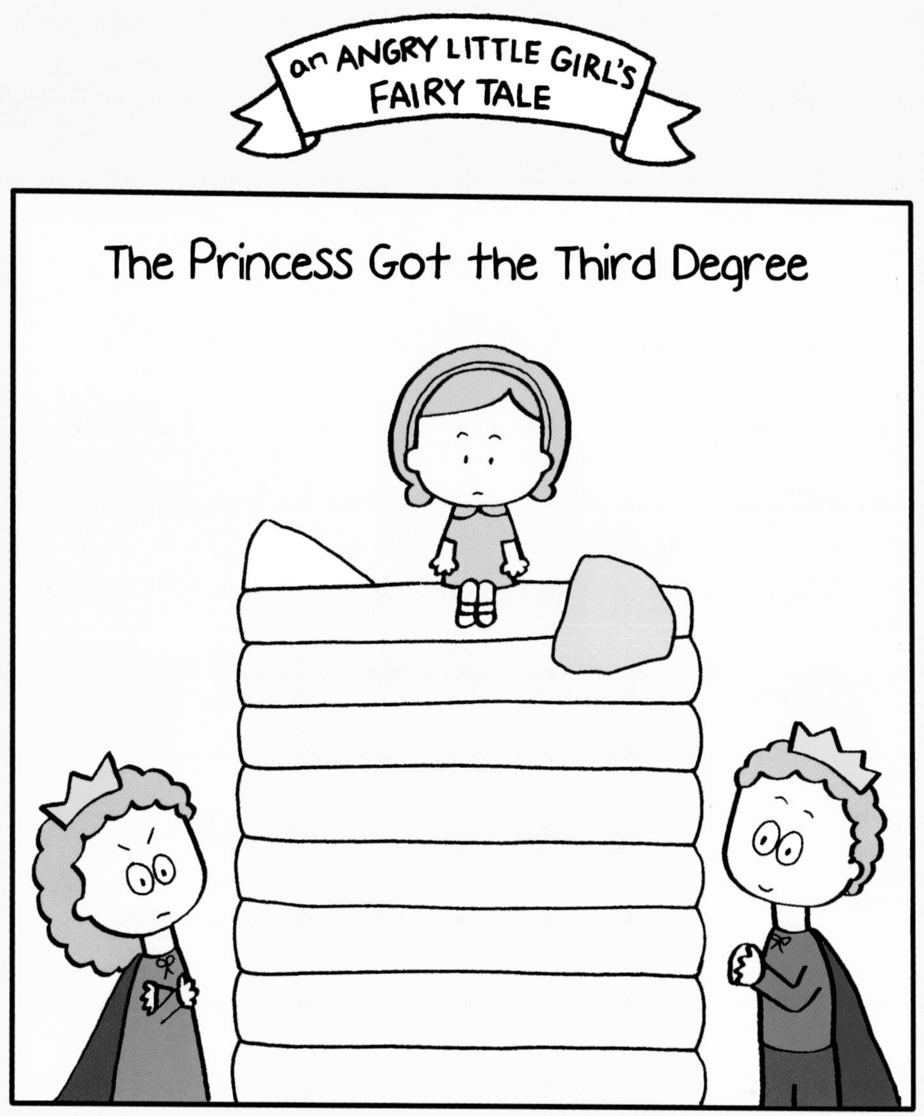

Starring

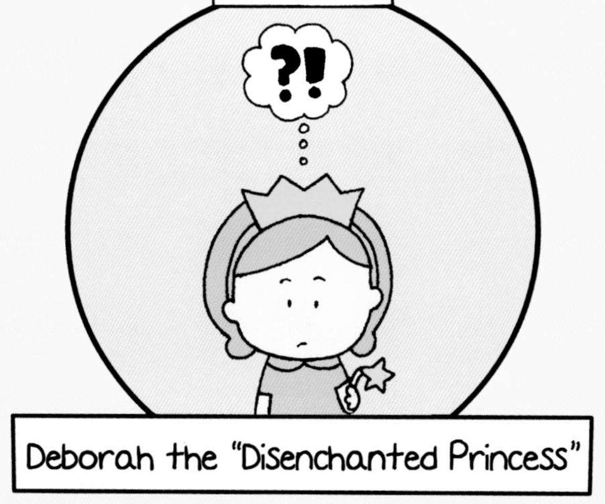
?!

Deborah the "Disenchanted Princess"

Once upon a time, there was a prince who wished to marry.

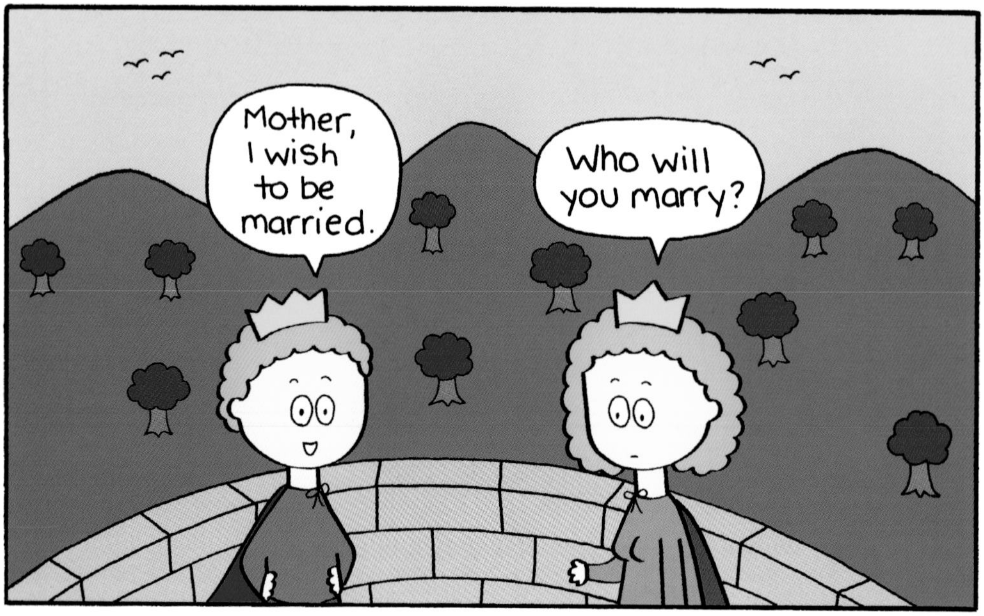
Mother, I wish to be married.
Who will you marry?

The prince traveled the world in search of his princess.

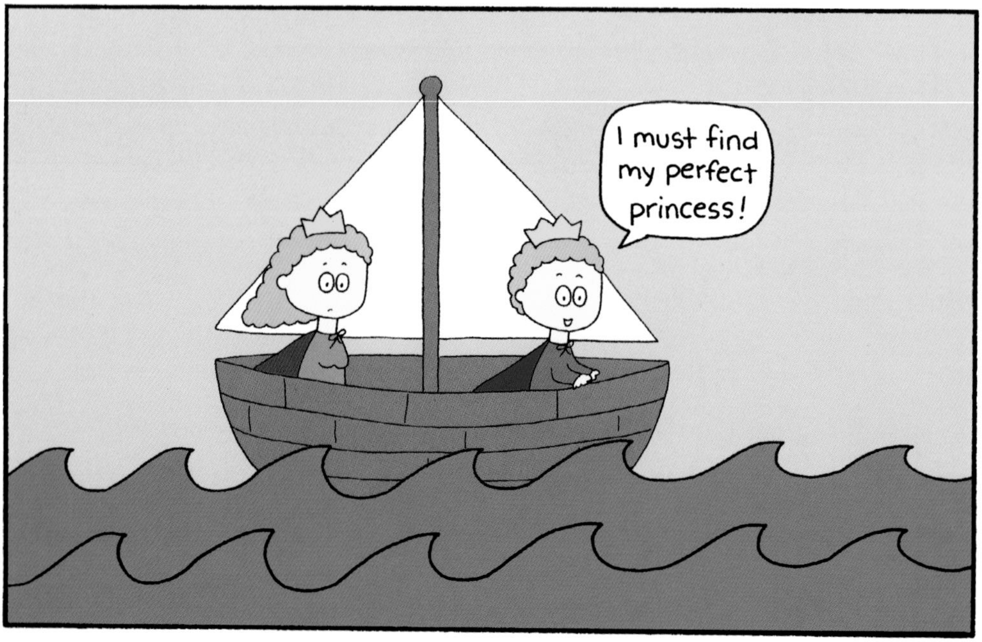
I must find my perfect princess!

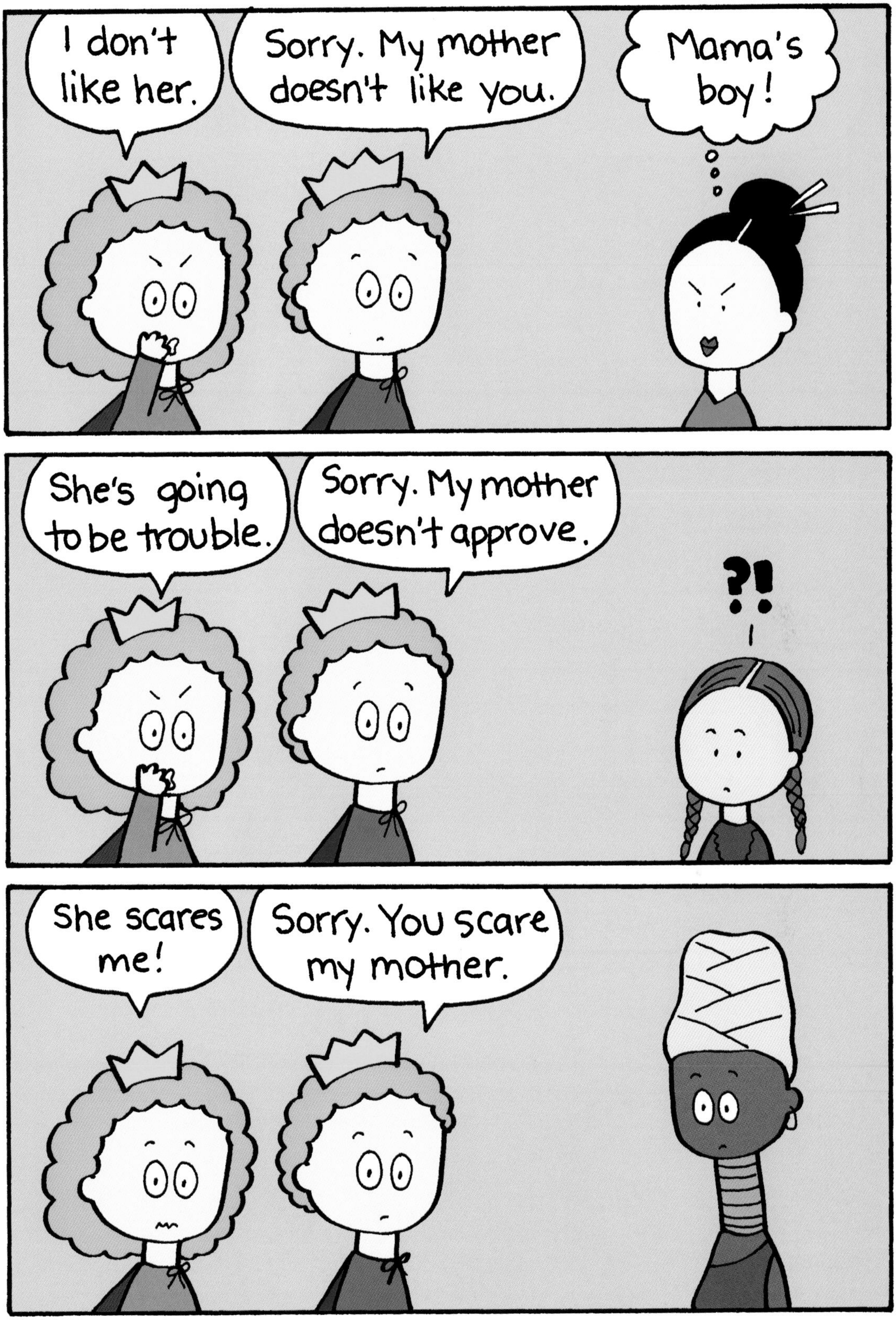
I don't like her.
Sorry. My mother doesn't like you.
Mama's boy!
She's going to be trouble.
Sorry. My mother doesn't approve.
?!
She scares me!
Sorry. You scare my mother.

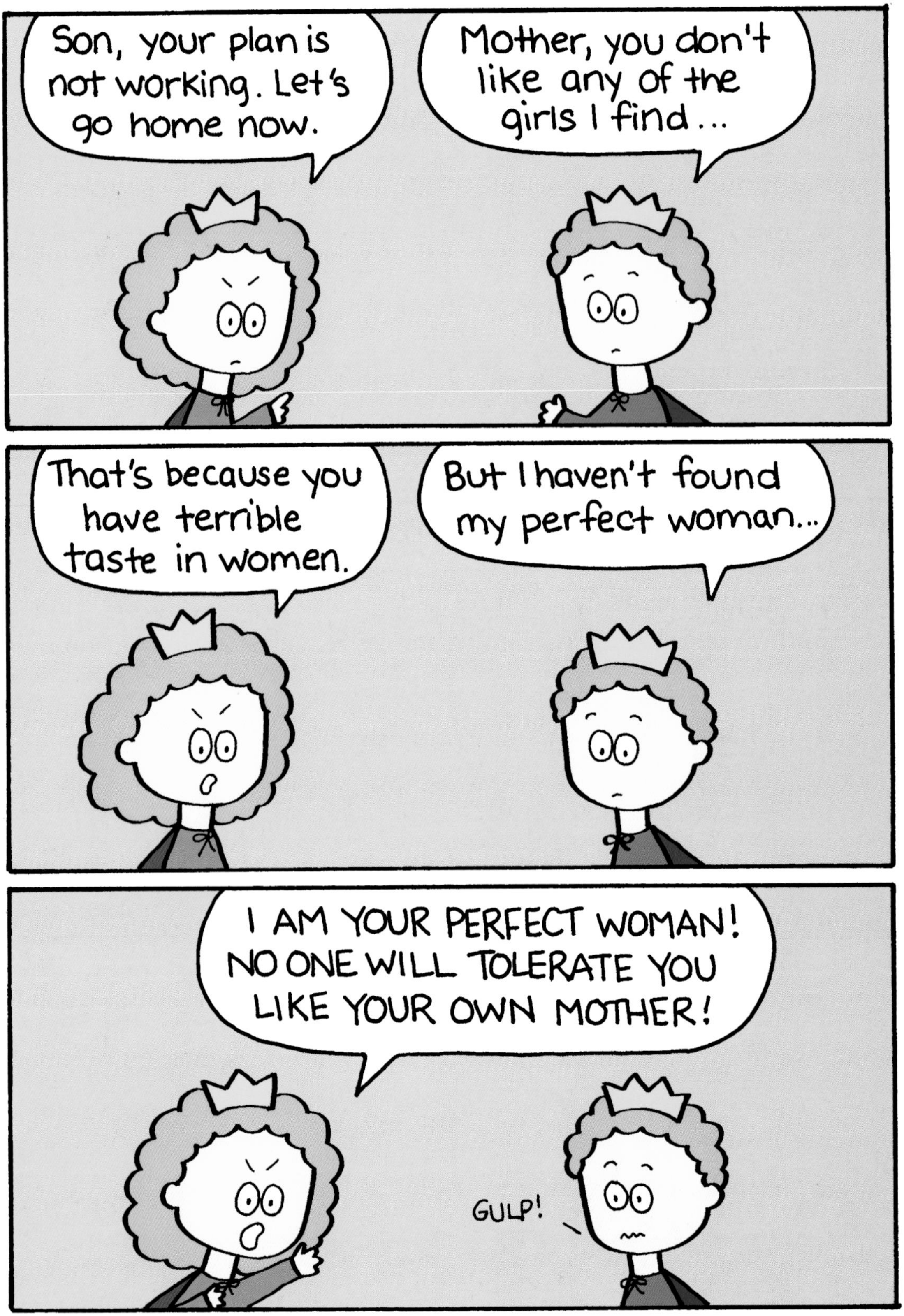

Son, your plan is not working. Let's go home now.
Mother, you don't like any of the girls I find...
That's because you have terrible taste in women.
But I haven't found my perfect woman...
I AM YOUR PERFECT WOMAN! NO ONE WILL TOLERATE YOU LIKE YOUR OWN MOTHER!
GULP!

The prince and his mother returned to their home.

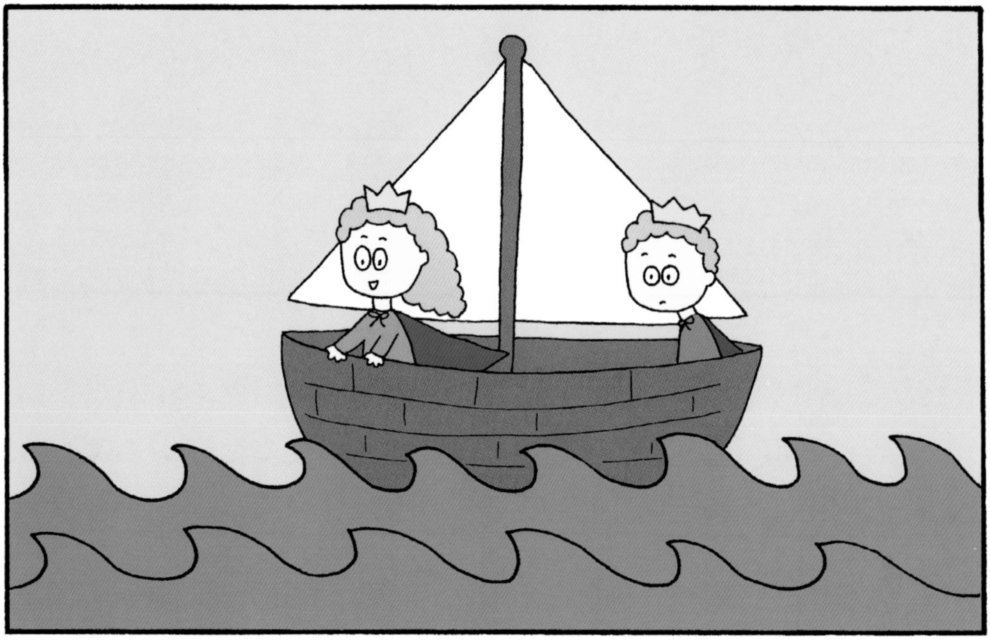

The prince was very unhappy.

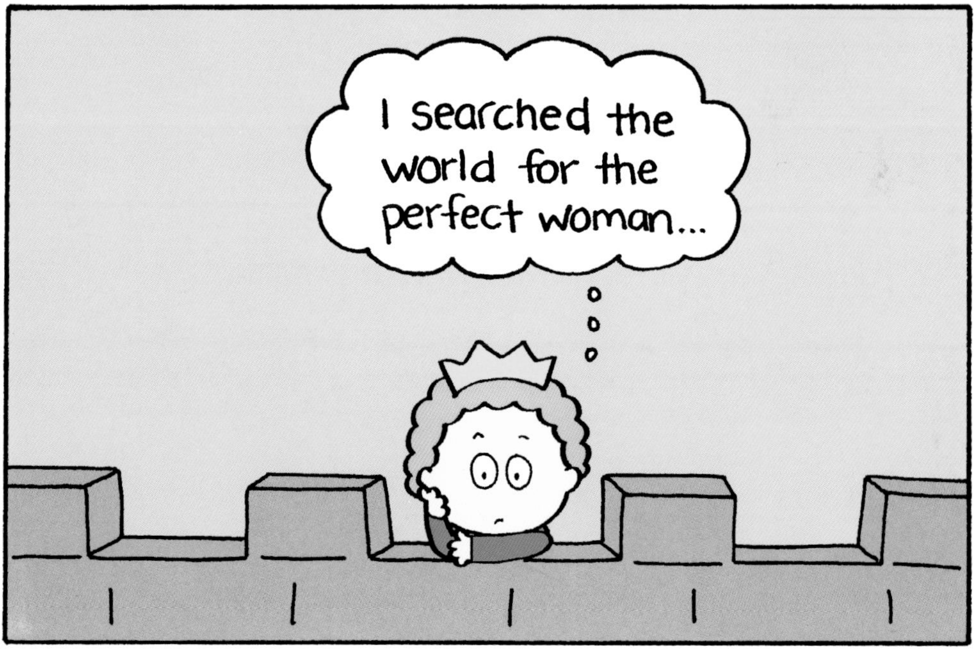
I searched the world for the perfect woman...

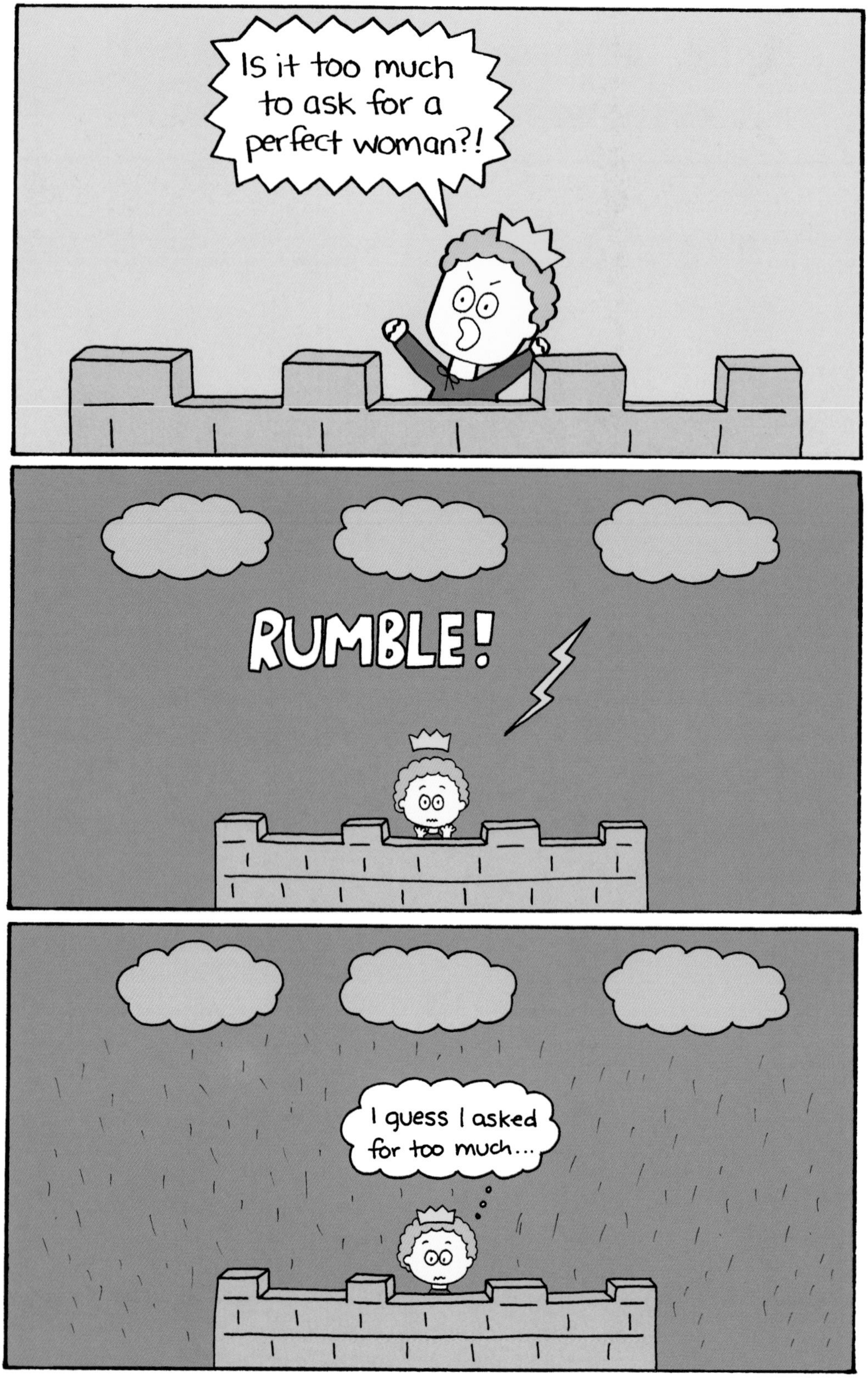

Is it too much to ask for a perfect woman?!
RUMBLE!
I guess I asked for too much...

A storm caught everyone by surprise, including a princess.

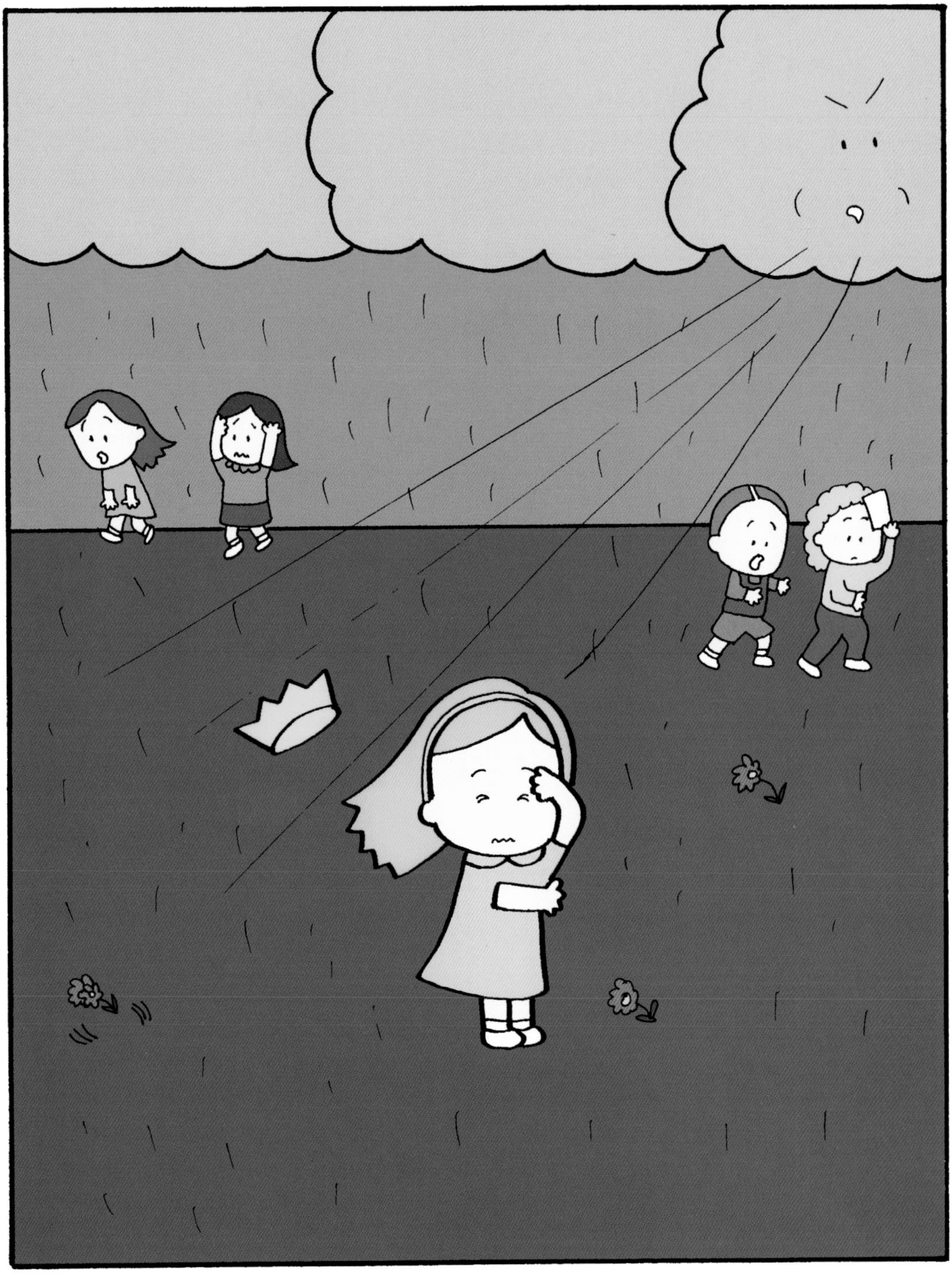

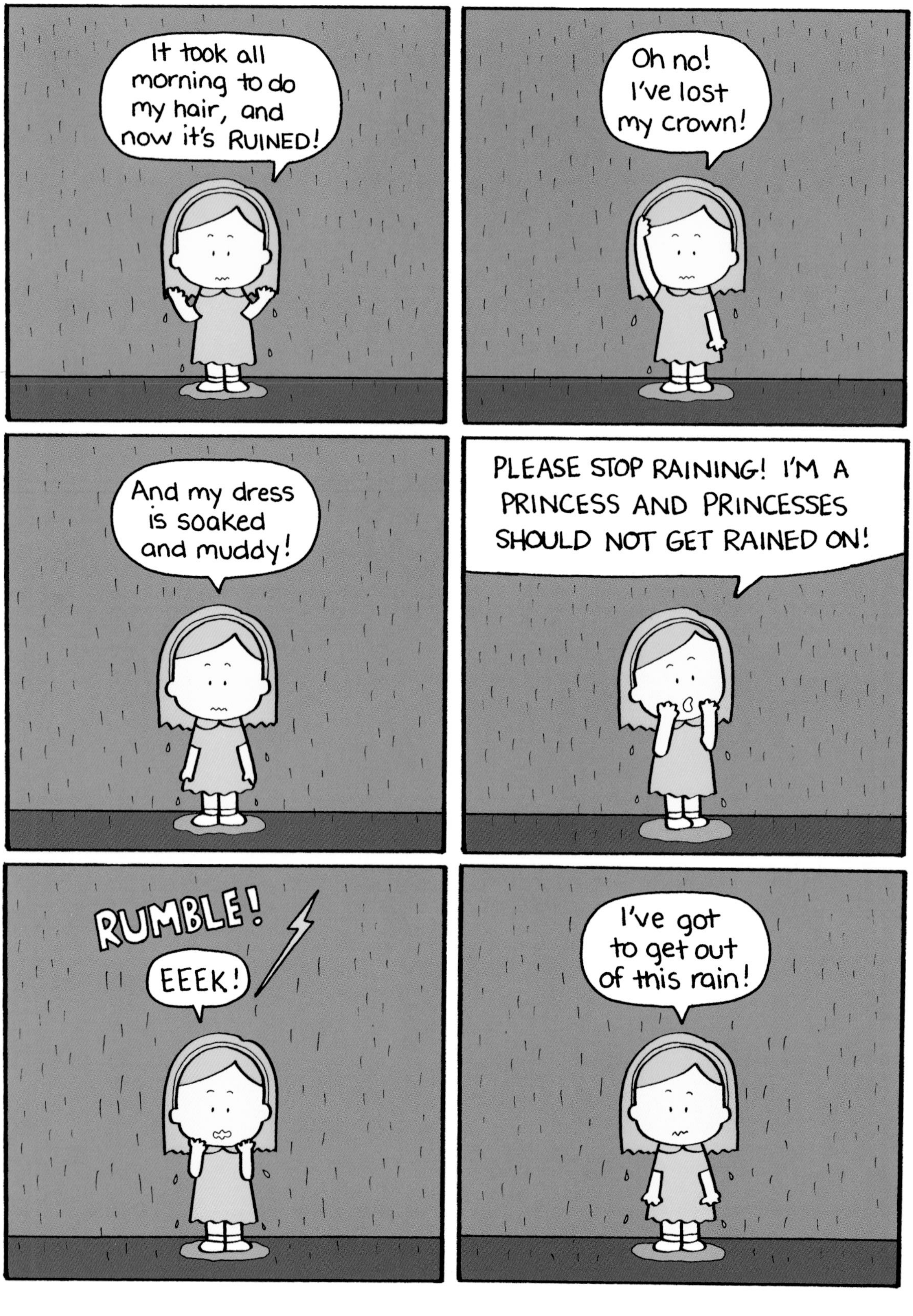
It took all morning to do my hair, and now it's RUINED!
Oh no! I've lost my crown!
And my dress is soaked and muddy!
PLEASE STOP RAINING! I'M A PRINCESS AND PRINCESSES SHOULD NOT GET RAINED ON!
RUMBLE!
EEEK!
I've got to get out of this rain!

The princess knocked on the prince's door.

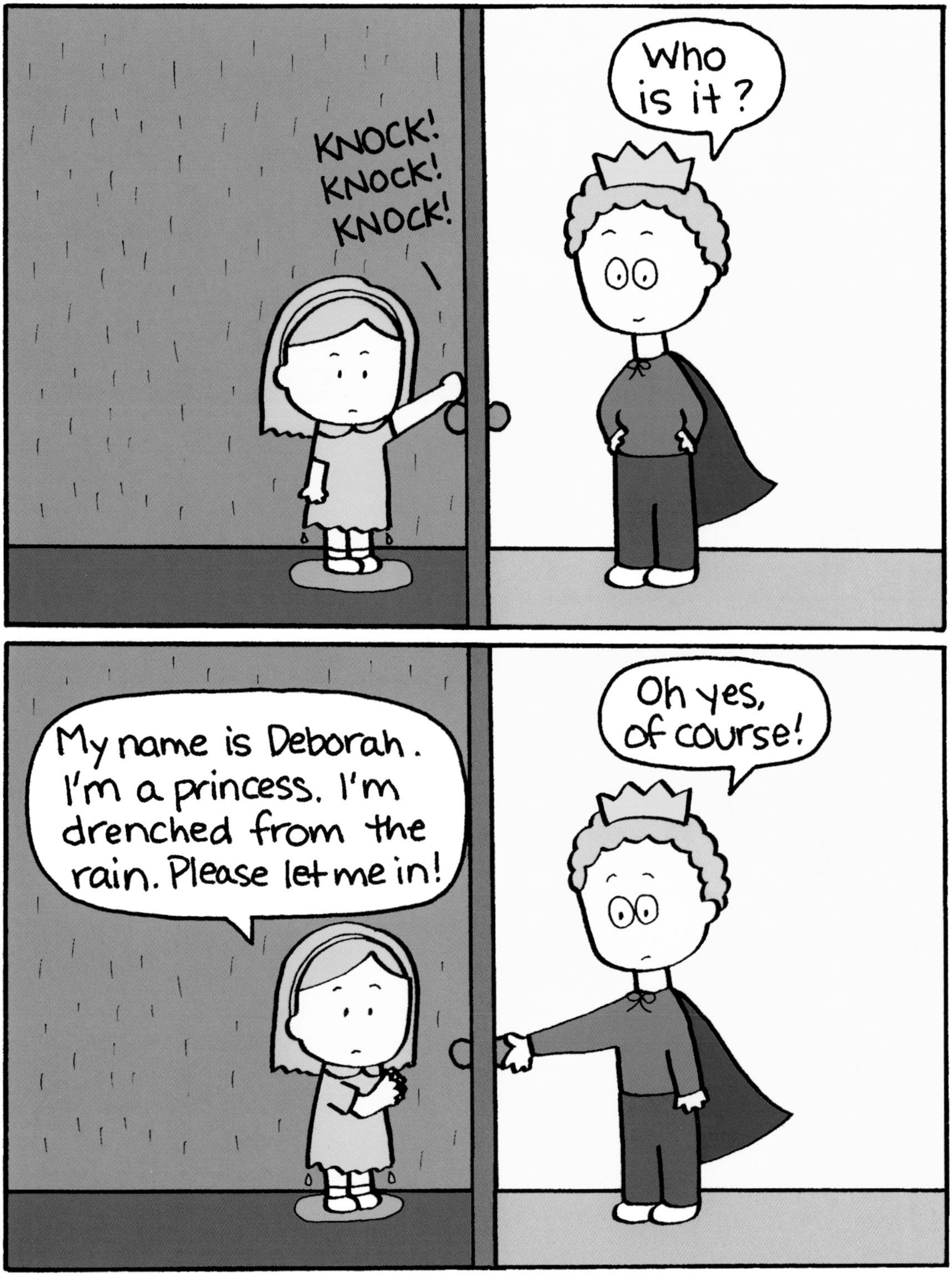
KNOCK!
KNOCK!
KNOCK!
Who is it?
My name is Deborah. I'm a princess. I'm drenched from the rain. Please let me in!
Oh yes, of course!

The prince and the princess were immediately smitten with each other.

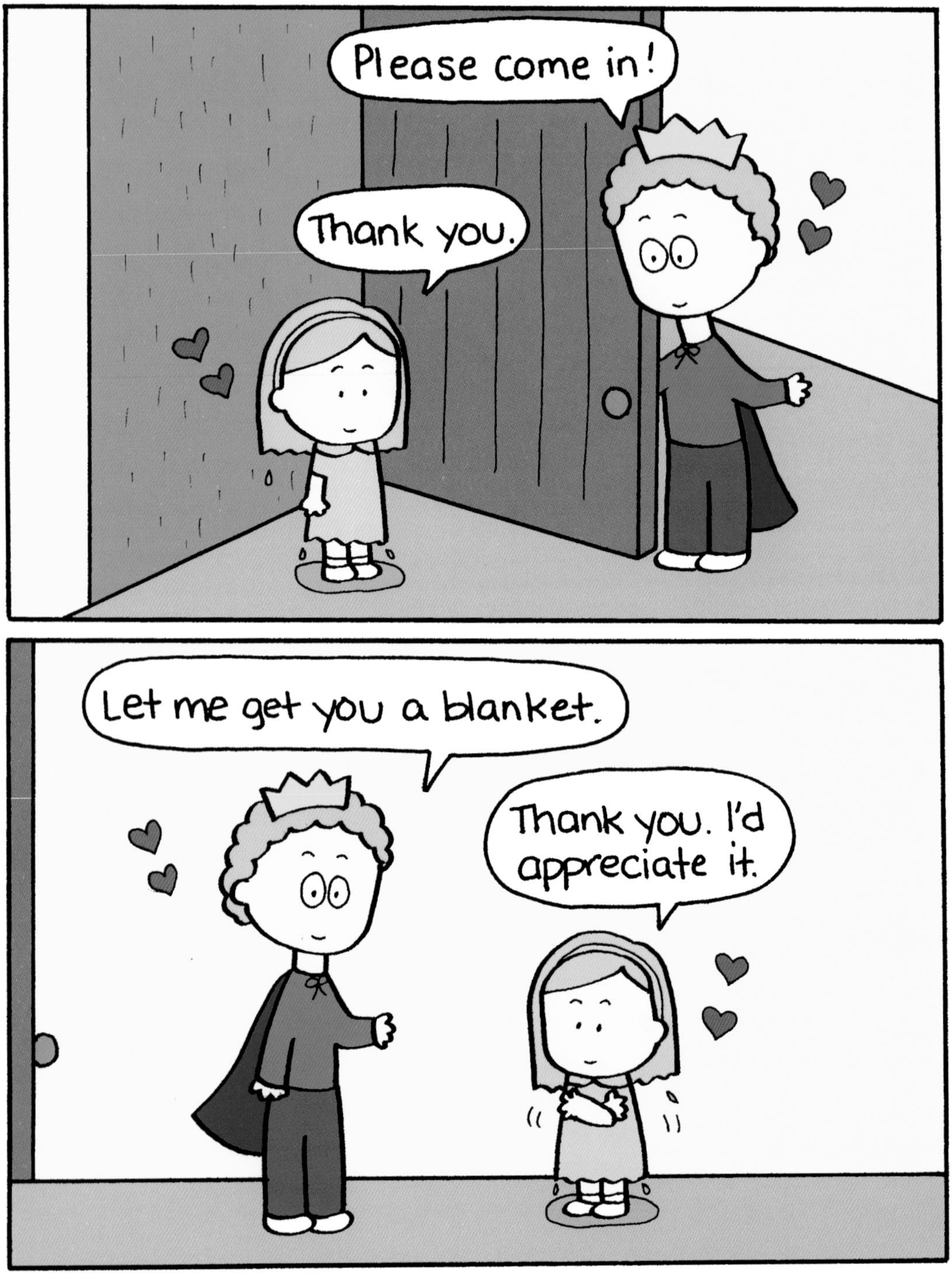
Please come in!
Thank you.
Let me get you a blanket.
Thank you. I'd appreciate it.

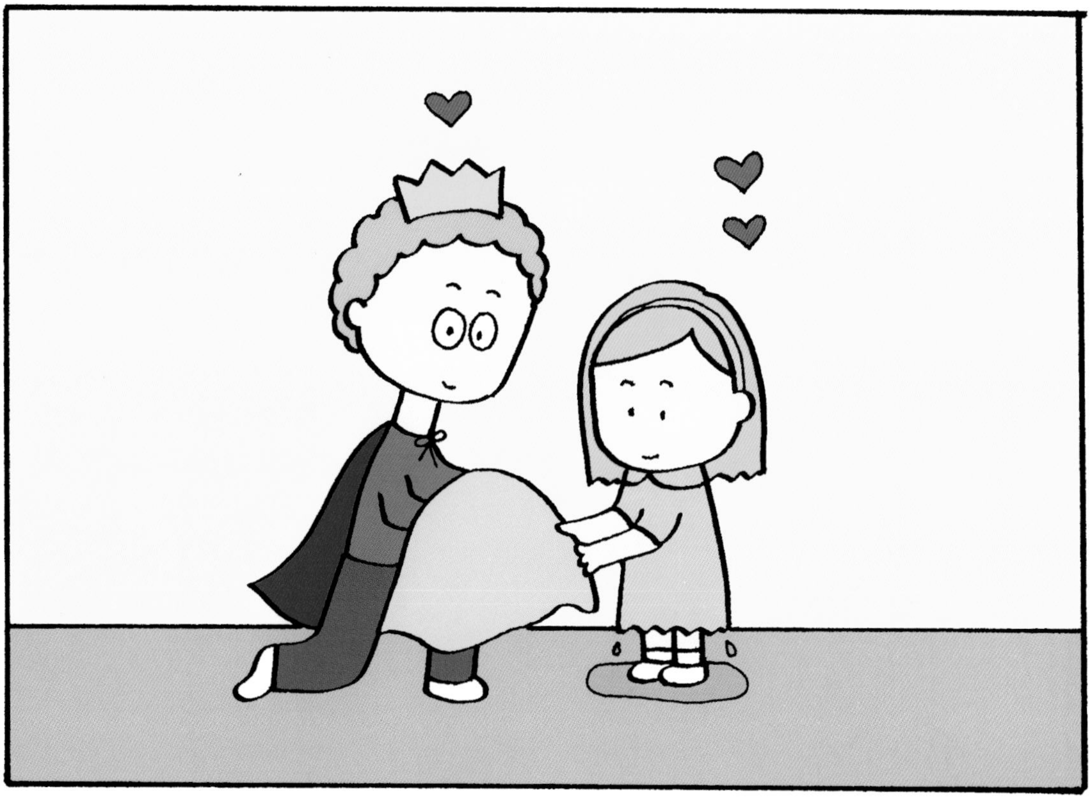

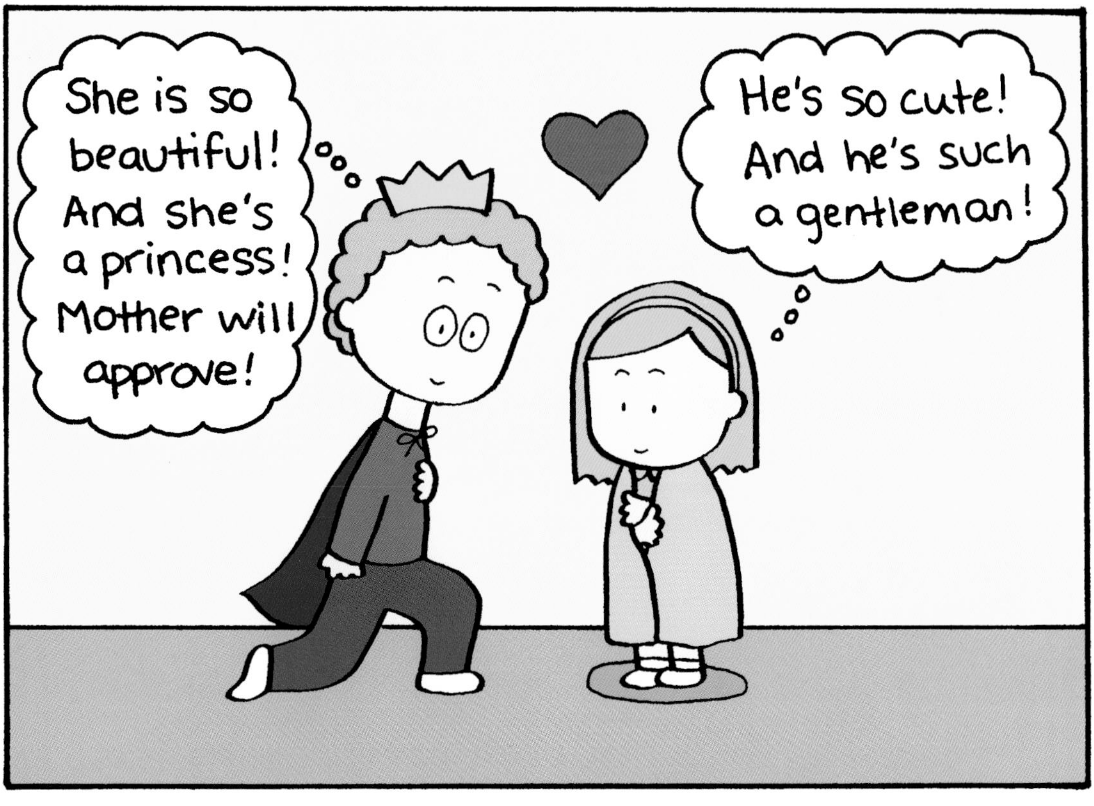
She is so beautiful! And she's a princess! Mother will approve!
He's so cute! And he's such a gentleman!

The prince told his mother about the princess, his newfound love.

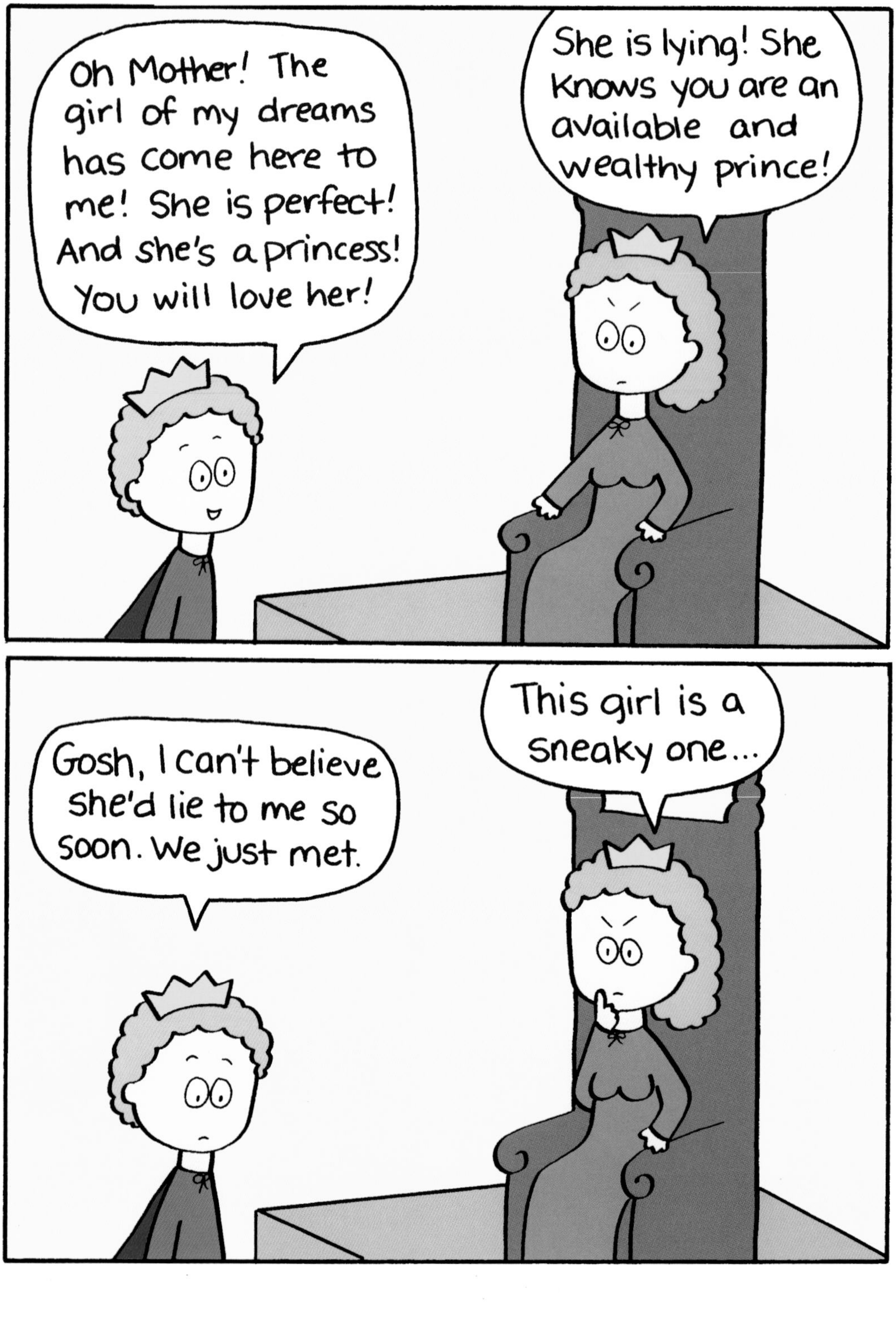
Oh Mother! The girl of my dreams has come here to me! She is perfect! And she's a princess! You will love her!
She is lying! She knows you are an available and wealthy prince!
Gosh, I can't believe she'd lie to me so soon. We just met.
This girl is a sneaky one...

The queen devised a plan to see if the girl really was a true princess.

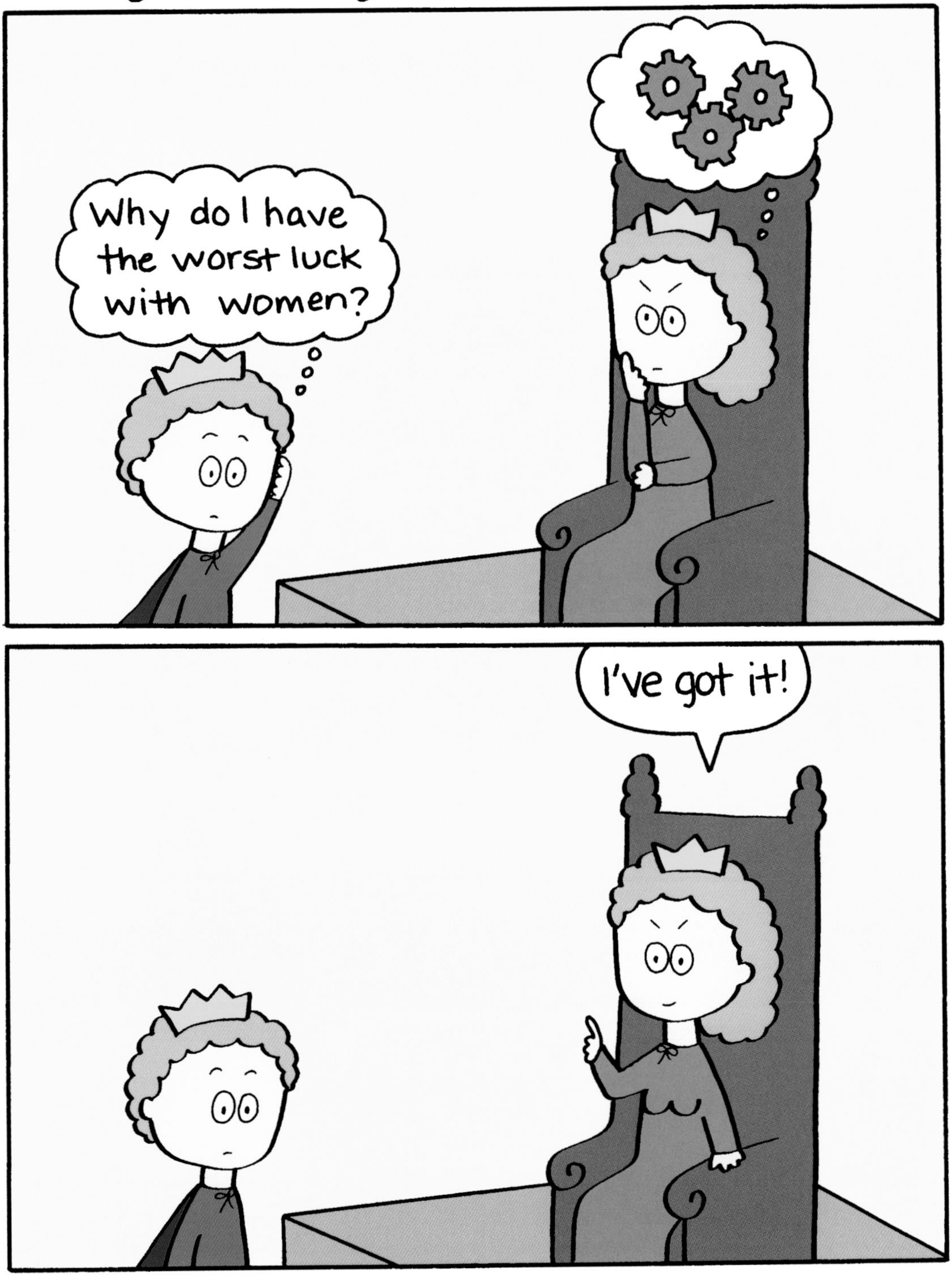
Why do I have the worst luck with women?
I've got it!

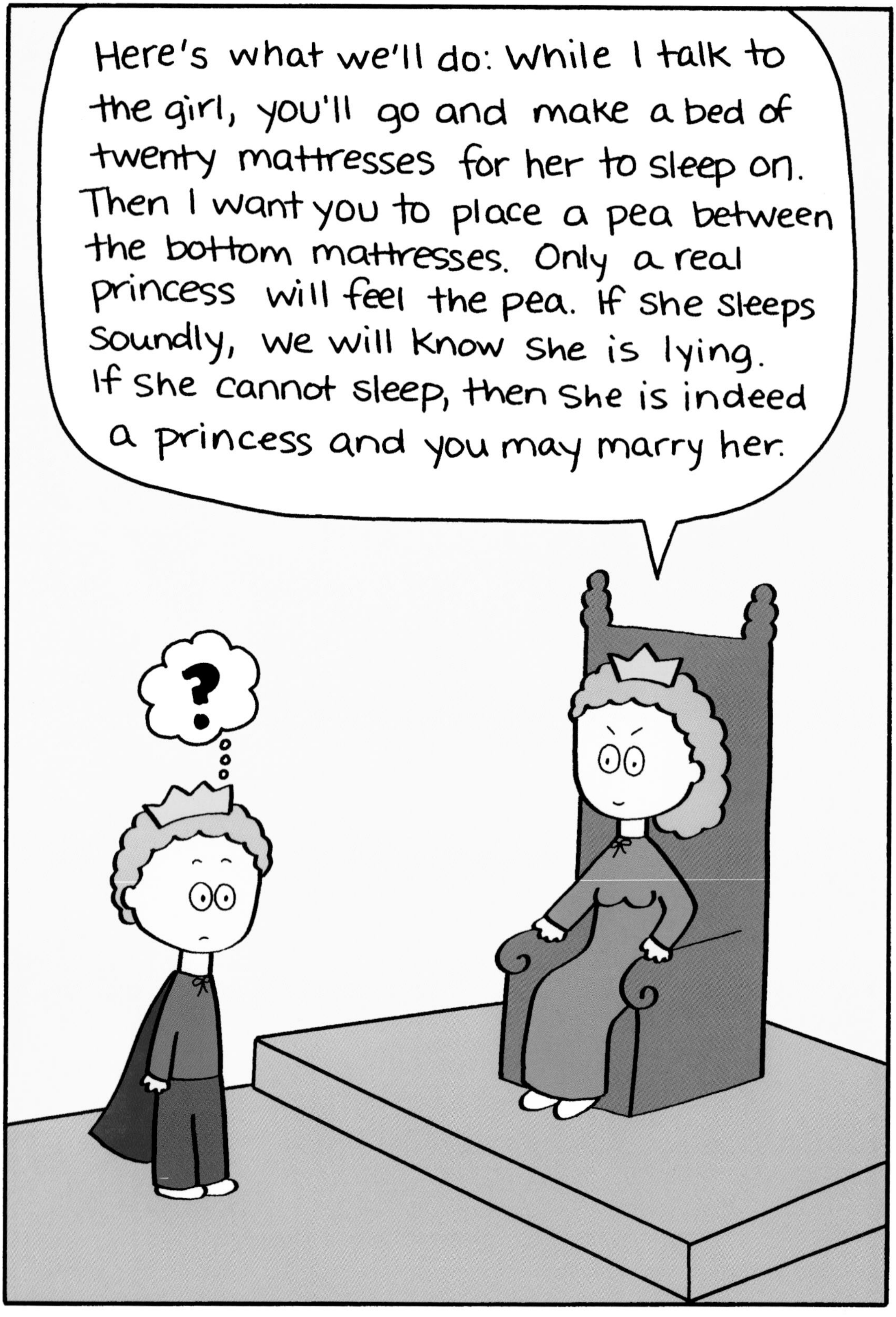
Here's what we'll do: While I talk to the girl, you'll go and make a bed of twenty mattresses for her to sleep on. Then I want you to place a pea between the bottom mattresses. Only a real princess will feel the pea. If she sleeps soundly, we will know she is lying. If she cannot sleep, then she is indeed a princess and you may marry her.
?

The queen went to speak to the girl.

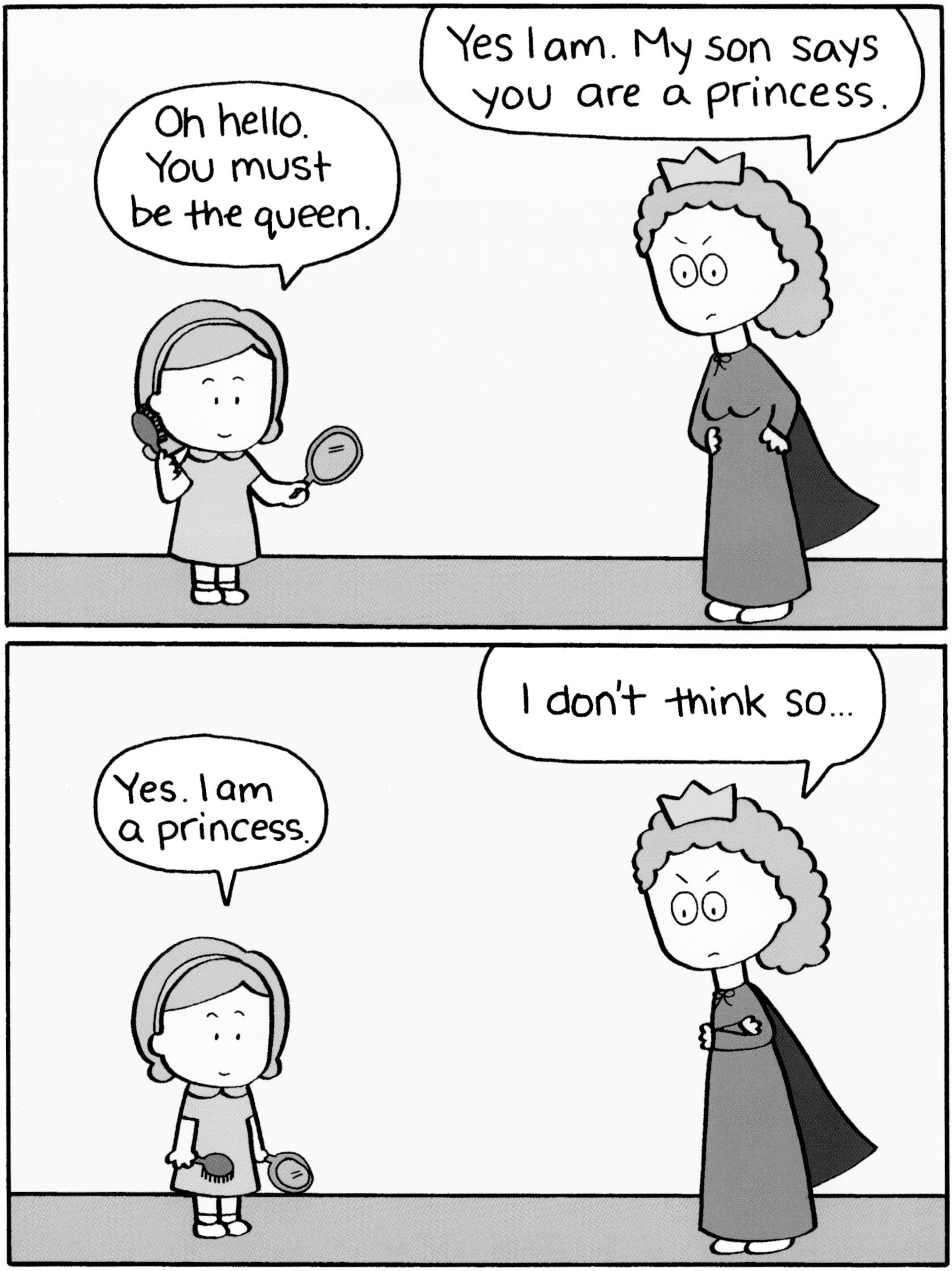
Oh hello. You must be the queen.
Yes I am. My son says you are a princess.
Yes. I am a princess.
I don't think so...

The prince made her bed and placed a pea underneath the mattresses.

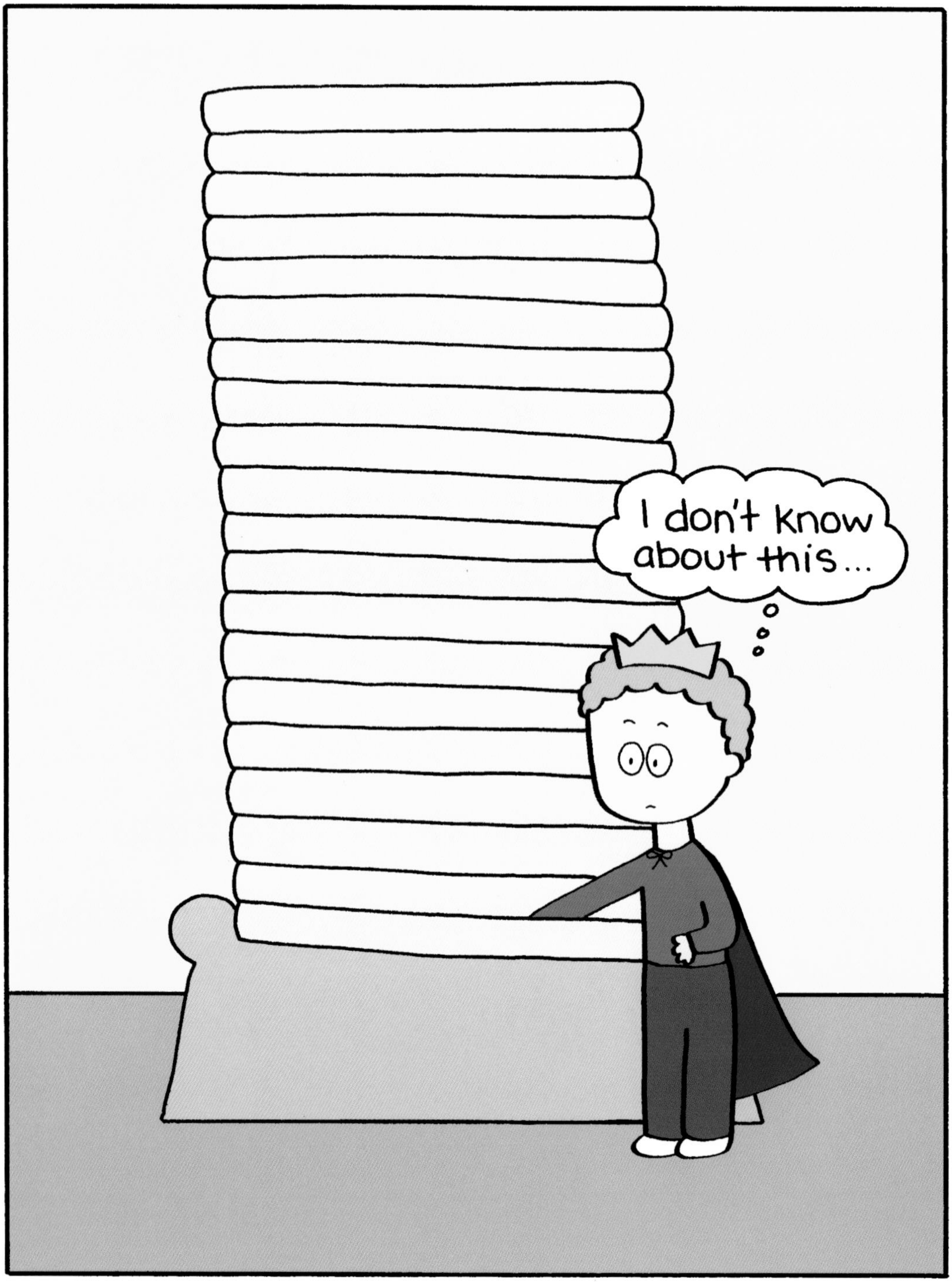
I don't know about this...

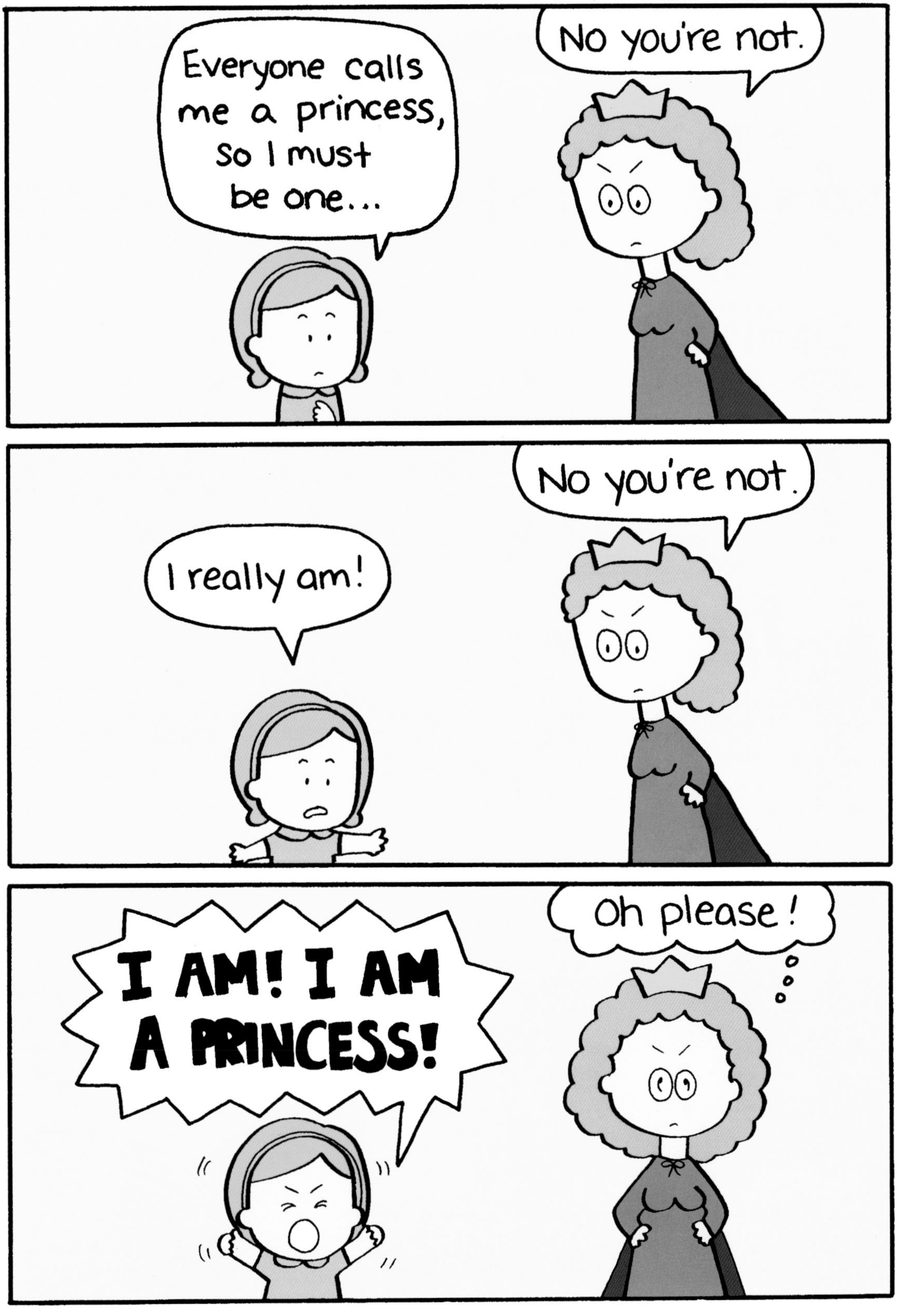
Everyone calls me a princess, so I must be one...
No you're not.
I really am!
No you're not.
I AM! I AM A PRINCESS!
Oh please!

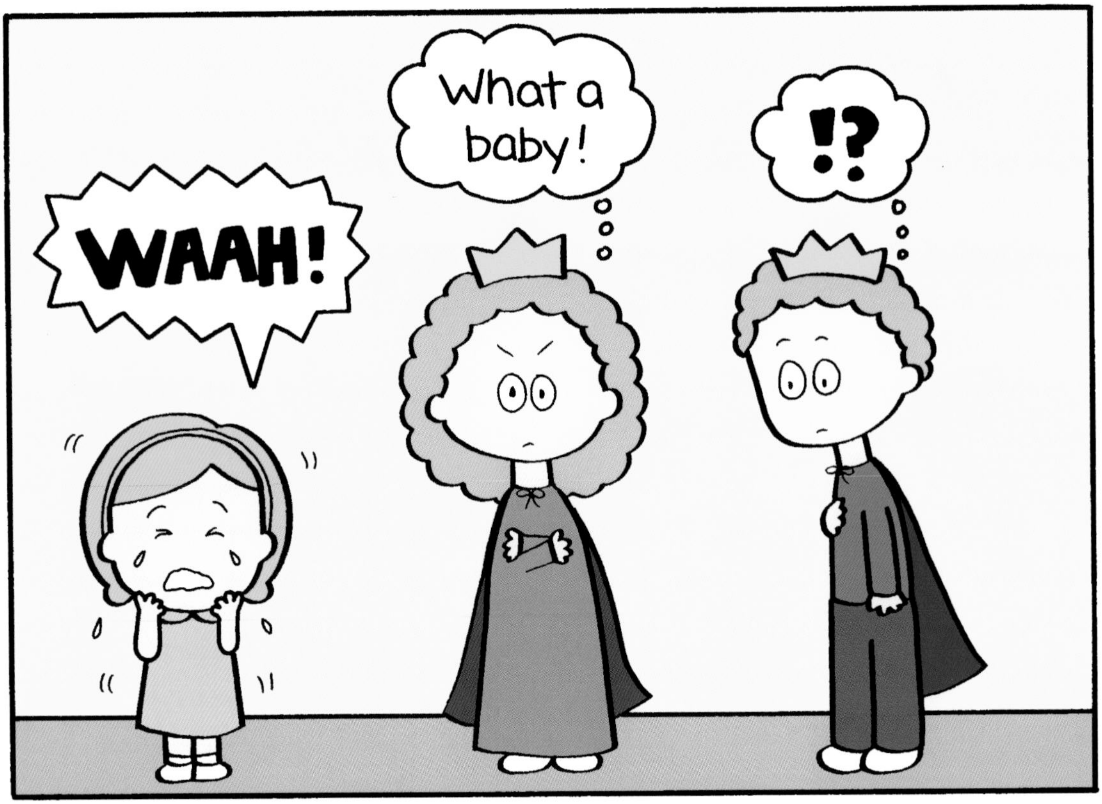
WAAH!
What a baby!
!?

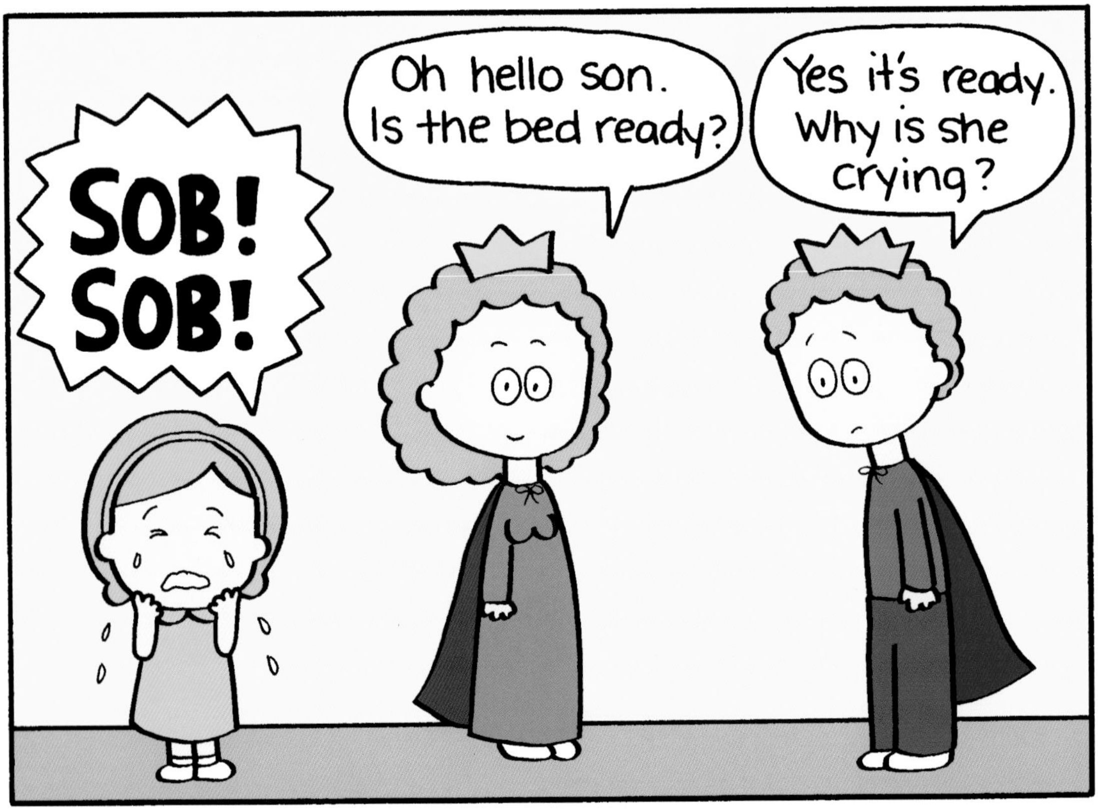
SOB! SOB!
Oh hello son. Is the bed ready?
Yes it's ready. Why is she crying?

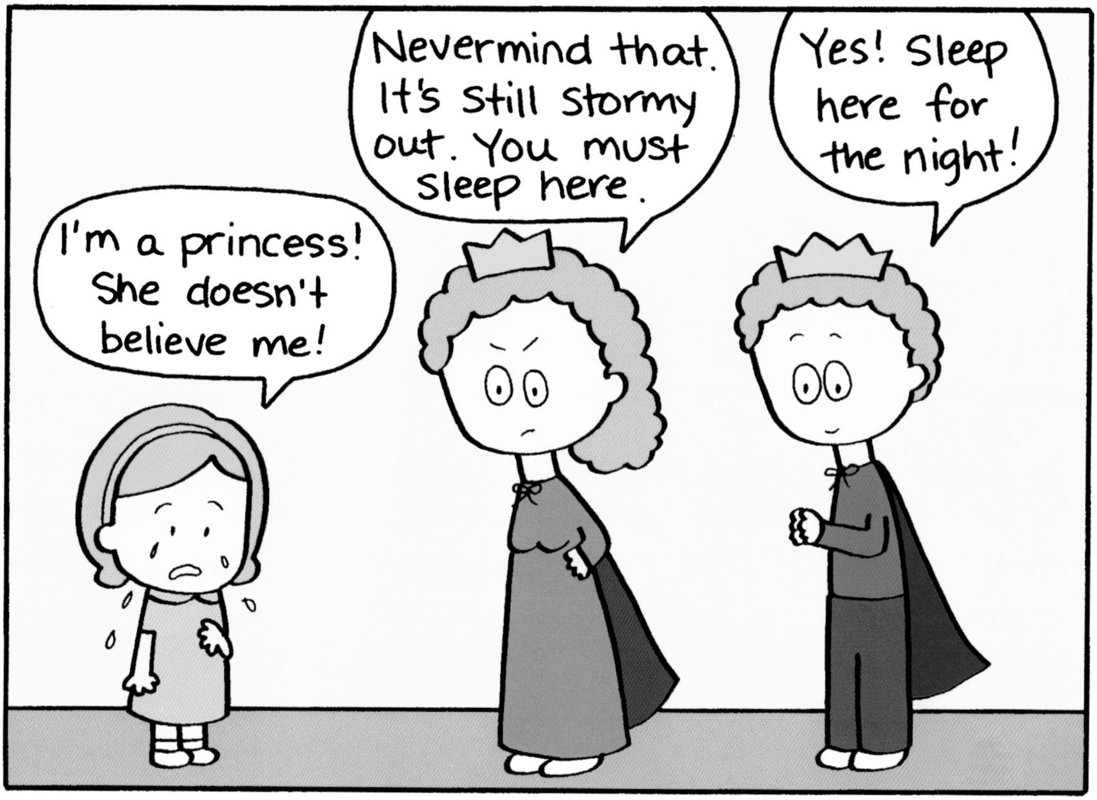
I'm a princess! She doesn't believe me!
Nevermind that. It's still stormy out. You must sleep here.
Yes! Sleep here for the night!

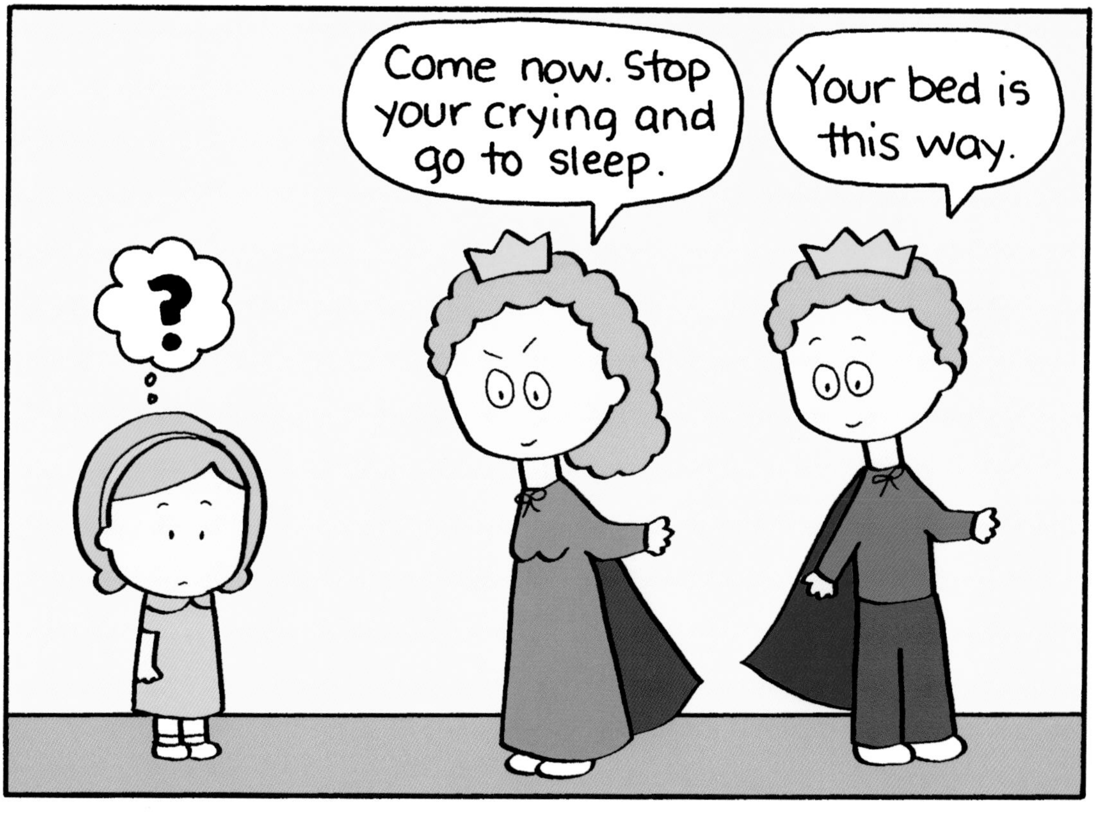
?
Come now. Stop your crying and go to sleep.
Your bed is this way.

The prince showed her to her bed.

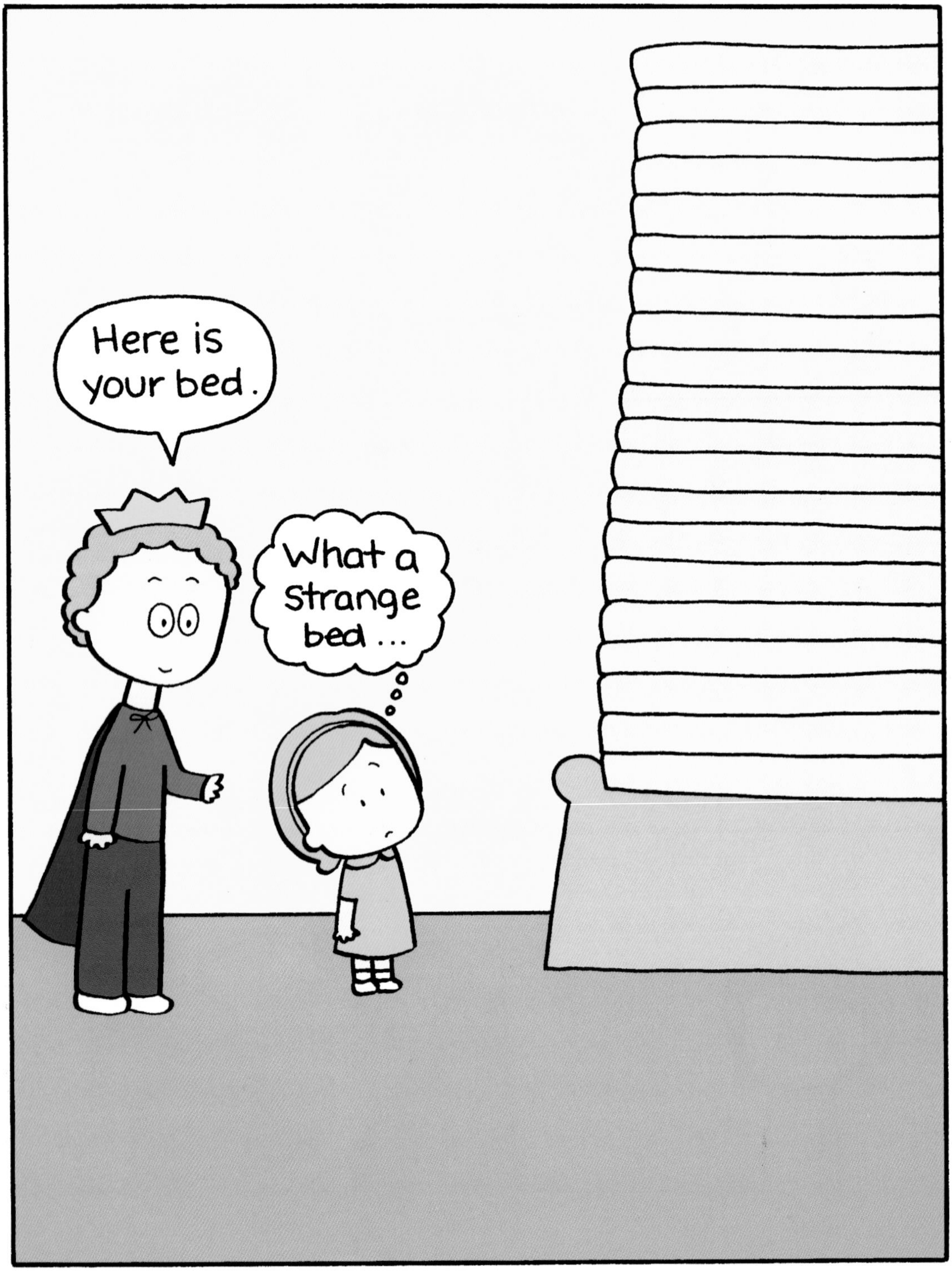

Here is your bed.
What a strange bed...

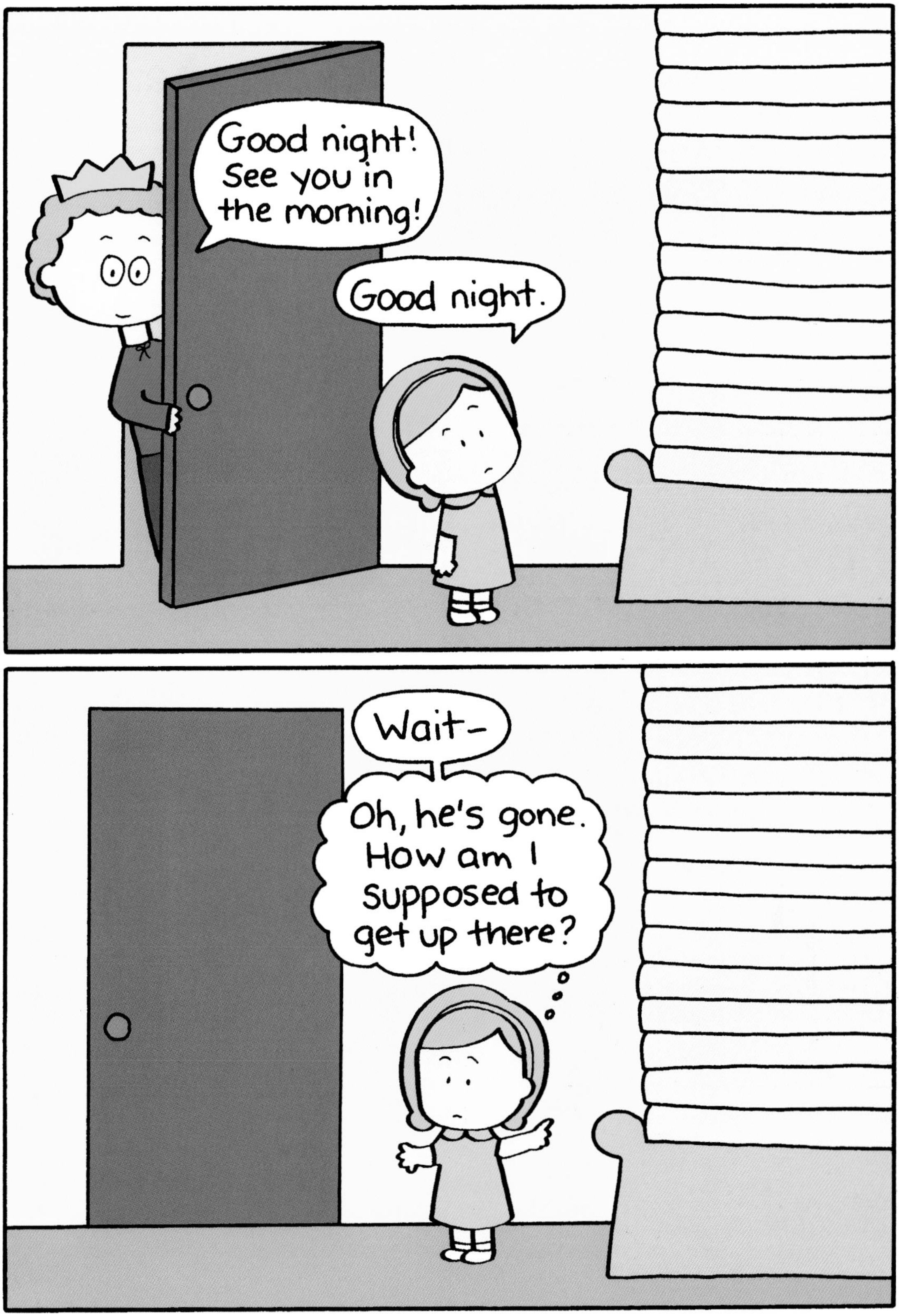
Good night! See you in the morning!
Good night.
Wait-
Oh, he's gone. How am I supposed to get up there?

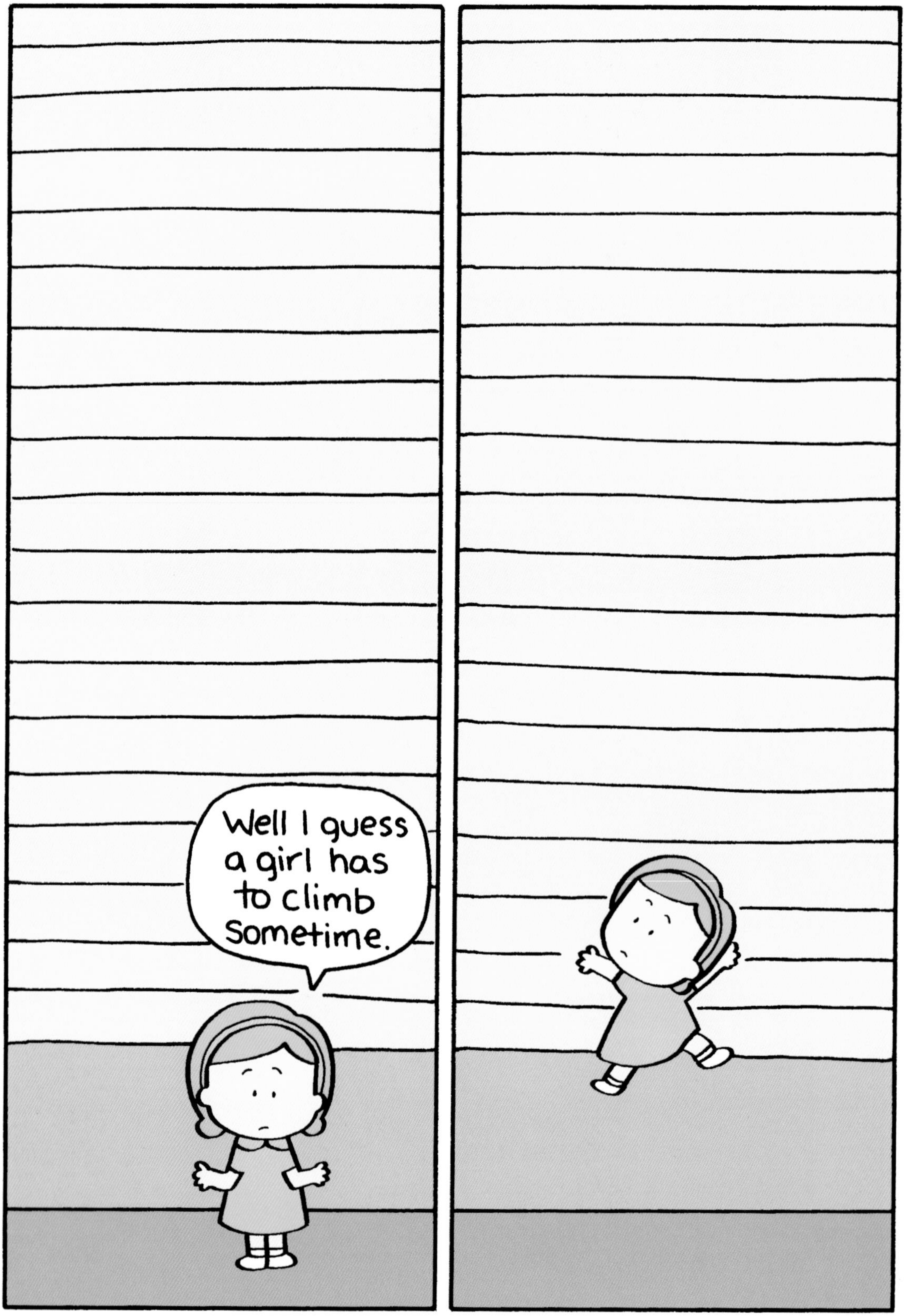
Well I guess a girl has to climb sometime.

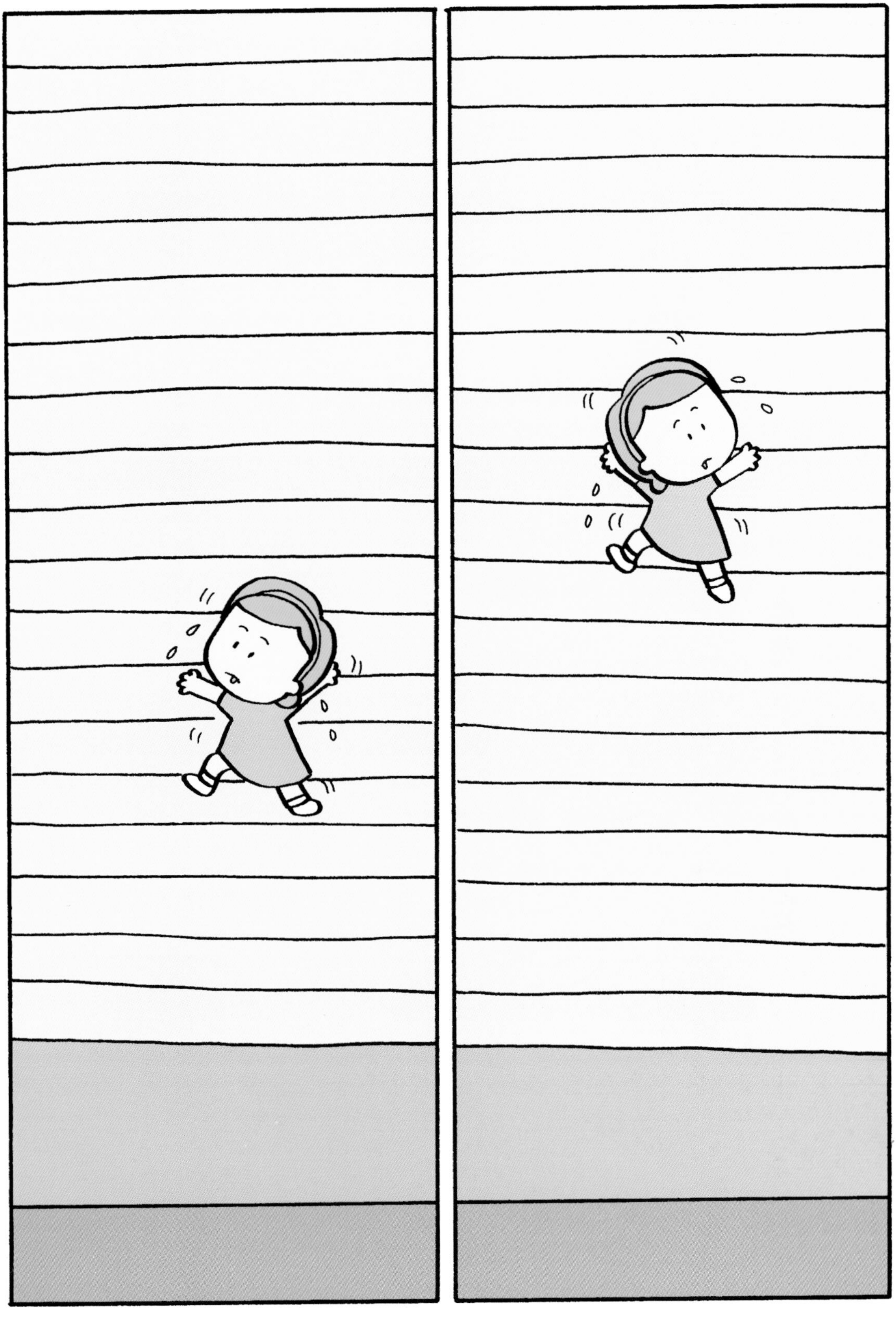

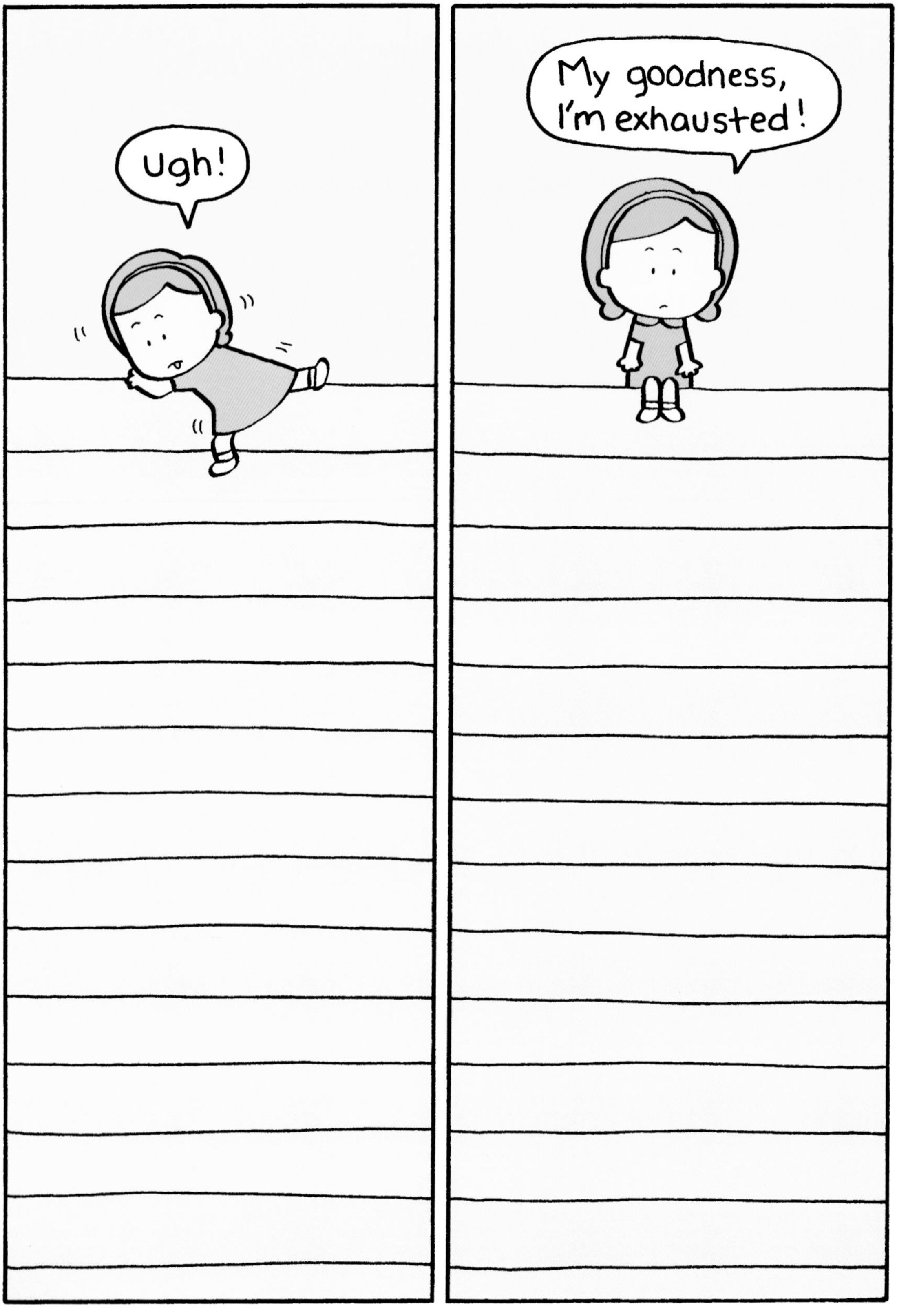
Ugh!
My goodness, I'm exhausted!

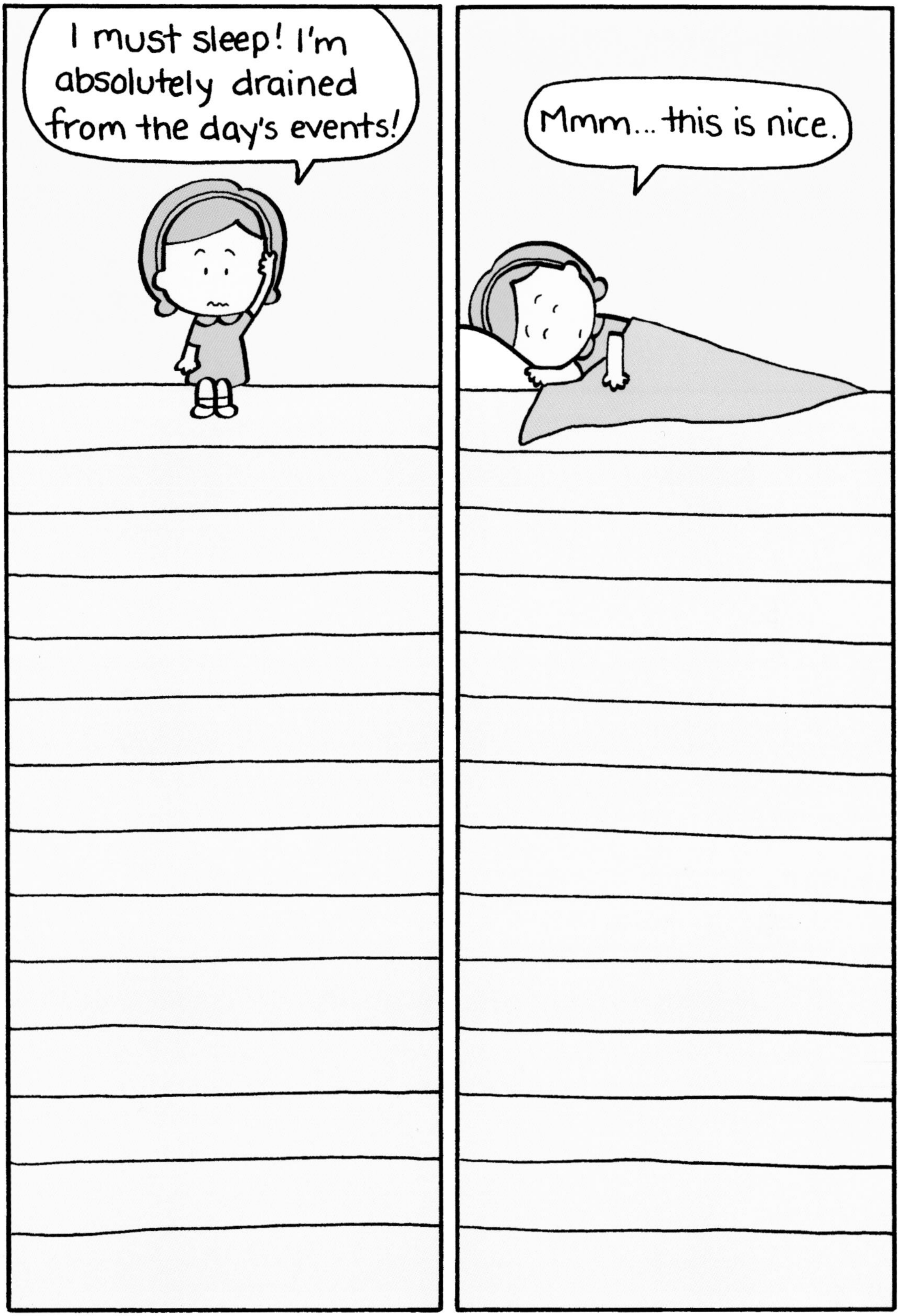
I must sleep! I'm absolutely drained from the day's events!
Mmm... this is nice.

The princess tossed and turned.

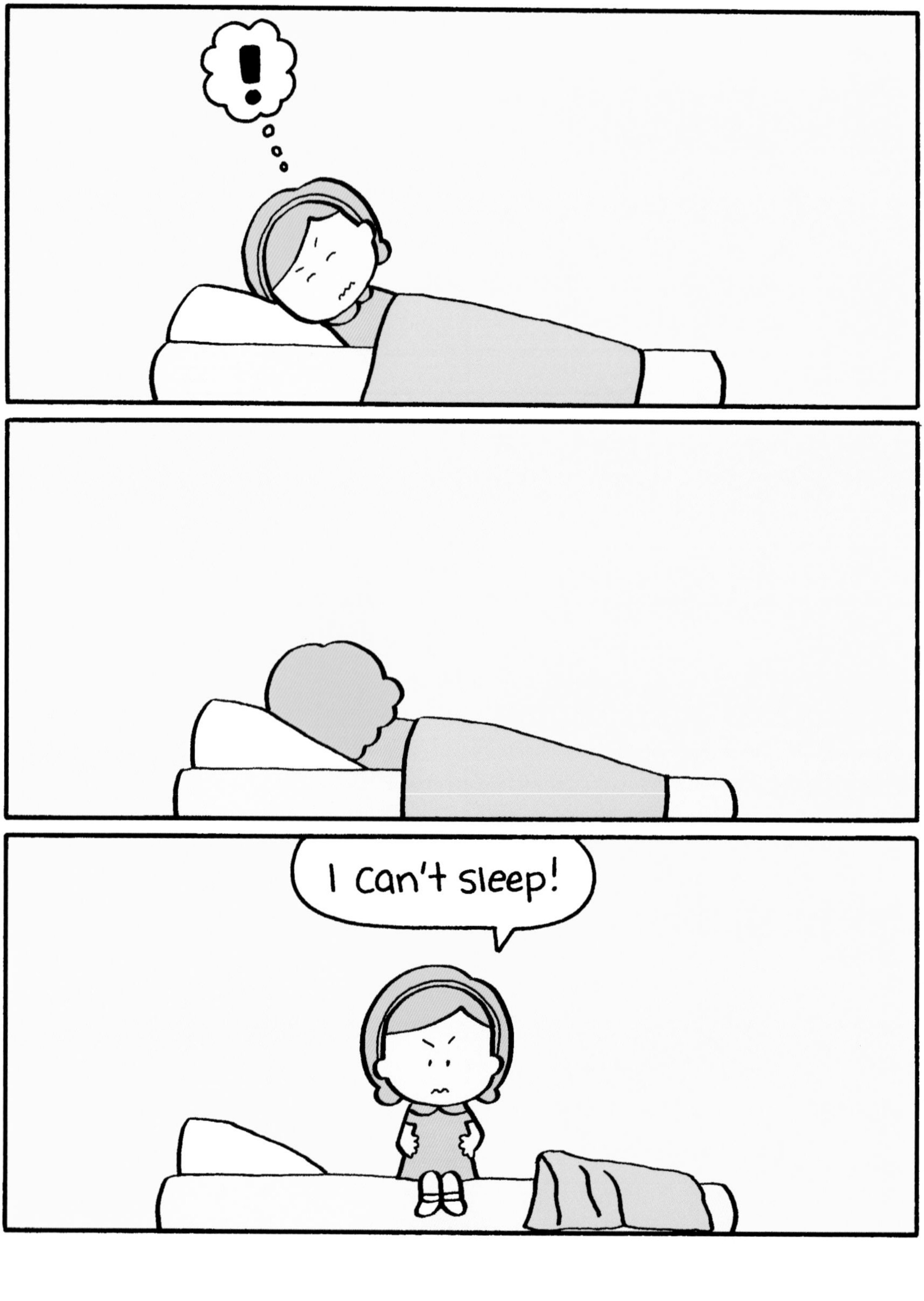
!
I can't sleep!

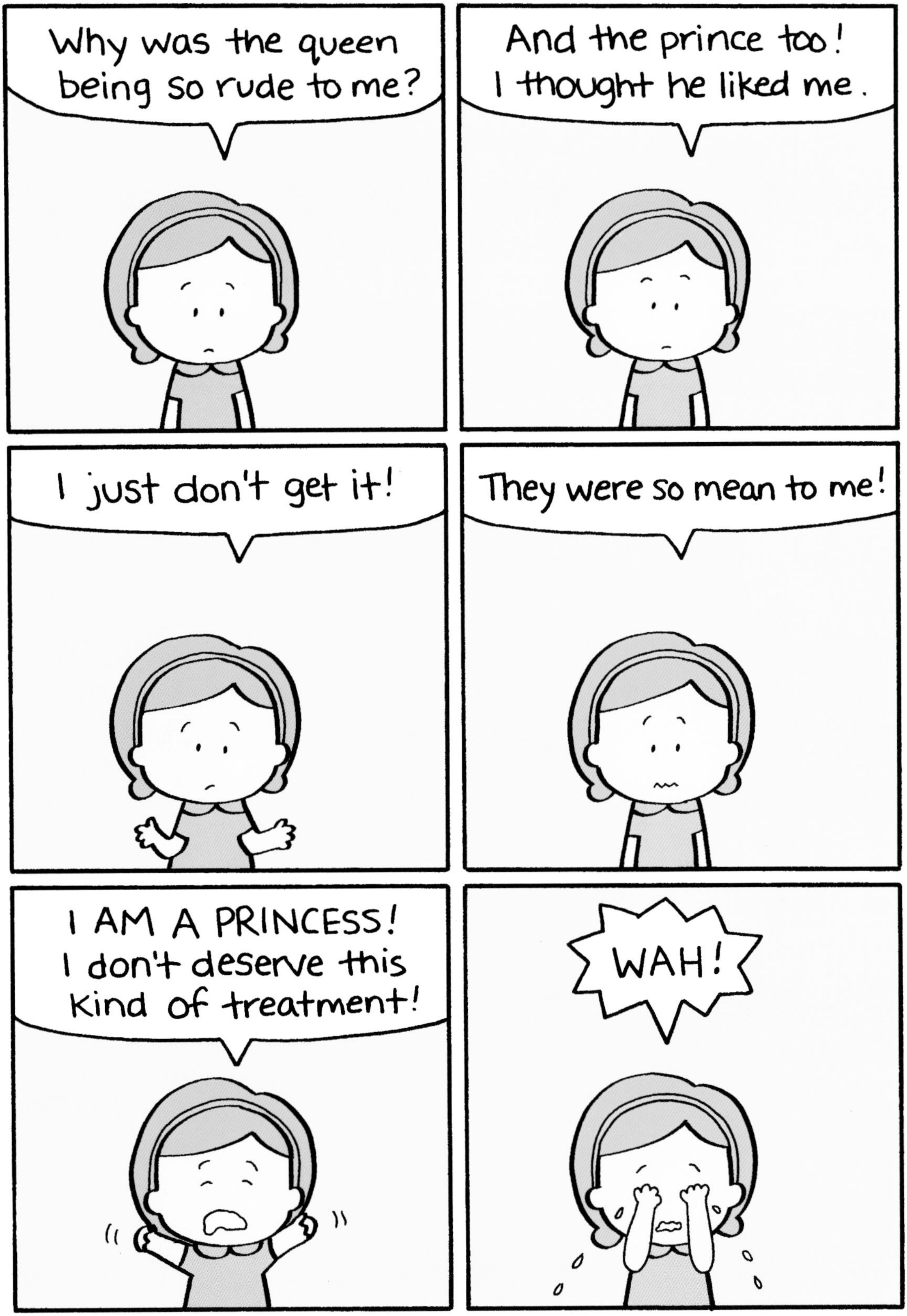
Why was the queen being so rude to me?
And the prince too! I thought he liked me.
I just don't get it!
They were so mean to me!
I AM A PRINCESS! I don't deserve this kind of treatment!
WAH!

The princess stayed up all night.

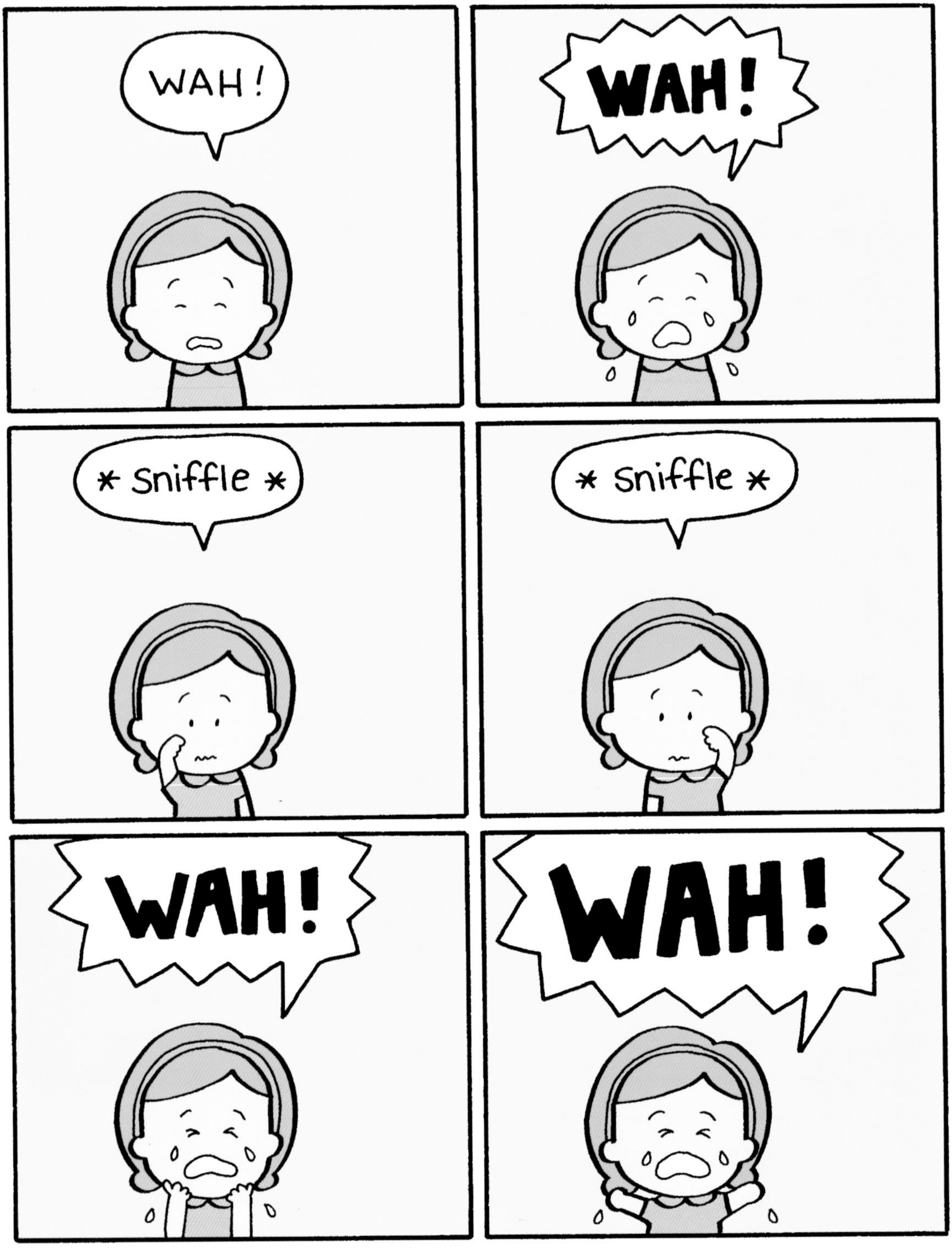
WAH!
WAH!
* sniffle *
* sniffle *
WAH!
WAH!

When morning broke, the prince and the queen went to the girl's room.

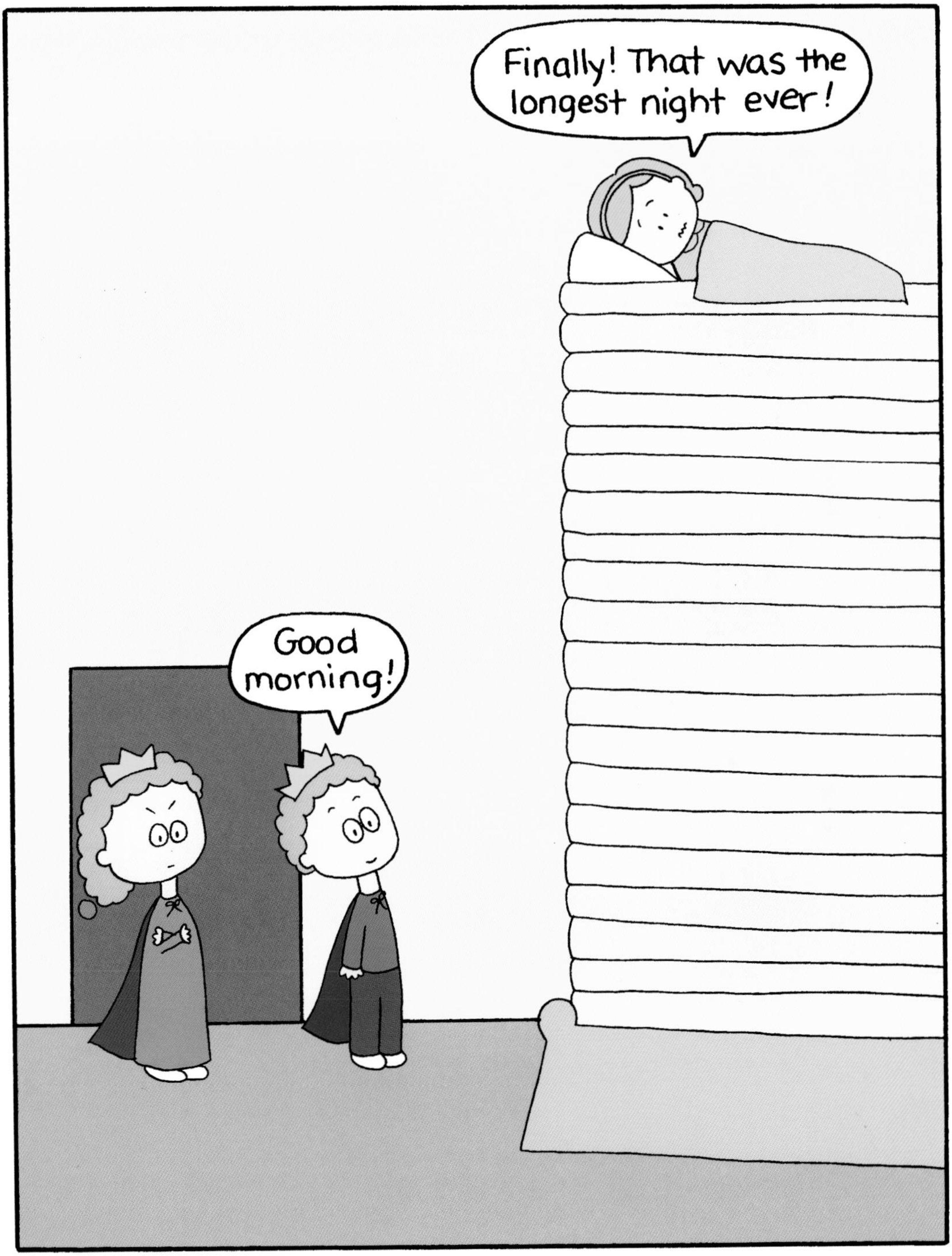
Finally! That was the longest night ever!
Good morning!

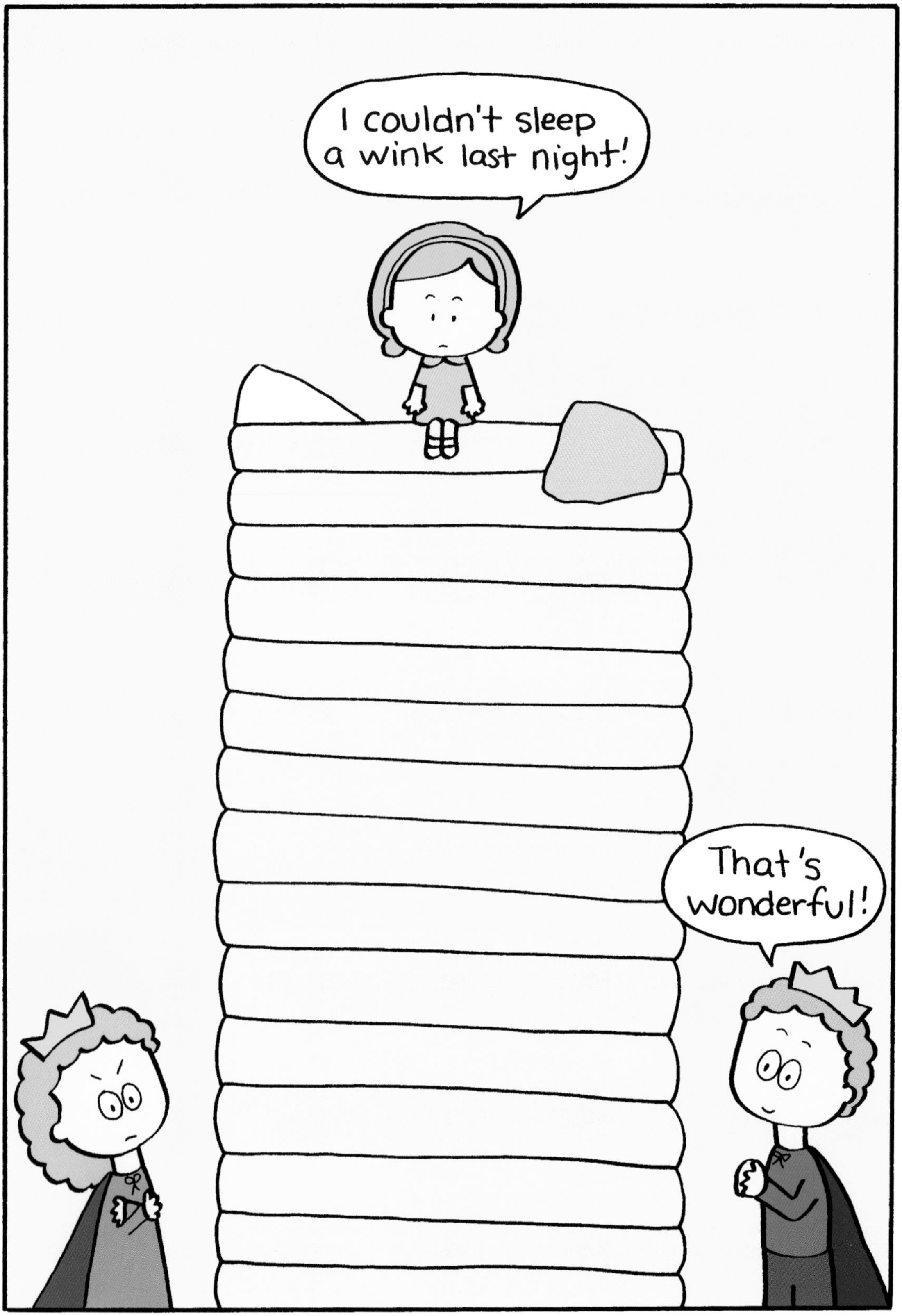
I couldn't sleep a wink last night!
That's wonderful!

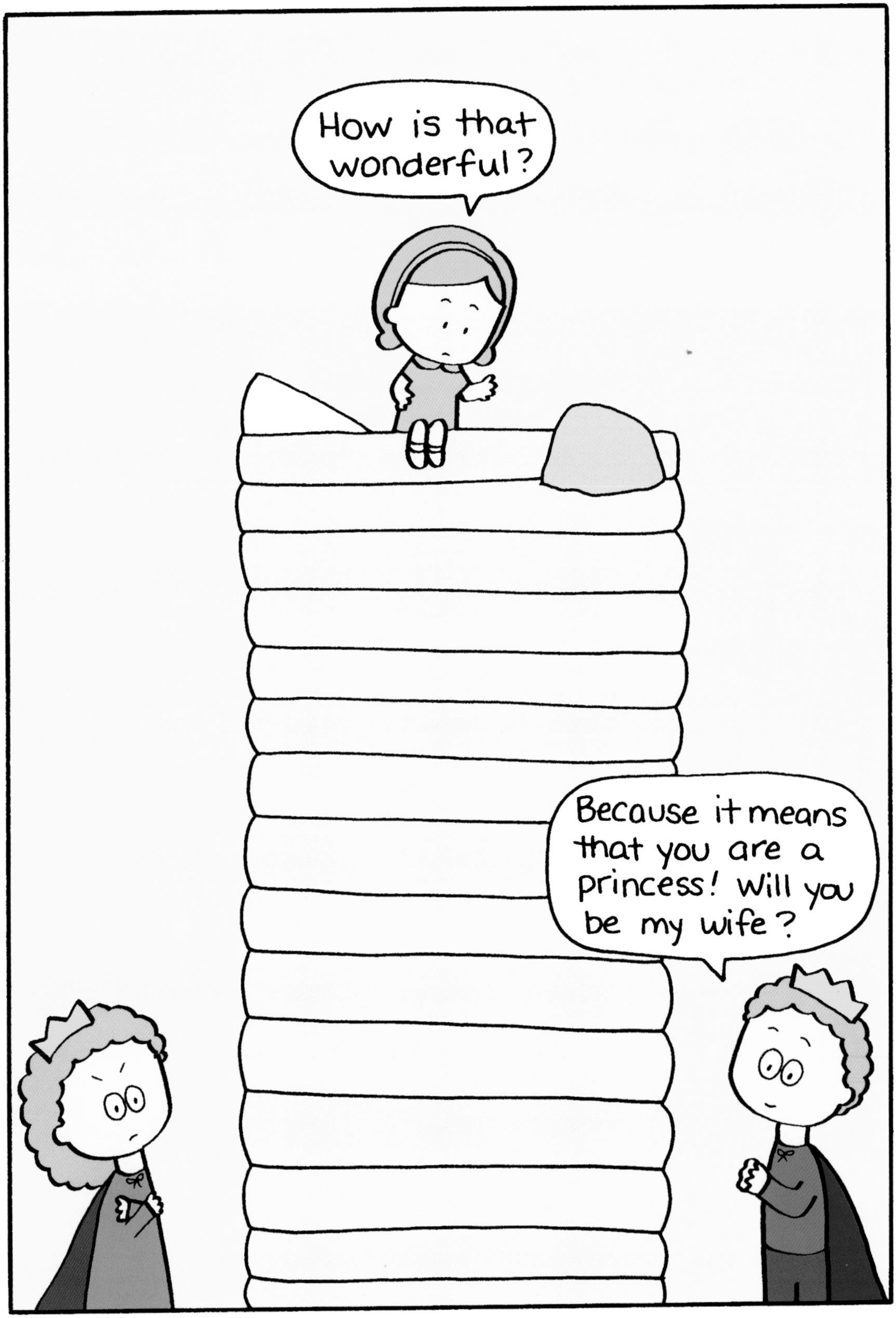
How is that wonderful?
Because it means that you are a princess! Will you be my wife?

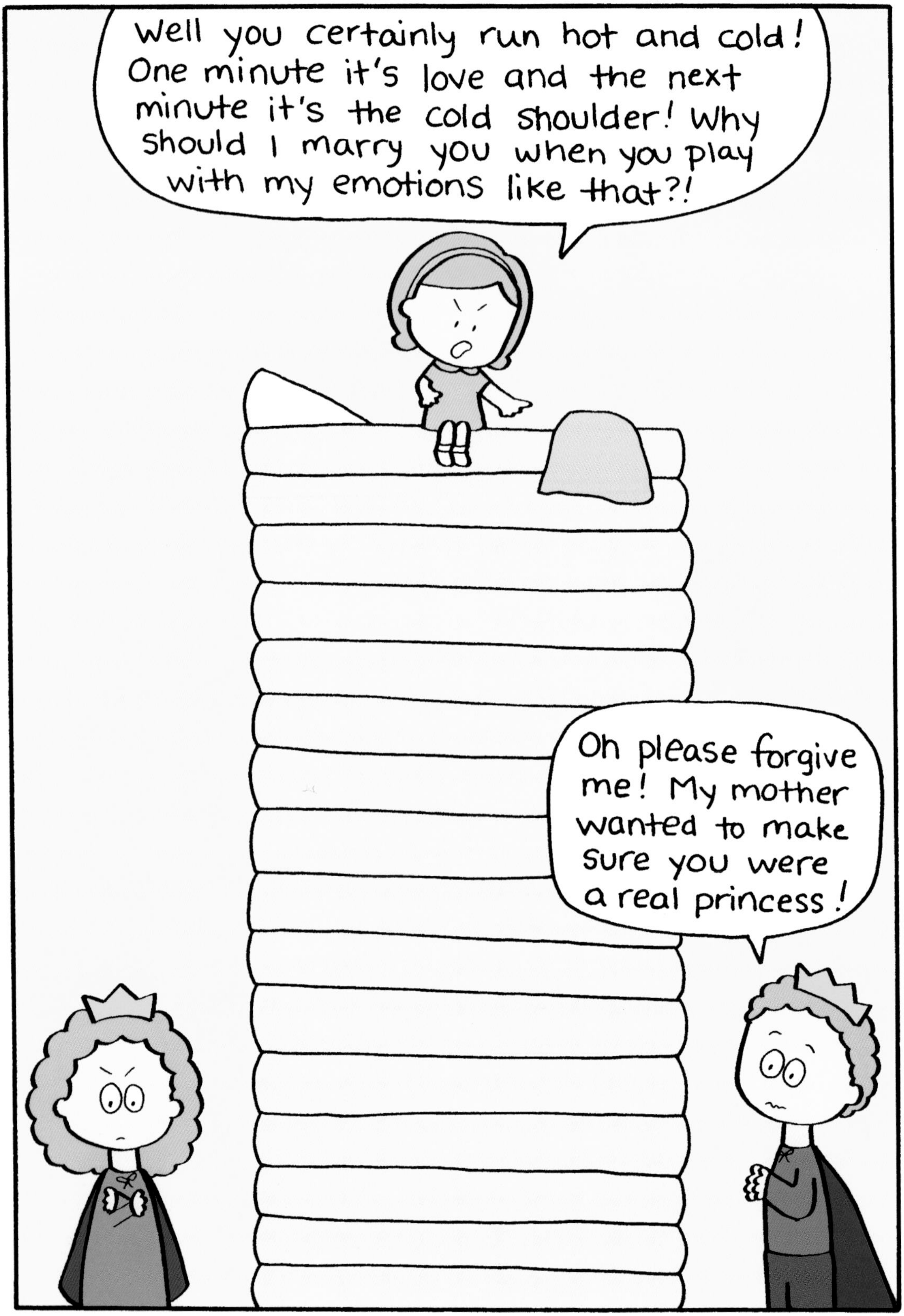
Well you certainly run hot and cold! One minute it's love and the next minute it's the cold shoulder! Why should I marry you when you play with my emotions like that?!
Oh please forgive me! My mother wanted to make sure you were a real princess!

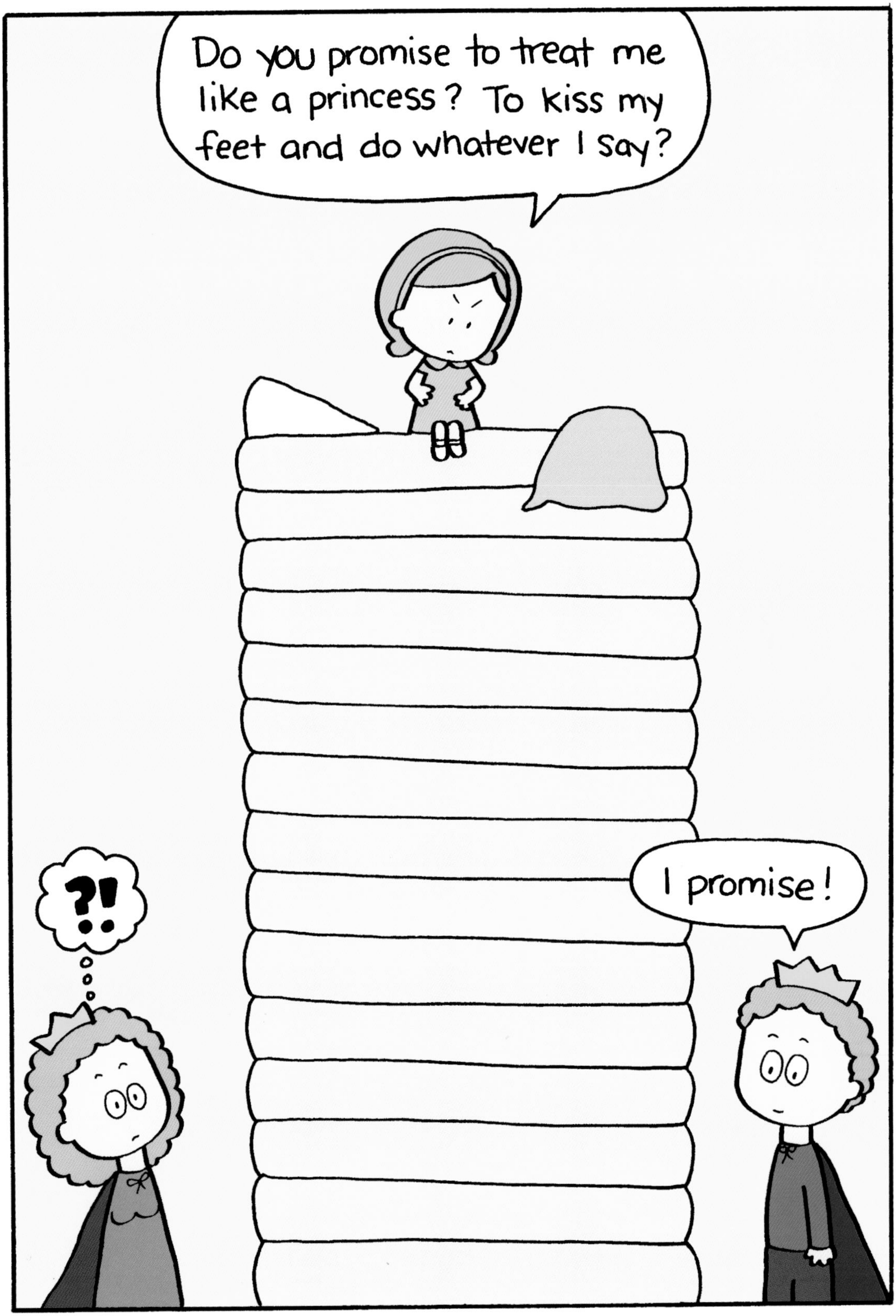
Do you promise to treat me like a princess? To kiss my feet and do whatever I say?
?!
I promise!

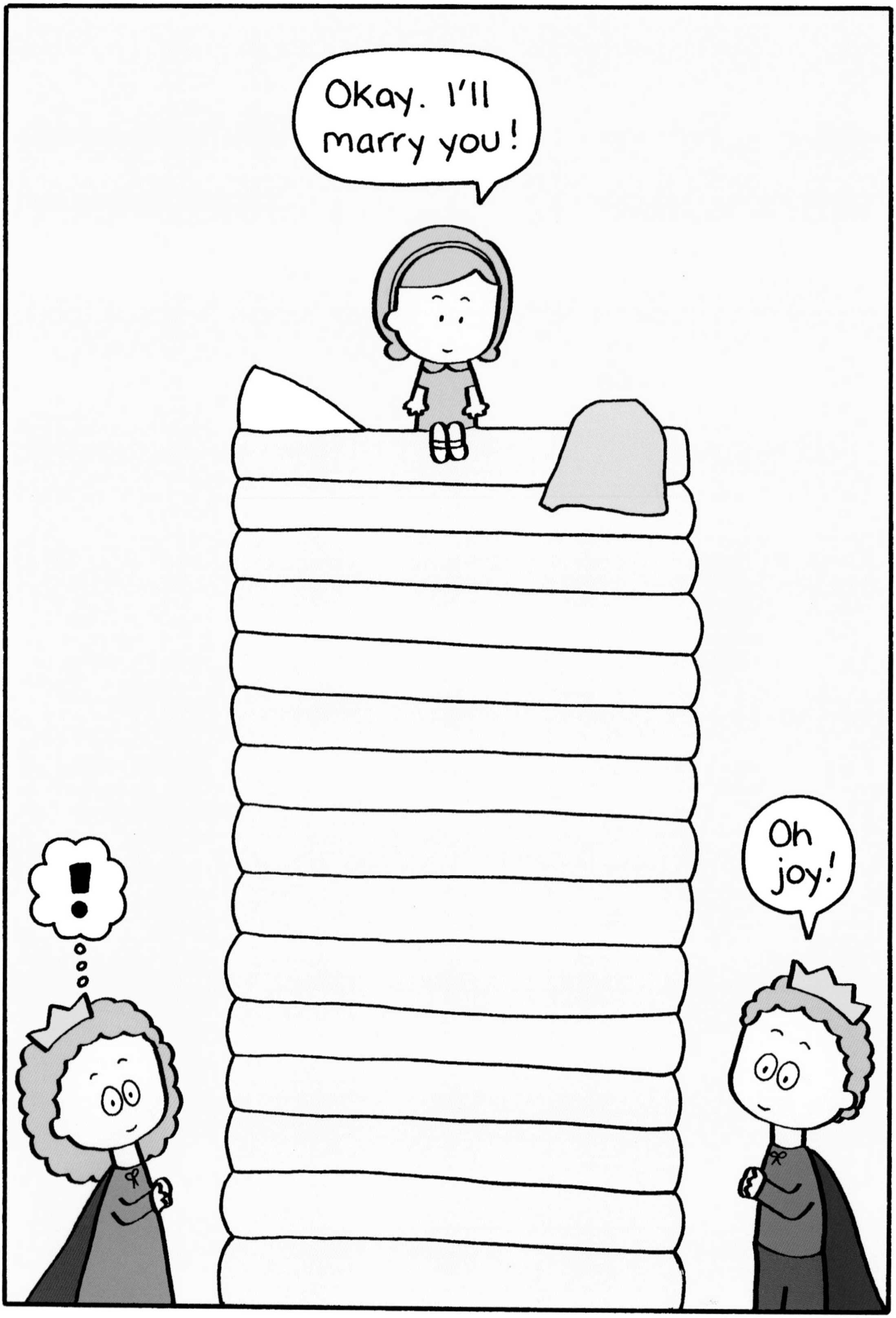
Okay. I'll marry you!
!
Oh joy!

The prince and the princess married.

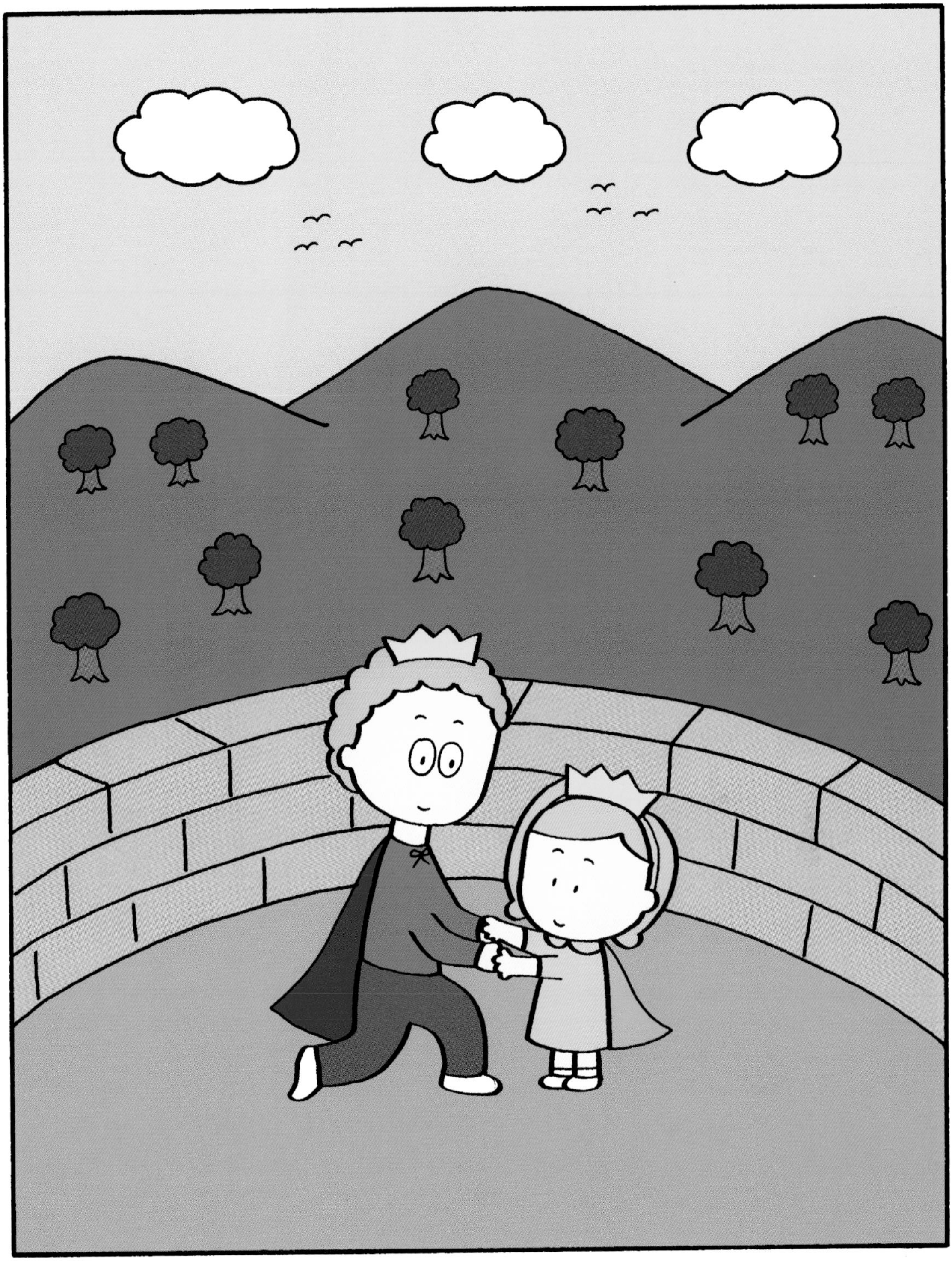

And they all lived happily ever after!

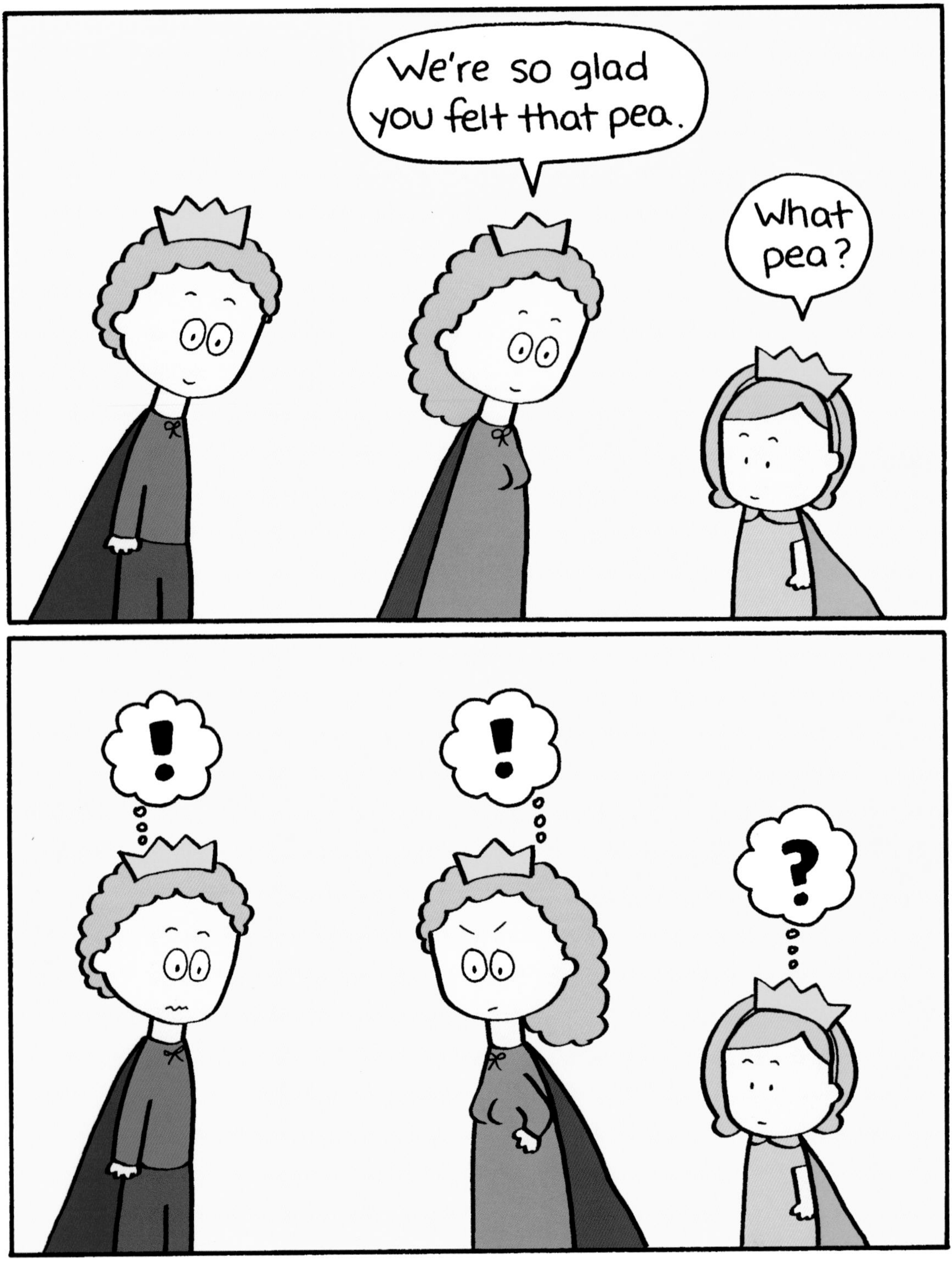
We're so glad you felt that pea.
What pea?
!
!
?

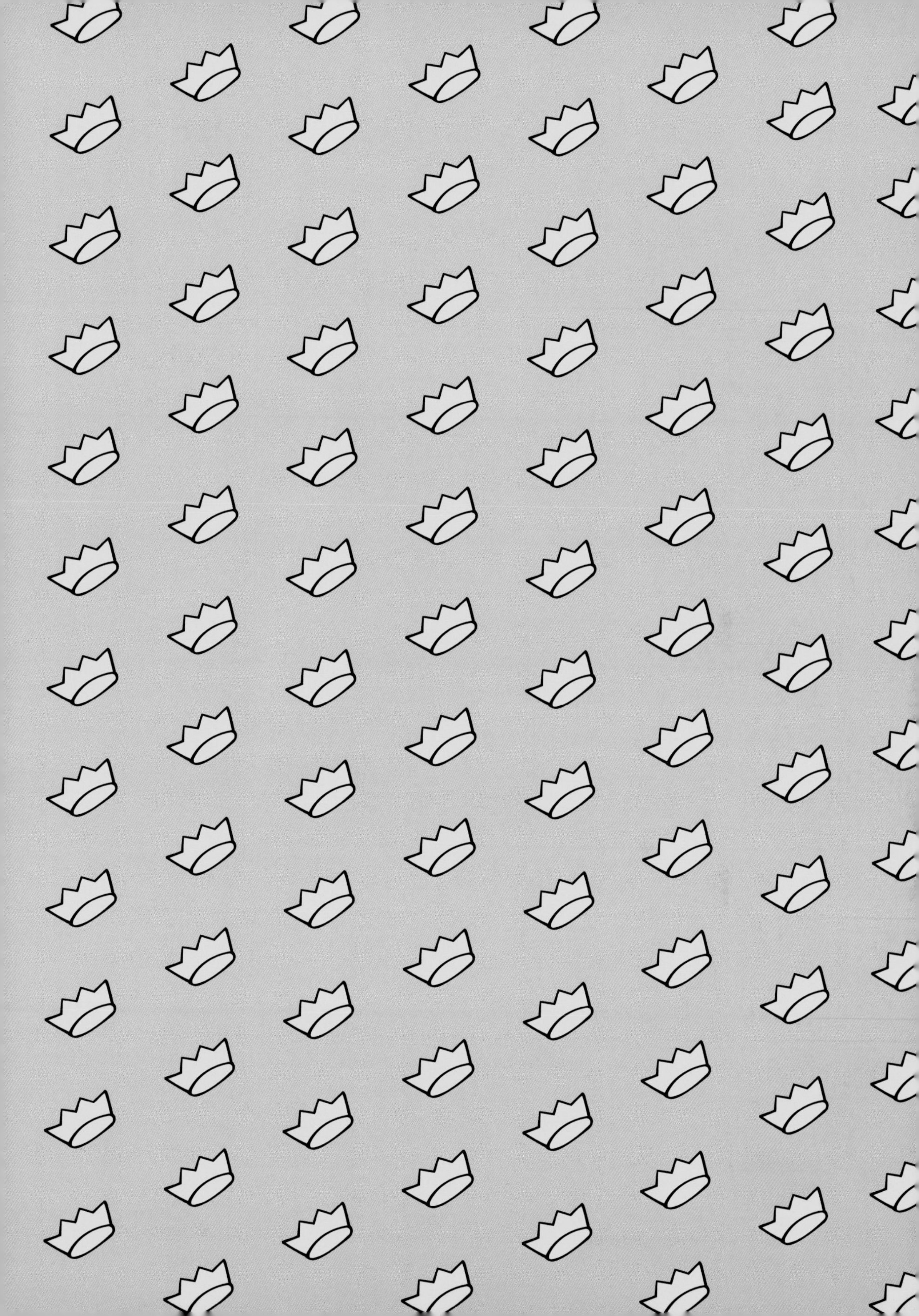

an ANGRY LITTLE GIRL'S FAIRY TALE

He's No Beauty in the Least
?!

Starring

?!

Maria the "Crazy Little Latina"

Once upon a time, a rich merchant lost his land and fortune.

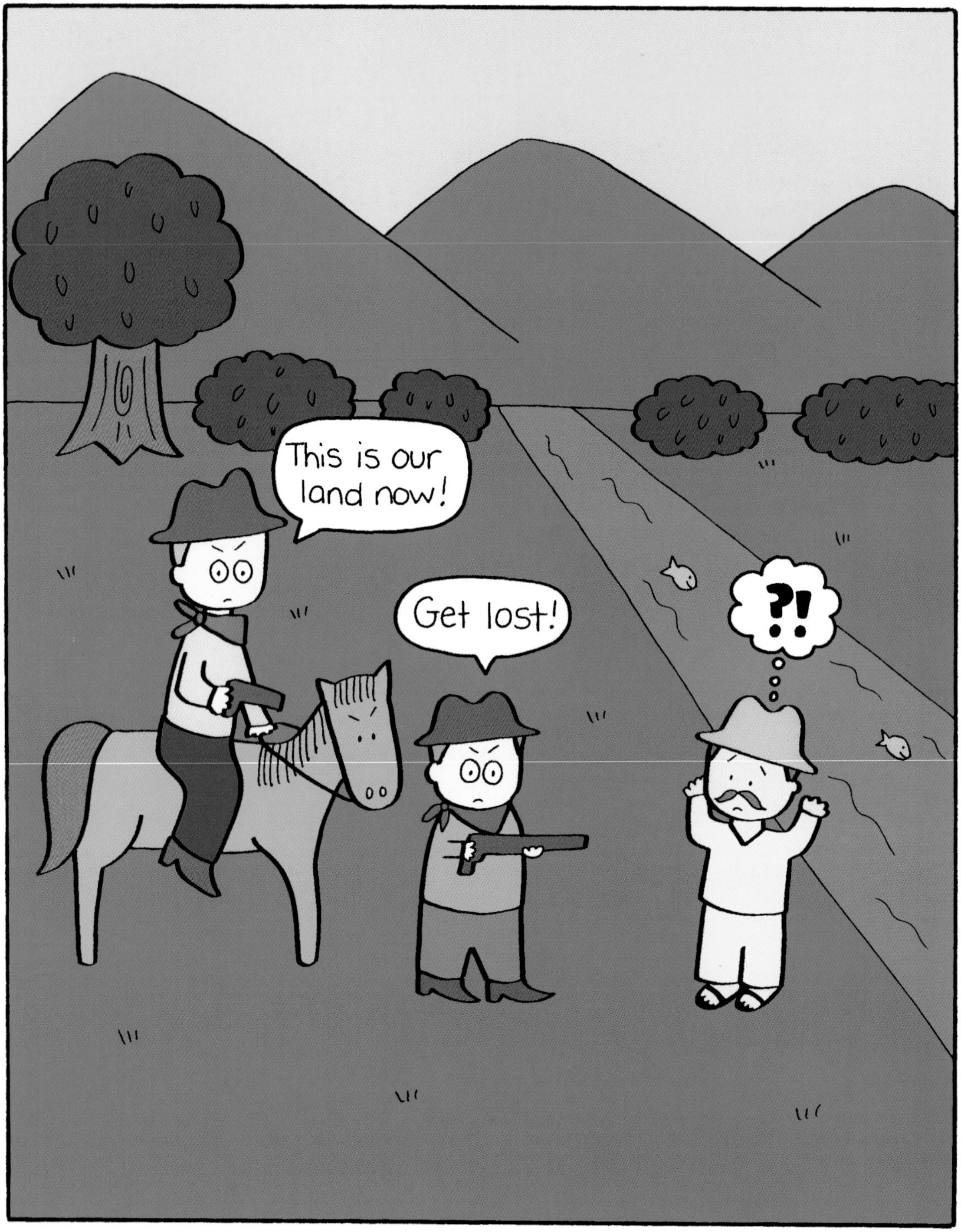
This is our land now!
Get lost!
?!

He moved with his family into a small cottage.

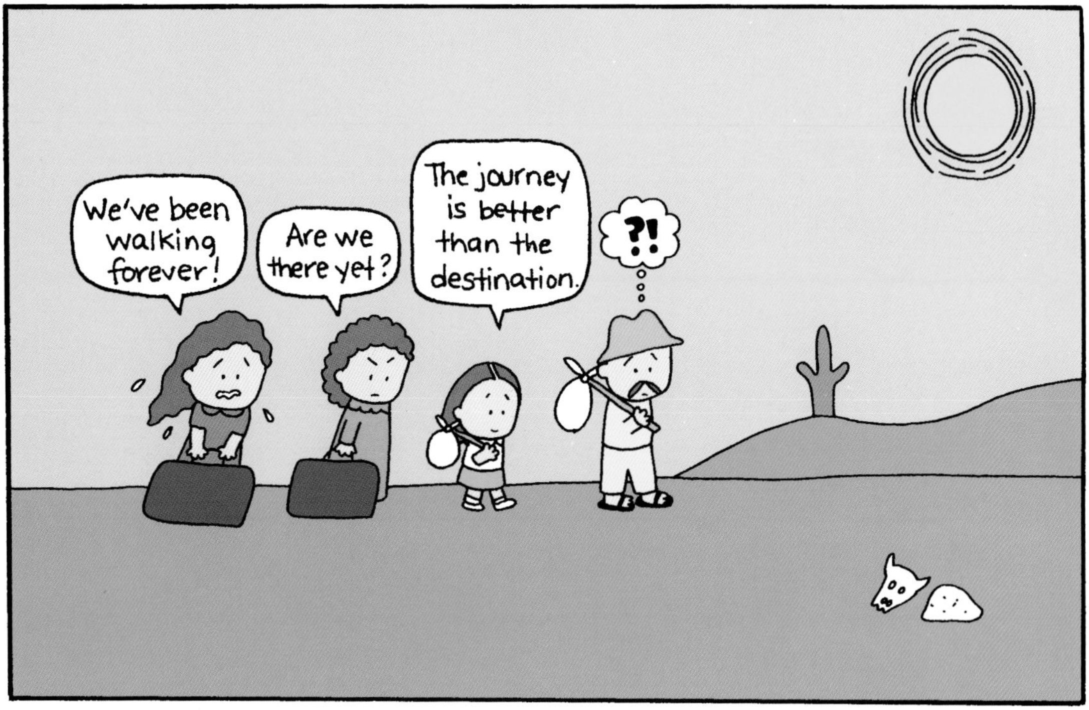
We've been walking forever!
Are we there yet?
The journey is better than the destination.
?!

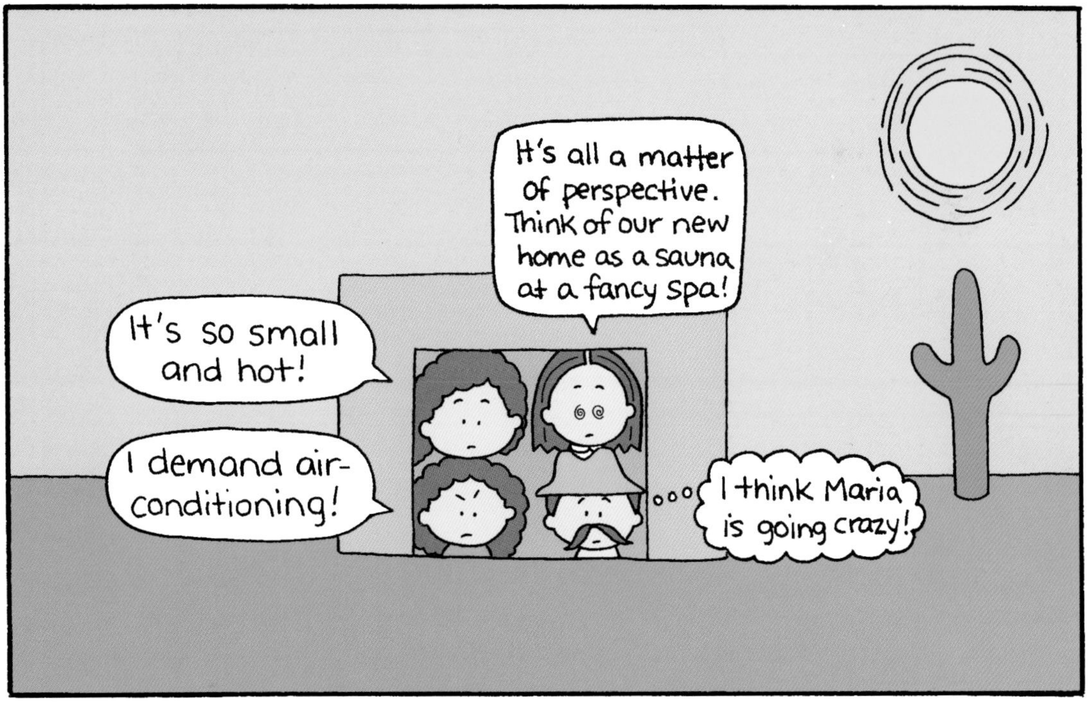
It's all a matter of perspective. Think of our new home as a sauna at a fancy spa!
It's so small and hot!
I demand air-conditioning!
I think Maria is going crazy!

He left his family to look for work.

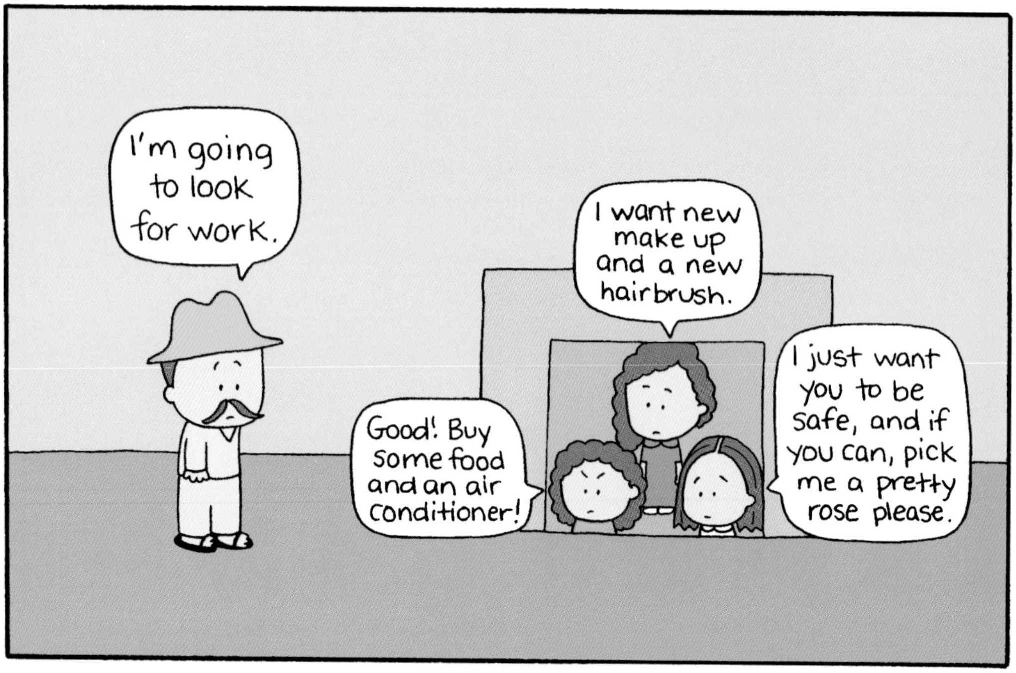
I'm going to look for work.
I want new make up and a new hairbrush.
Good! Buy some food and an air conditioner!
I just want you to be safe, and if you can, pick me a pretty rose please.

He walked...

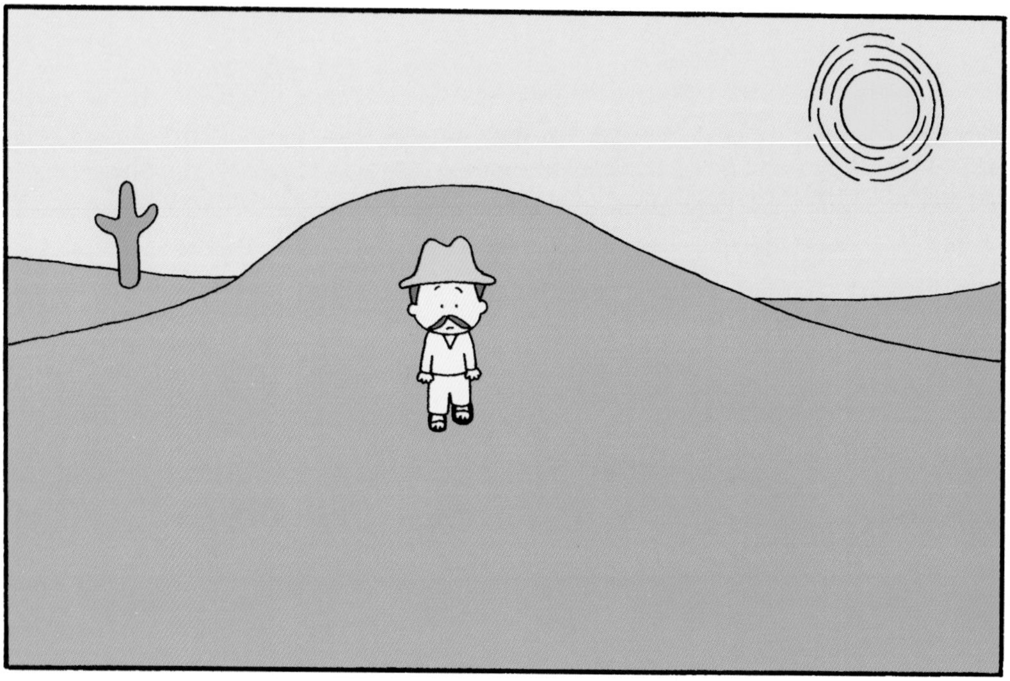

And walked...

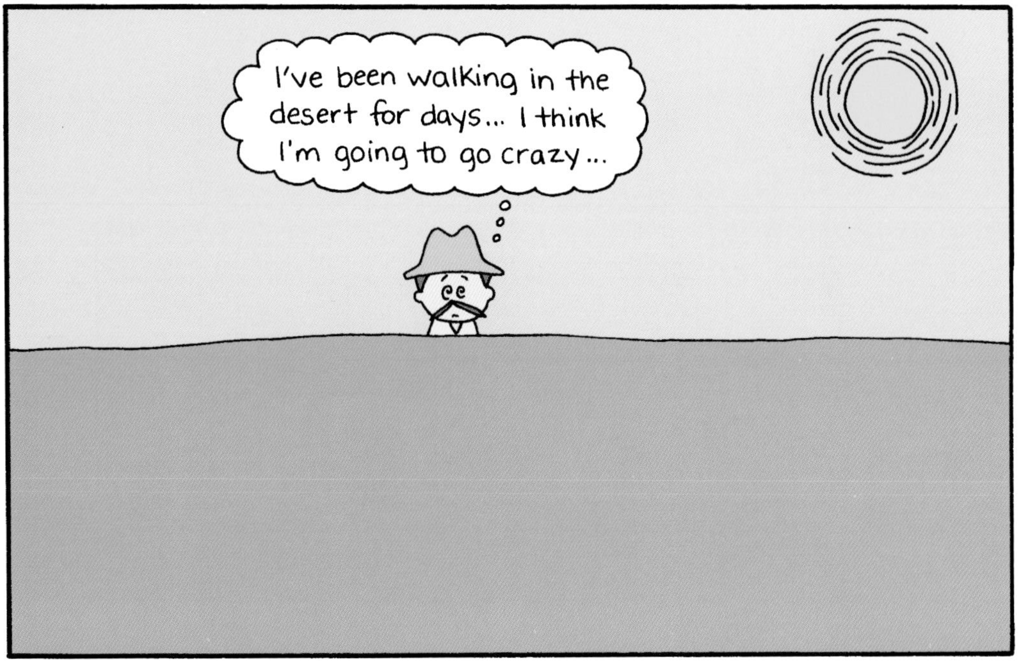
I've been walking in the desert for days... I think I'm going to go crazy...

And walked...

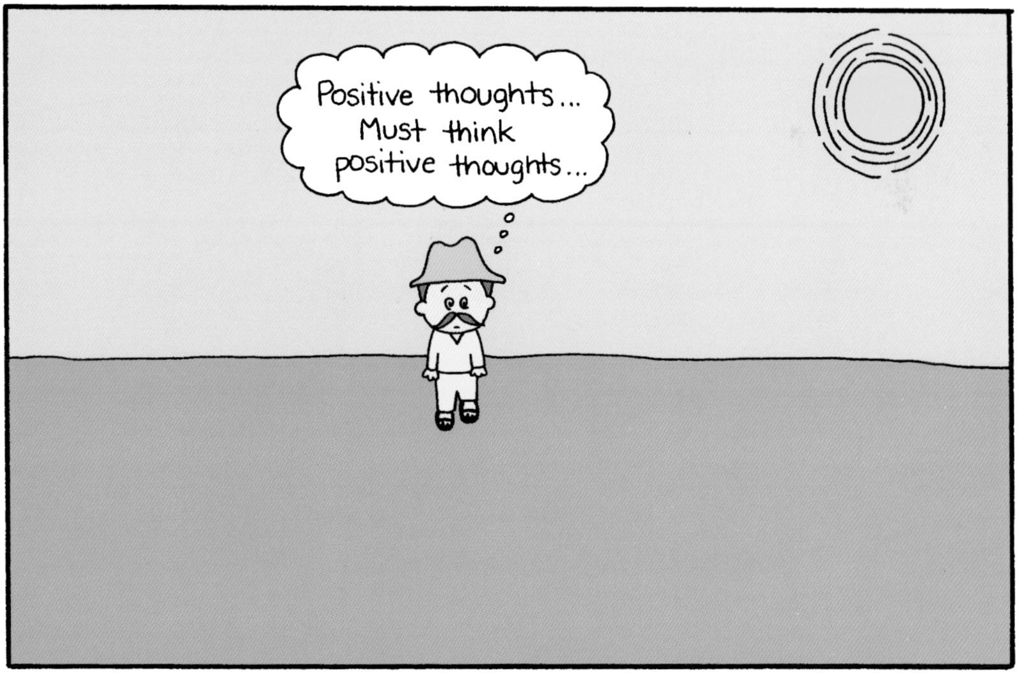
Positive thoughts... Must think positive thoughts...

He came upon a busy town.

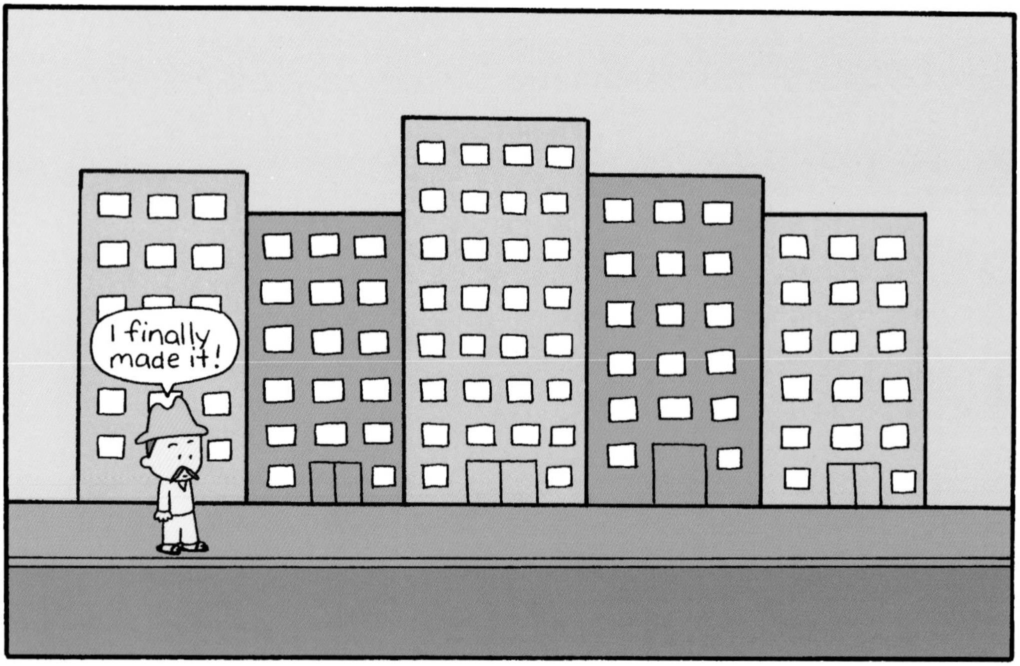
I finally made it!

He found a job and worked hard.

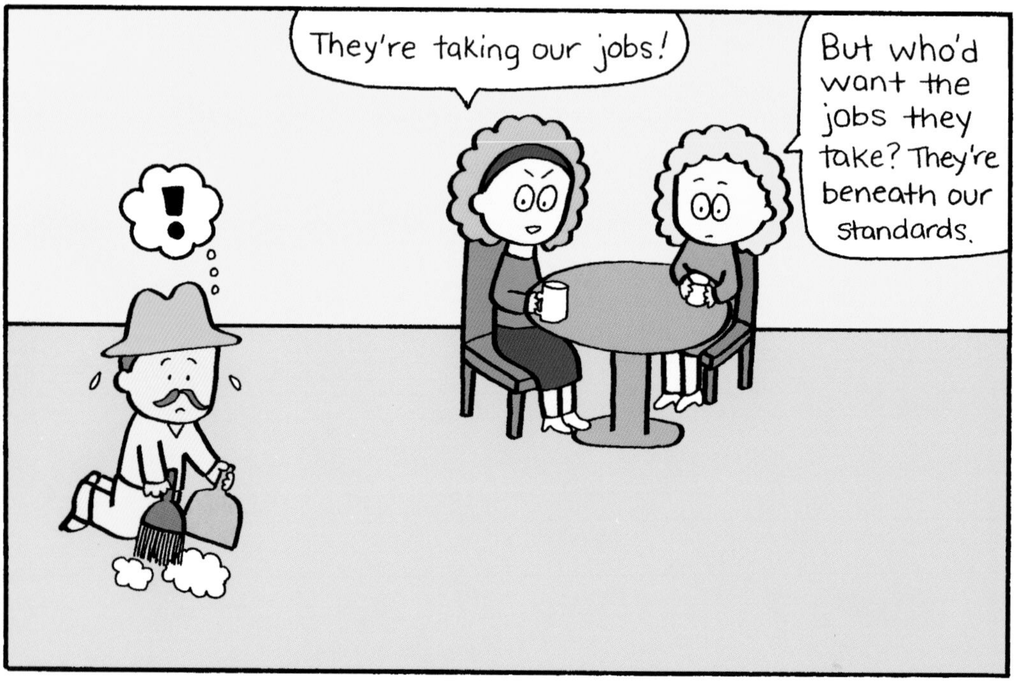
They're taking our jobs!
But who'd want the jobs they take? They're beneath our standards.

He earned enough money to buy the things his daughters needed.

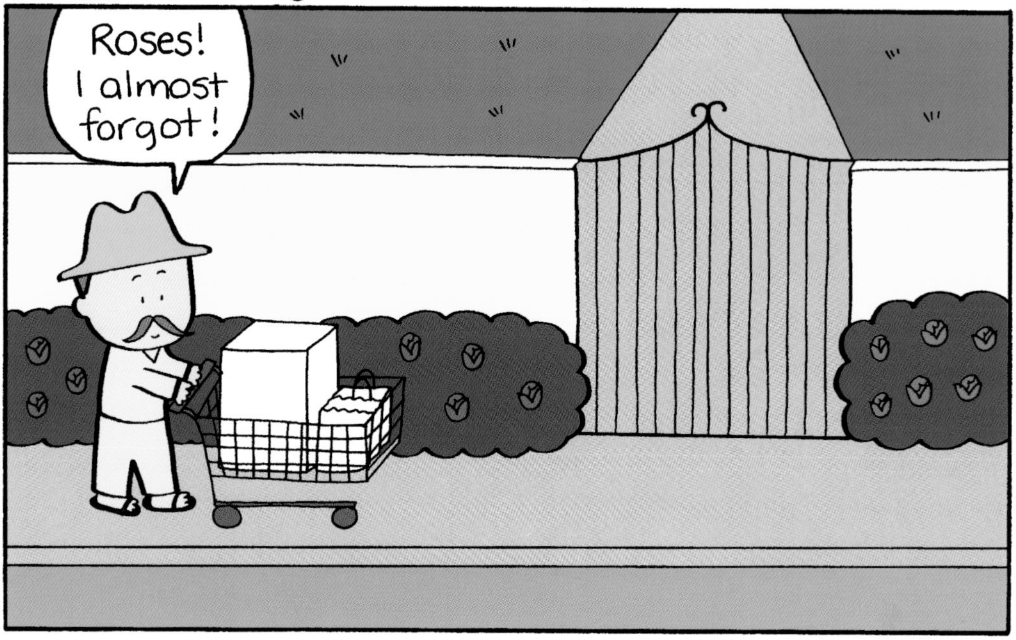
Roses! I almost forgot!

He remembered to pick a rose for his daughter, but he collapsed!

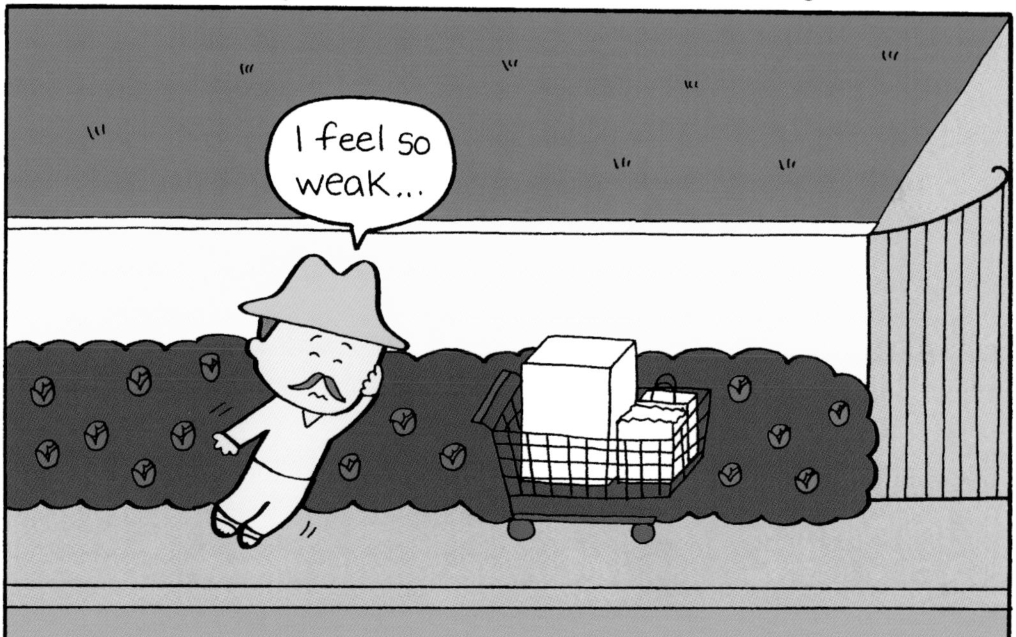
I feel so weak...

A beast took pity on the man.

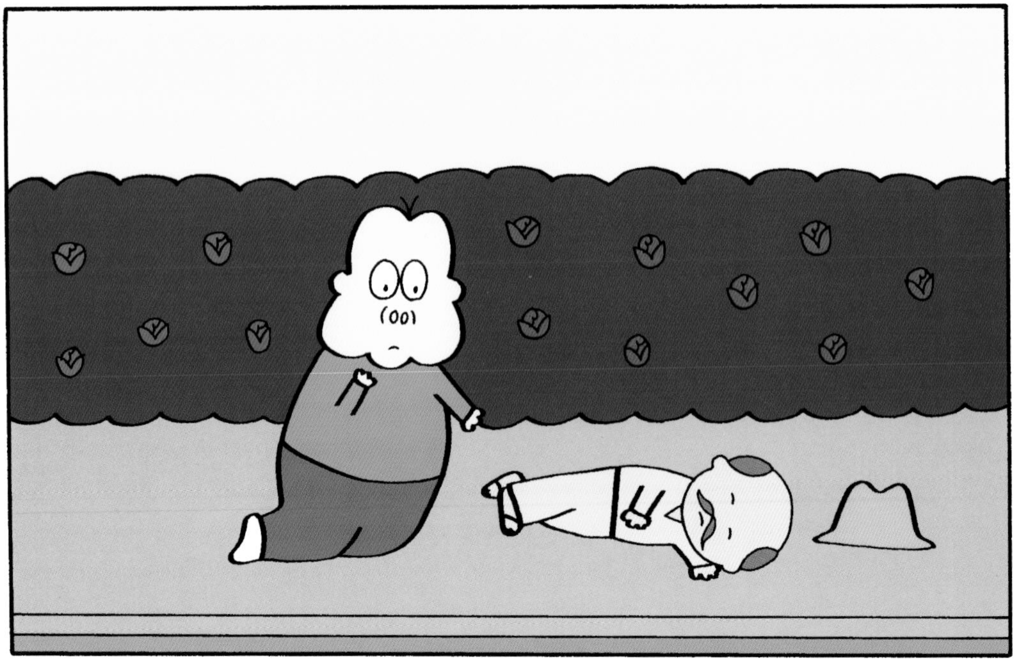

The beast let the man sleep peacefully in his home.

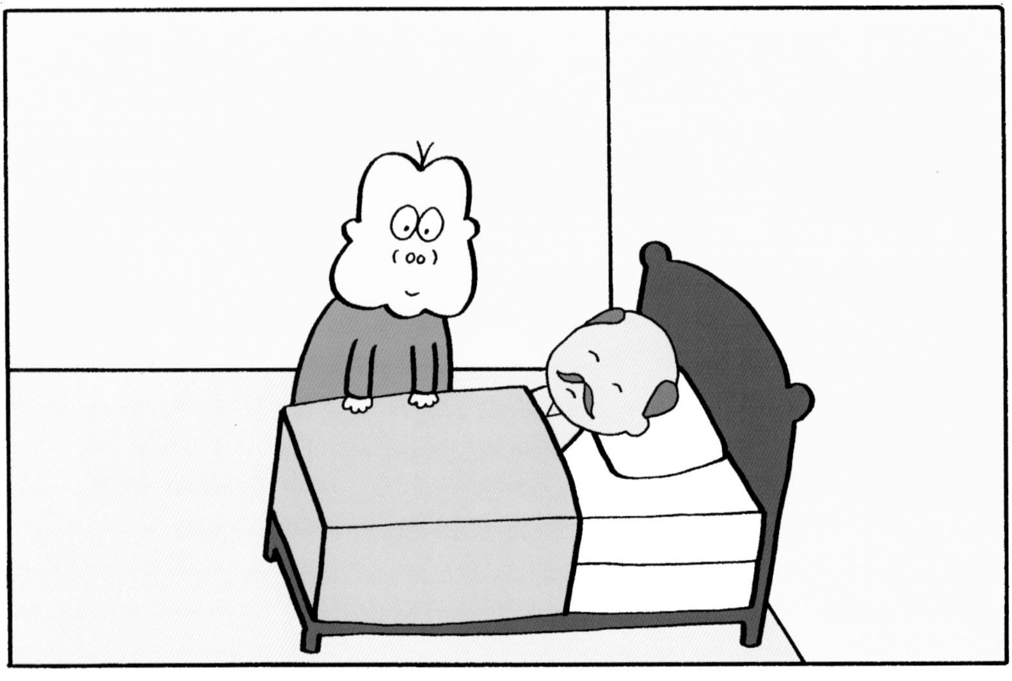

The merchant felt much better.

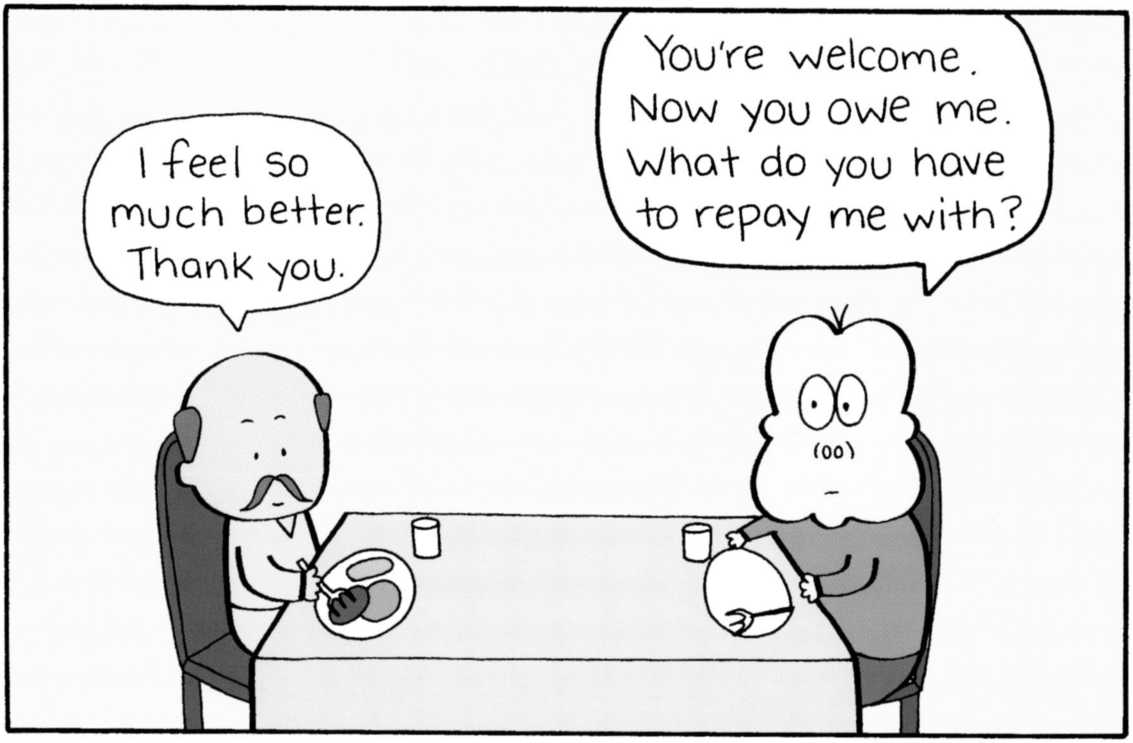
I feel so much better. Thank you.
You're welcome. Now you owe me. What do you have to repay me with?

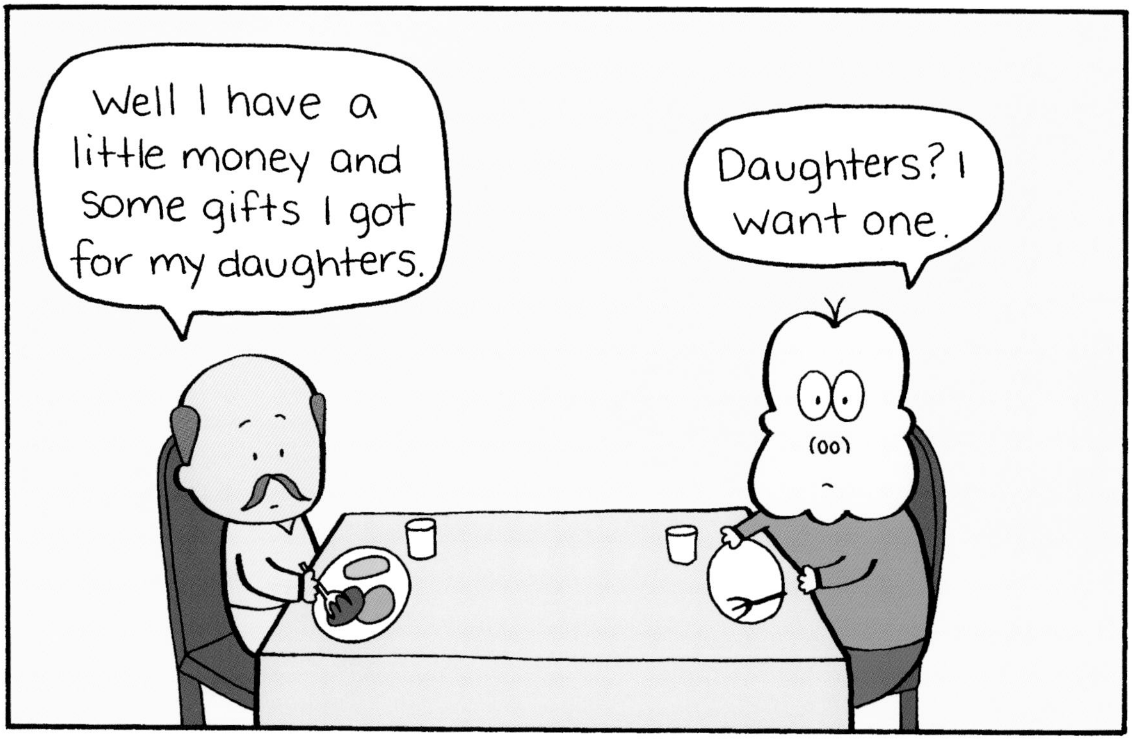
Well I have a little money and some gifts I got for my daughters.
Daughters? I want one.

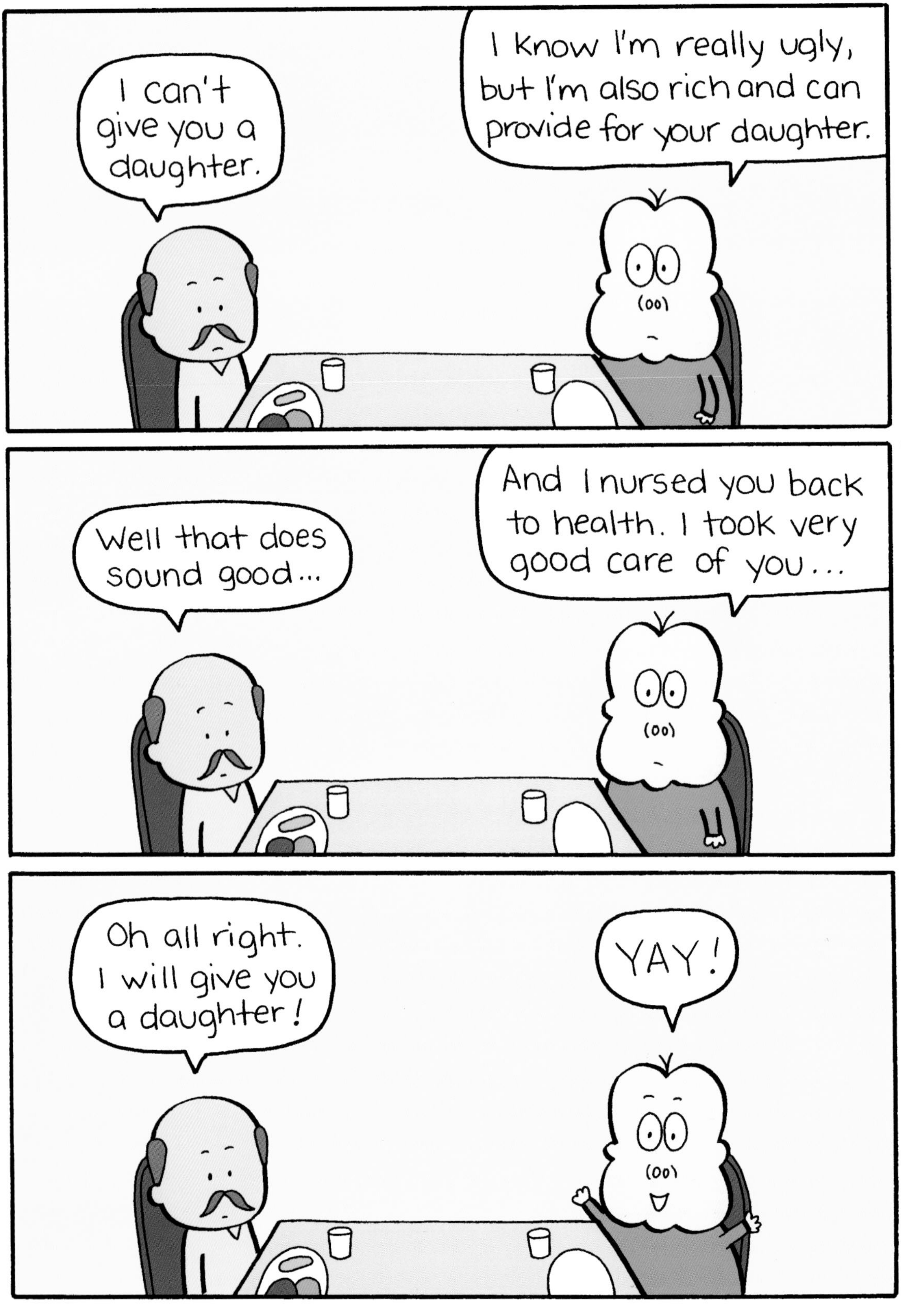
I can't give you a daughter.
I know I'm really ugly, but I'm also rich and can provide for your daughter.
Well that does sound good...
And I nursed you back to health. I took very good care of you...
Oh all right. I will give you a daughter!
YAY!

The merchant returned home to get a daughter for the beast.

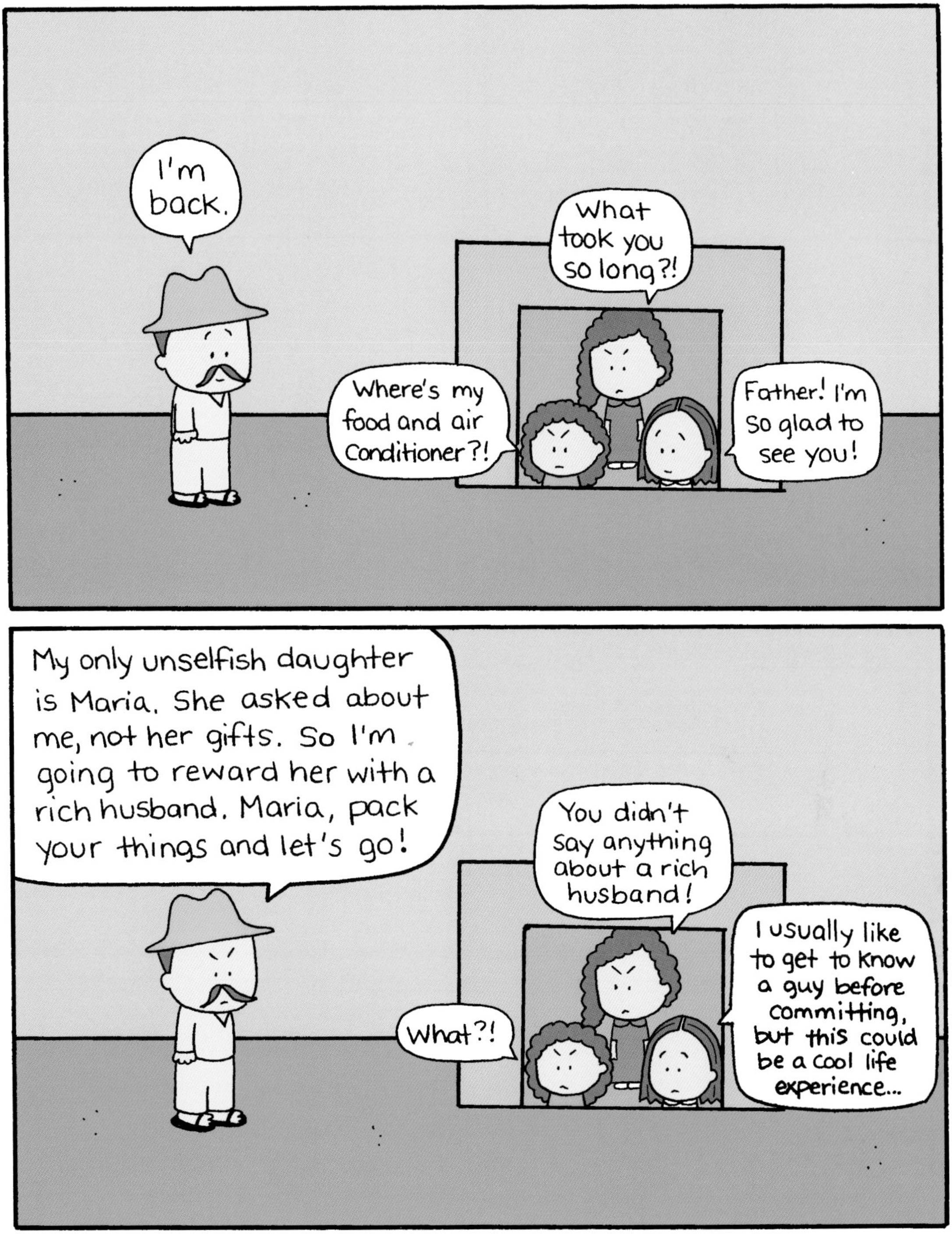
I'm back.
What took you so long?!
Where's my food and air conditioner?!
Father! I'm so glad to see you!
My only unselfish daughter is Maria. She asked about me, not her gifts. So I'm going to reward her with a rich husband. Maria, pack your things and let's go!
You didn't say anything about a rich husband!
What?!
I usually like to get to know a guy before committing, but this could be a cool life experience...

Meanwhile, the beast excitedly prepared for their arrival.

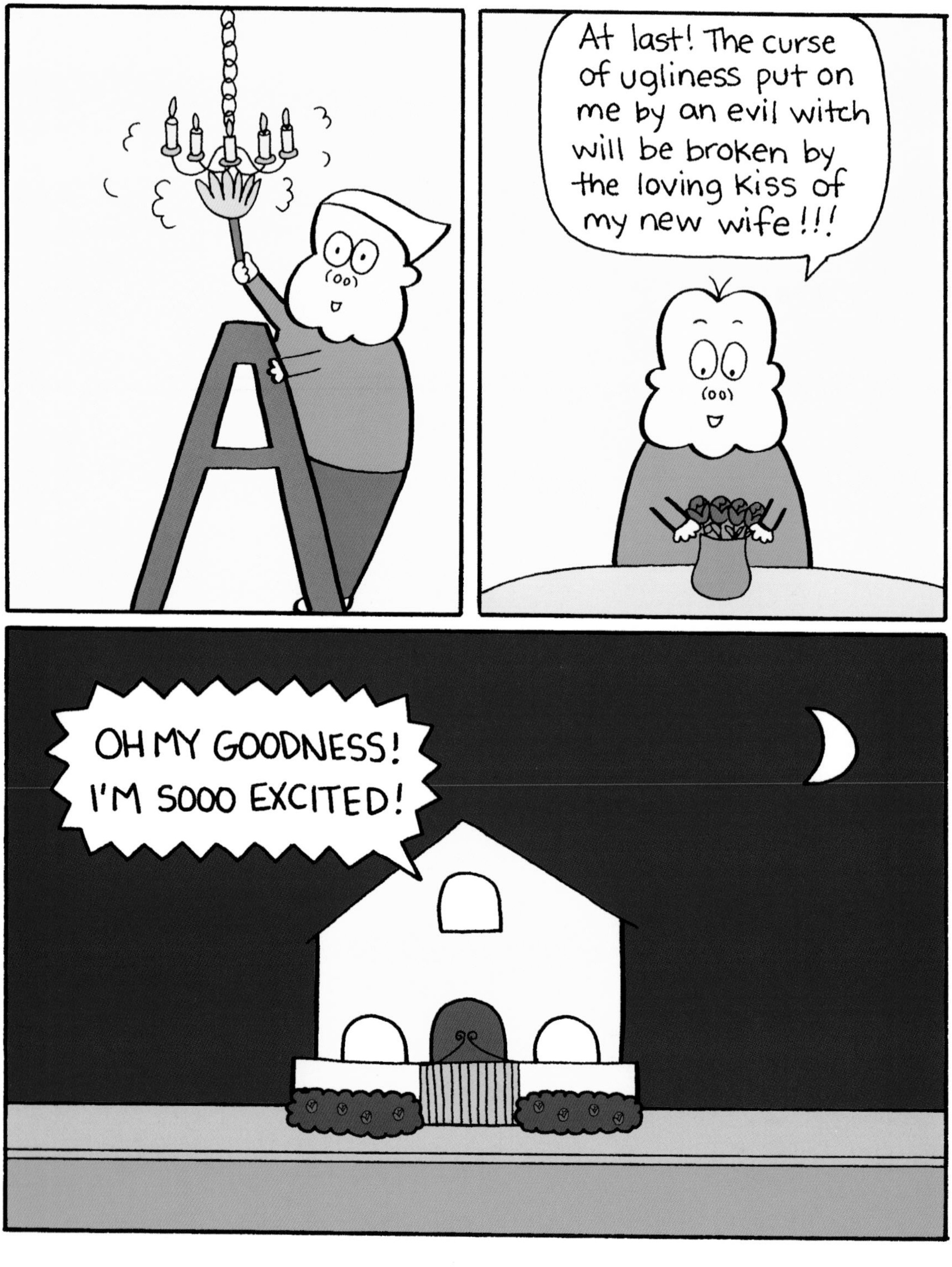
At last! The curse of ugliness put on me by an evil witch will be broken by the loving kiss of my new wife!!!
OH MY GOODNESS! I'M SOOO EXCITED!

The merchant and his daughter finally arrived at the beast's home.

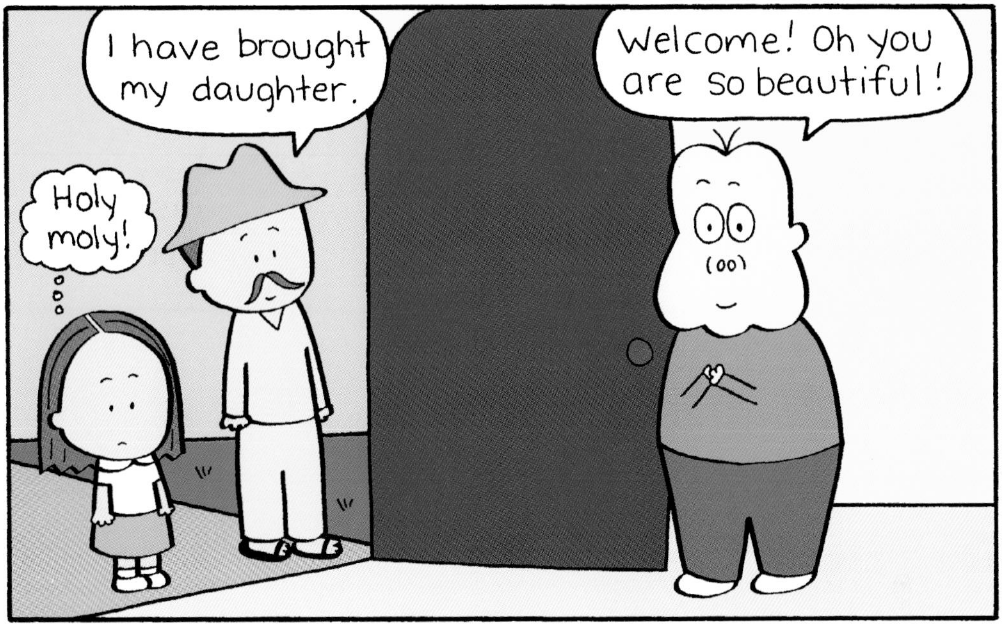
I have brought my daughter.
Holy moly!
Welcome! Oh you are so beautiful!
(oo)

The beast thought the merchant's daughter was very beautiful.

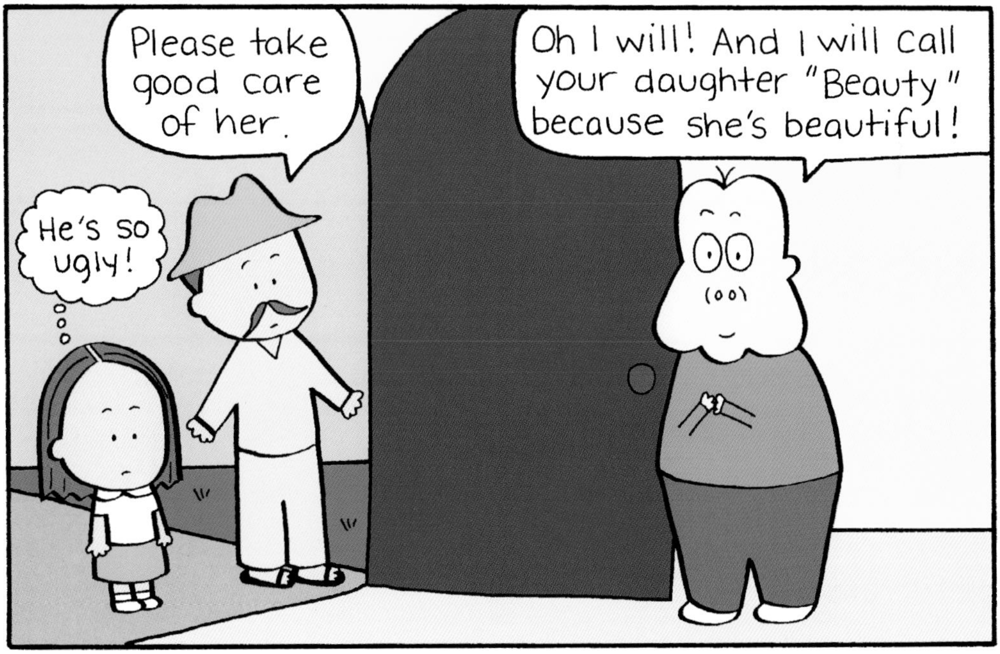
Please take good care of her.
He's so ugly!
Oh I will! And I will call your daughter "Beauty" because she's beautiful!
(oo)

Beauty was scared and began to cry.

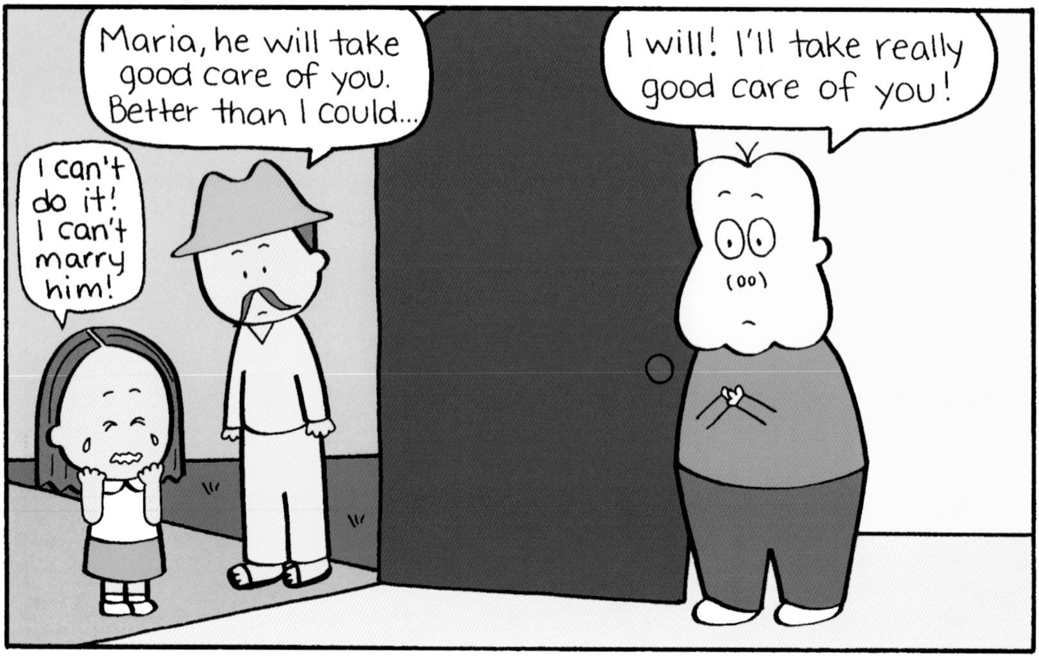
Maria, he will take good care of you. Better than I could...
I will! I'll take really good care of you!
I can't do it! I can't marry him!

The beast felt very bad.

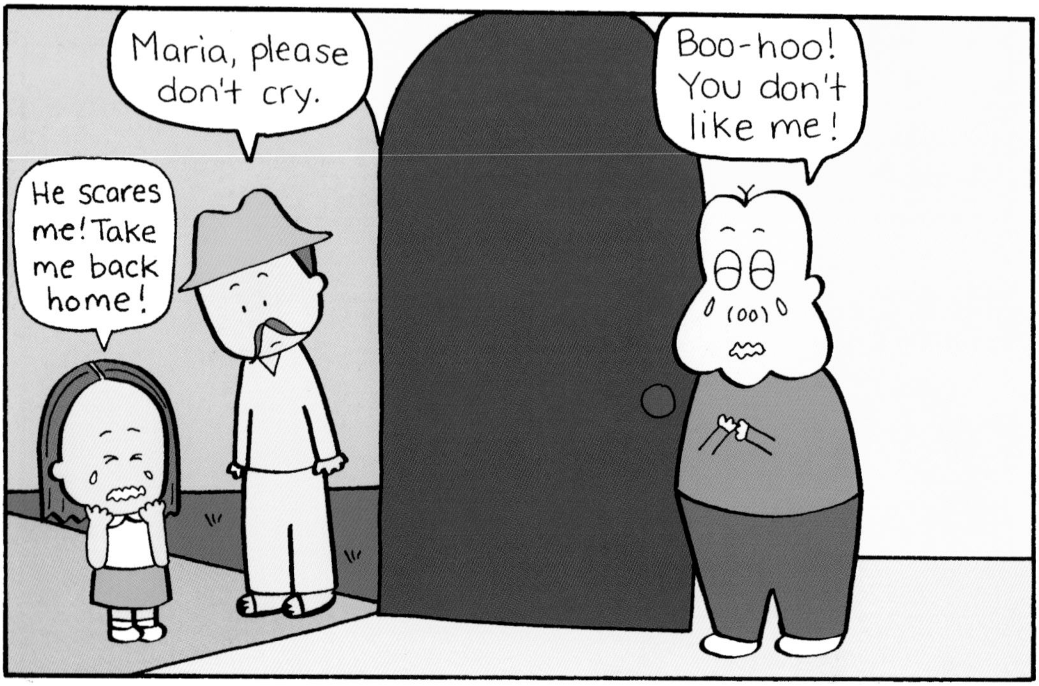
Maria, please don't cry.
Boo-hoo! You don't like me!
He scares me! Take me back home!

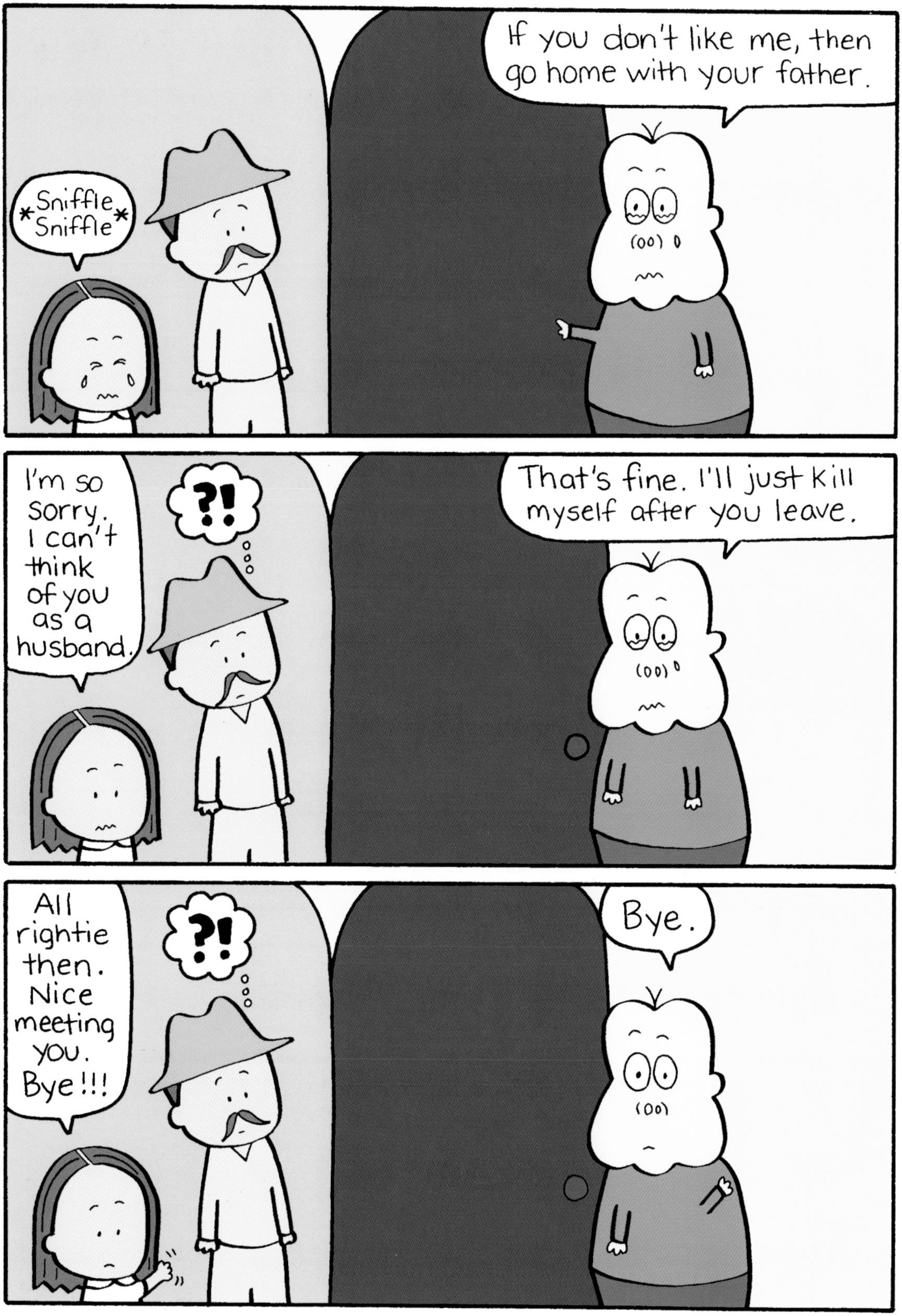
If you don't like me, then go home with your father.
Sniffle Sniffle
I'm so sorry. I can't think of you as a husband.
?!
That's fine. I'll just kill myself after you leave.
All rightie then. Nice meeting you. Bye!!!
?!
Bye.

Beauty went home with her father.

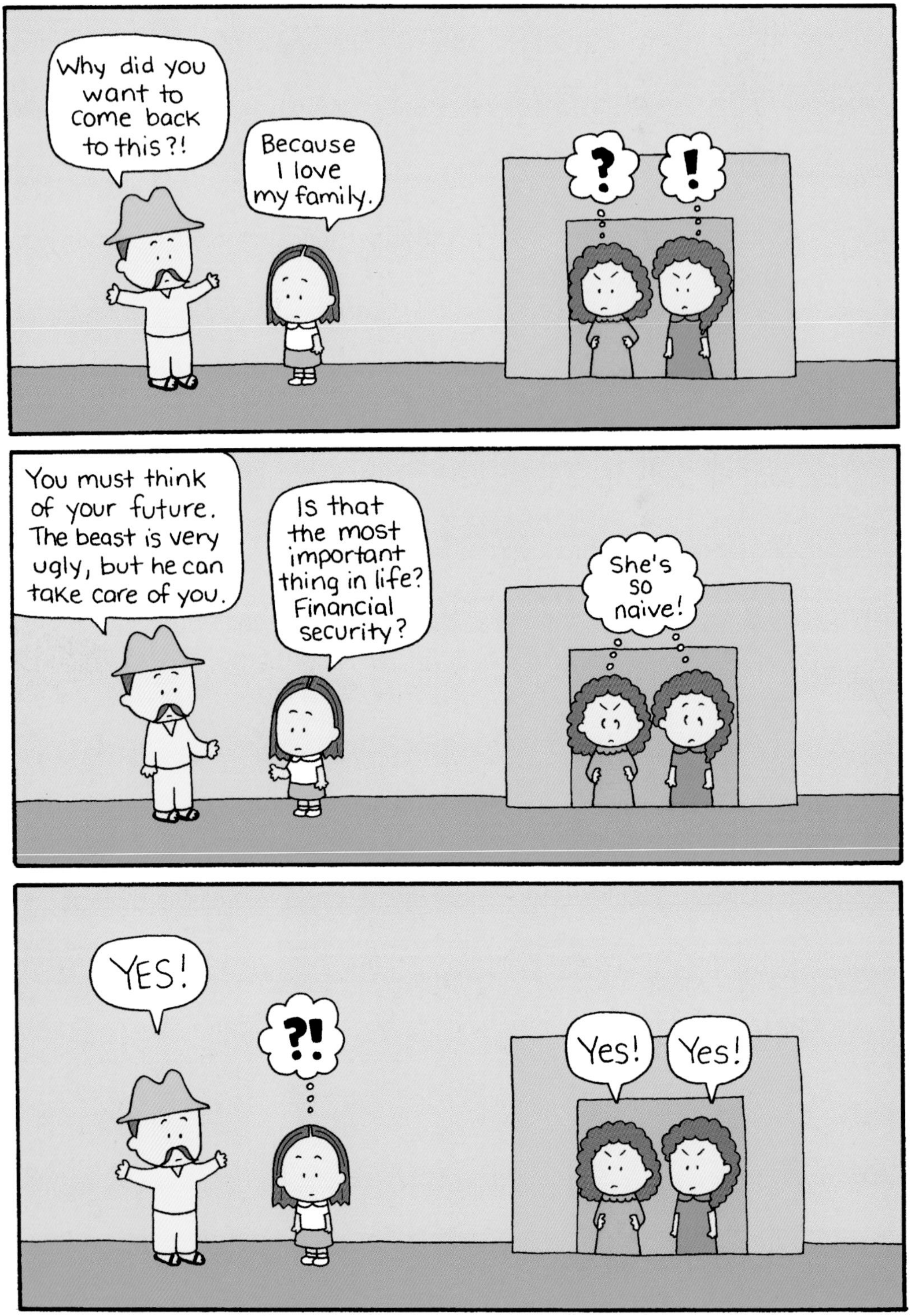
Why did you want to come back to this?!
Because I love my family.
?
!
You must think of your future. The beast is very ugly, but he can take care of you.
Is that the most important thing in life? Financial security?
She's so naive!
YES!
?!
Yes!
Yes!

Beauty thought about the beast.

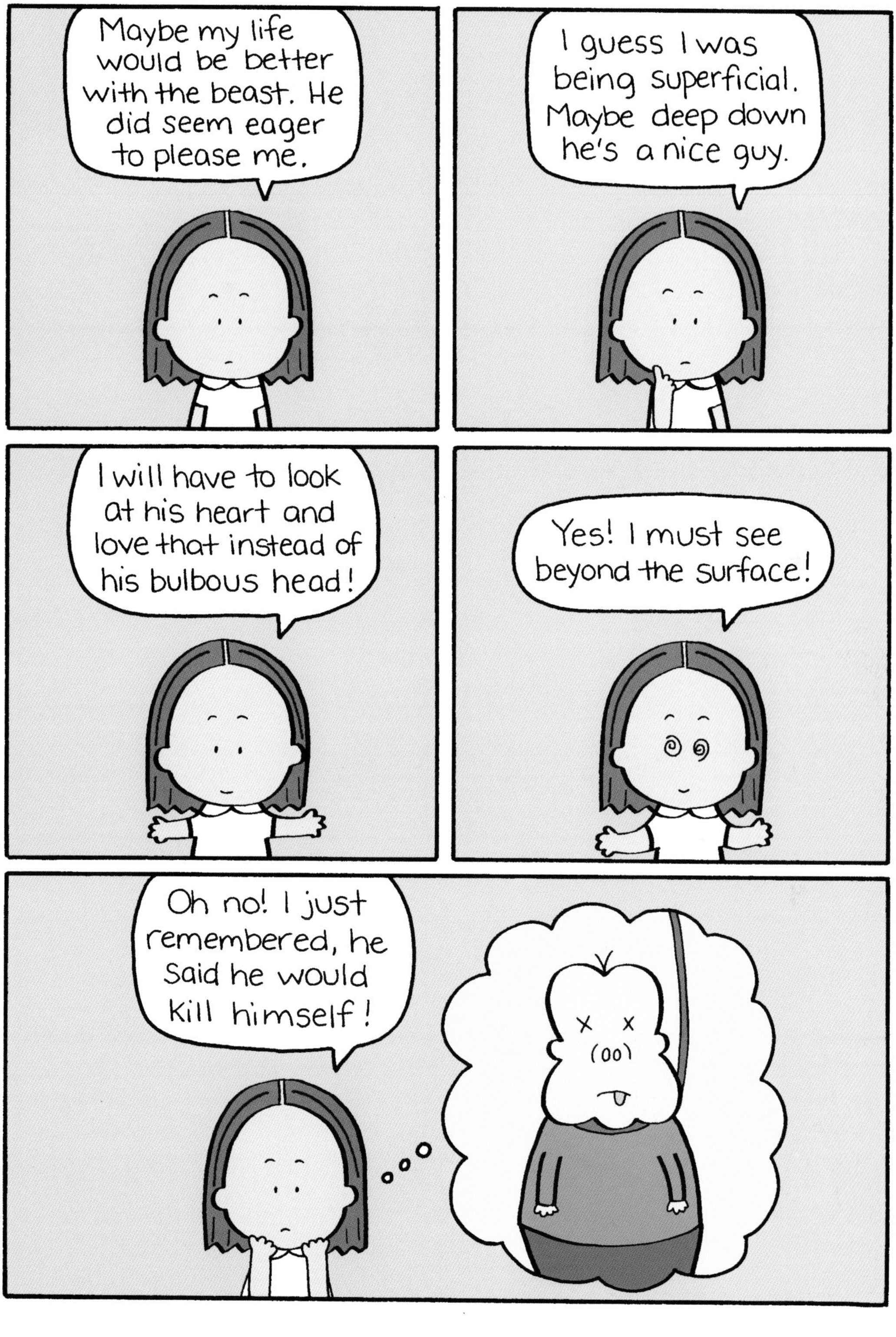
Maybe my life would be better with the beast. He did seem eager to please me.
I guess I was being superficial. Maybe deep down he's a nice guy.
I will have to look at his heart and love that instead of his bulbous head!
Yes! I must see beyond the surface!
Oh no! I just remembered, he said he would kill himself!

Beauty raced to the beast's home.

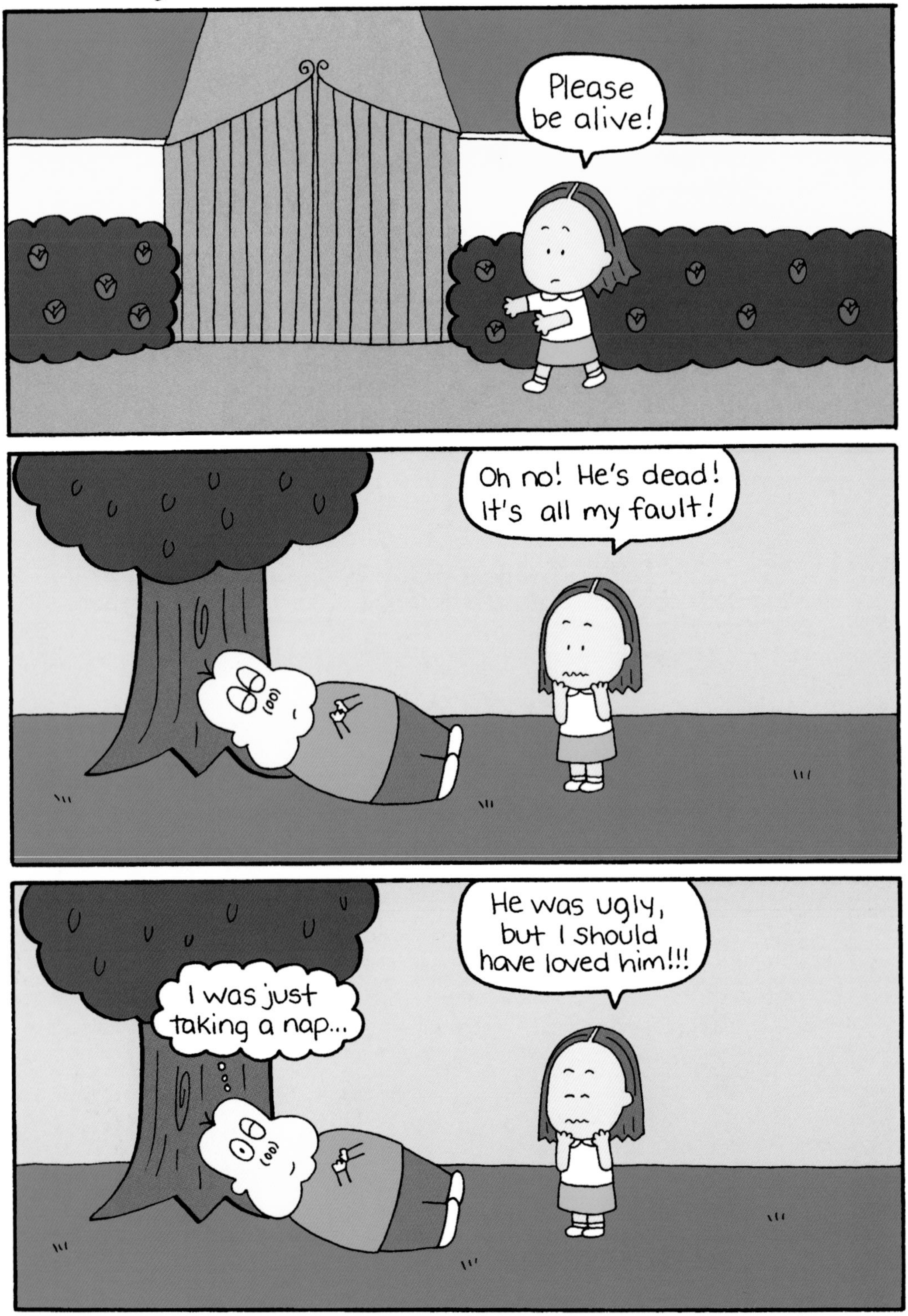
Please be alive!
Oh no! He's dead! It's all my fault!
He was ugly, but I should have loved him!!!
I was just taking a nap...

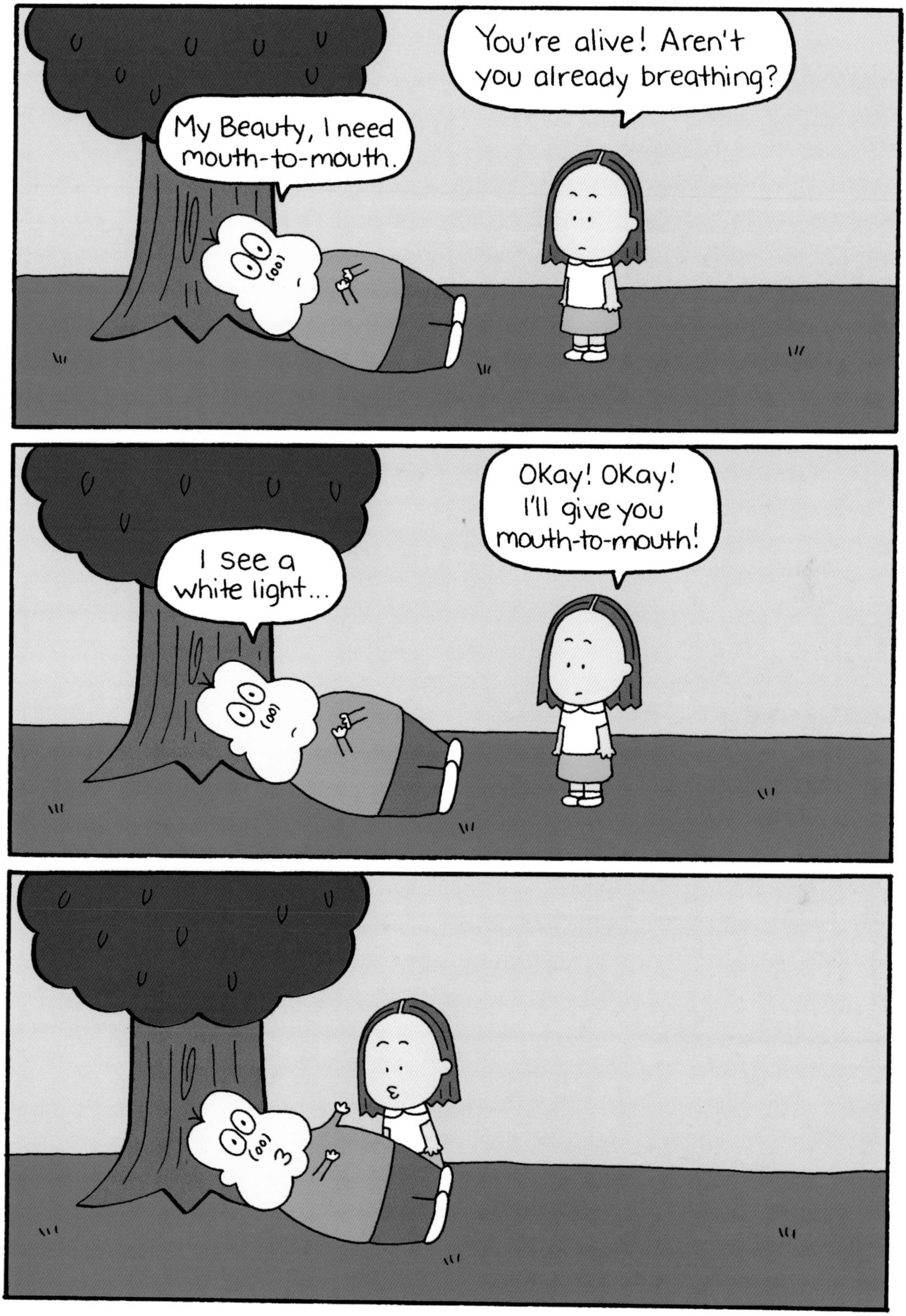
My Beauty, I need mouth-to-mouth.
You're alive! Aren't you already breathing?
I see a white light...
OKay! OKay! I'll give you mouth-to-mouth!

When Beauty kissed the beast, he turned into a handsome man.

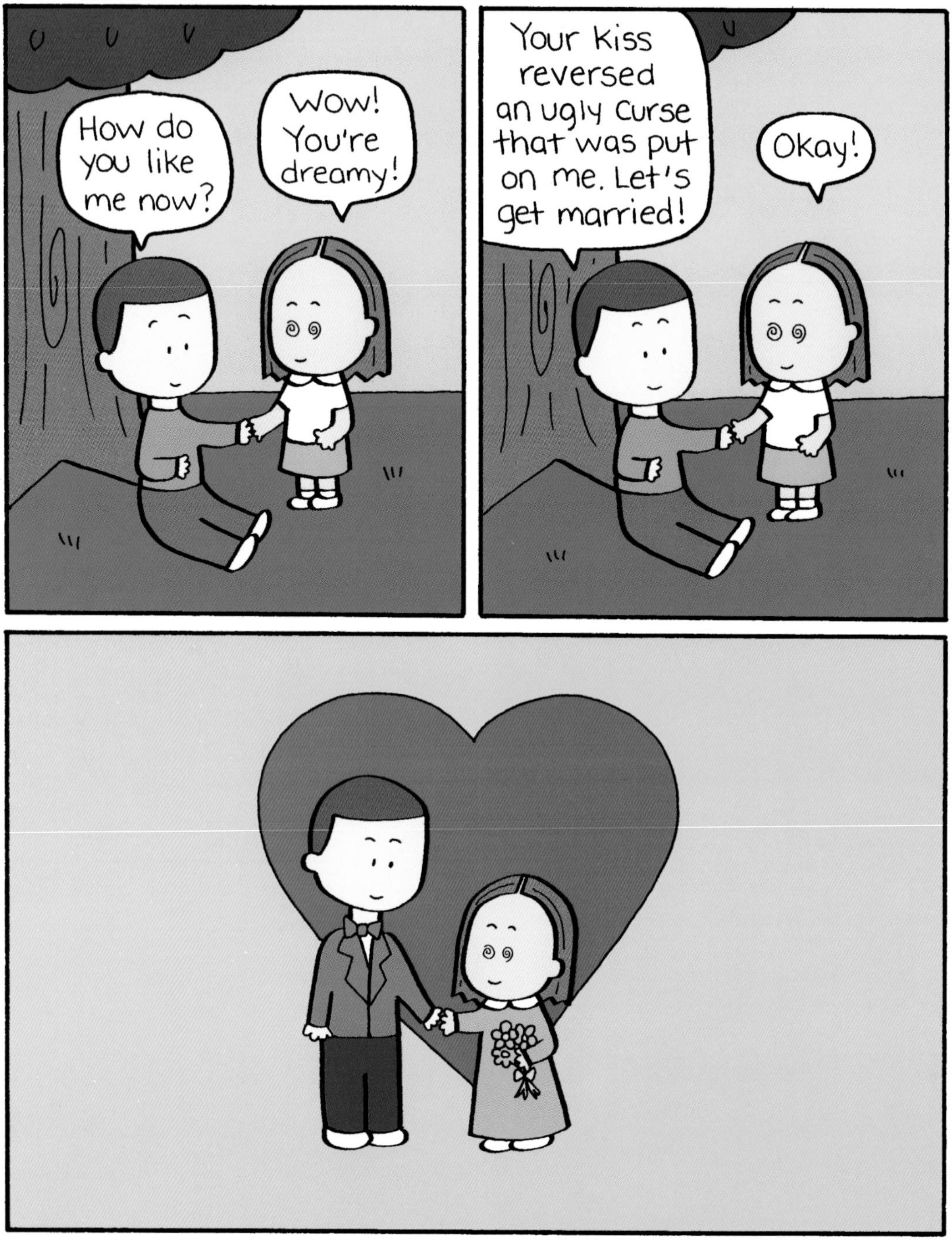
How do you like me now?
Wow! You're dreamy!
Your kiss reversed an ugly curse that was put on me. Let's get married!
Okay!

And they lived happily ever after!

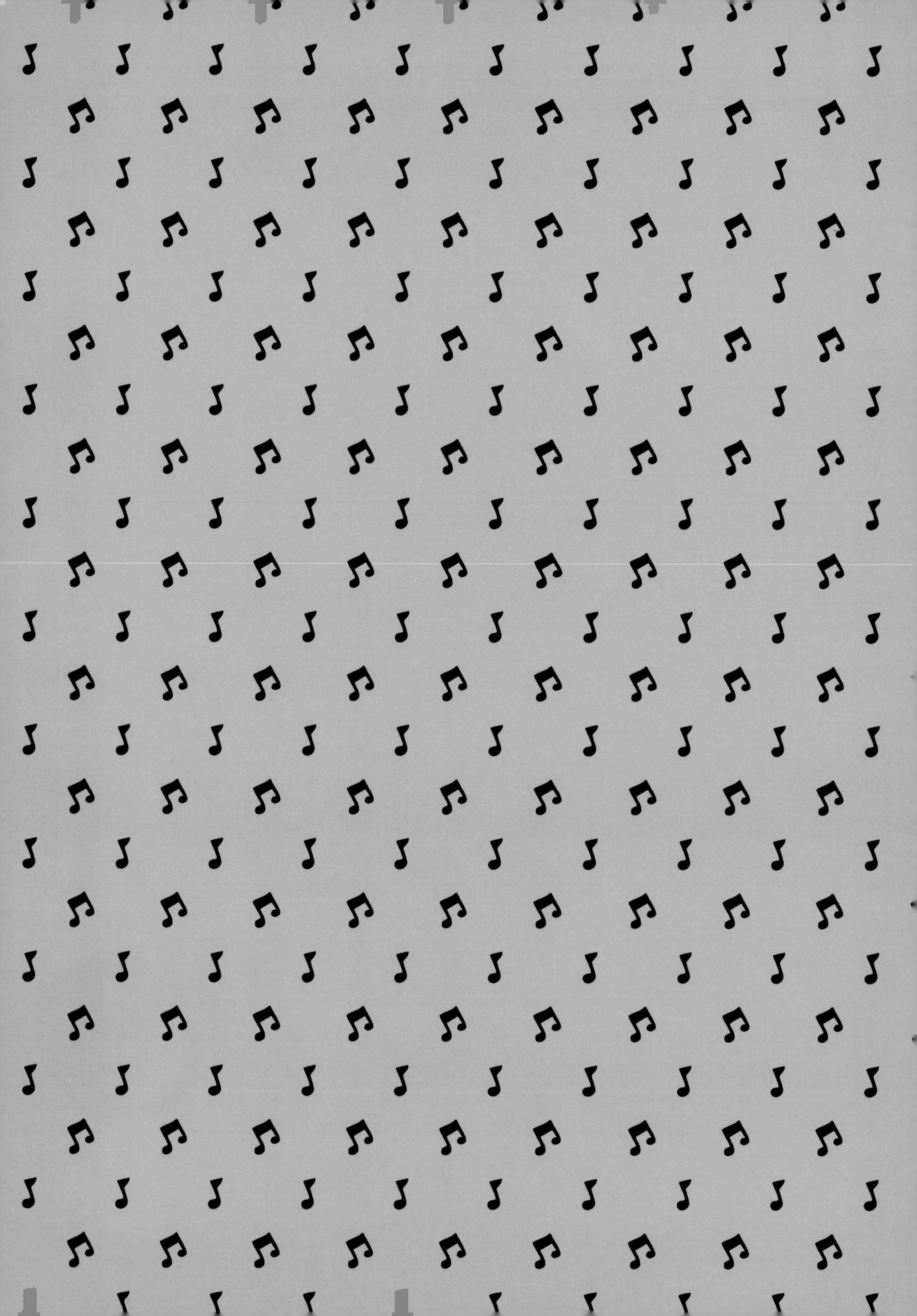

an ANGRY LITTLE GIRL'S FAIRY TALE

RapPunsWell

Starring

Wanda the "Fresh Little Soul Sistah"

Once there was a couple...

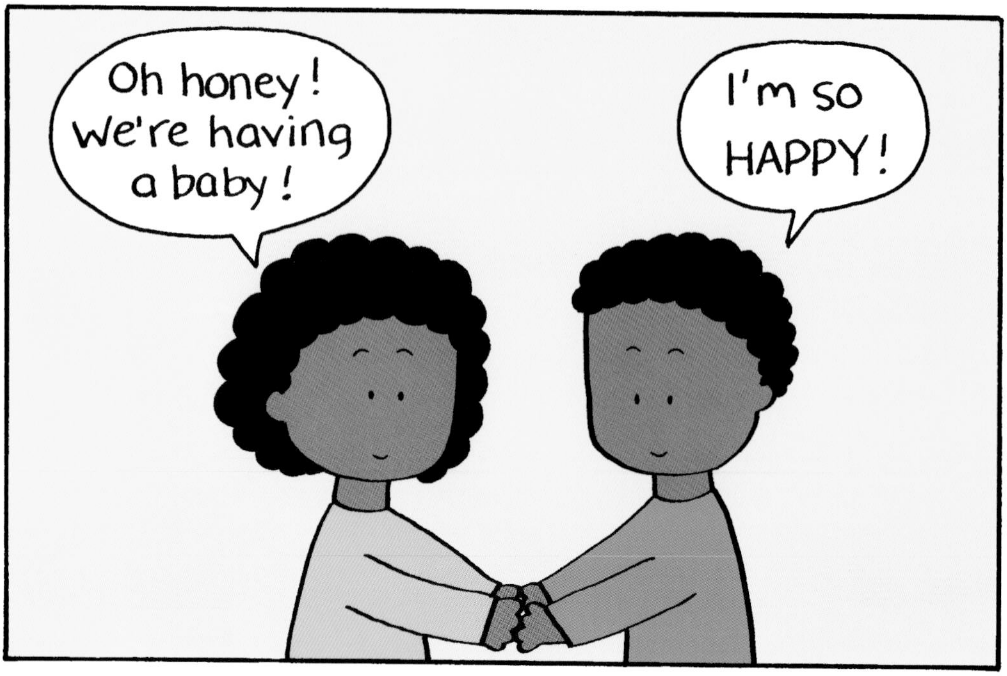
Oh honey! We're having a baby!
I'm so HAPPY!

The mother-to-be began to eat a lot.

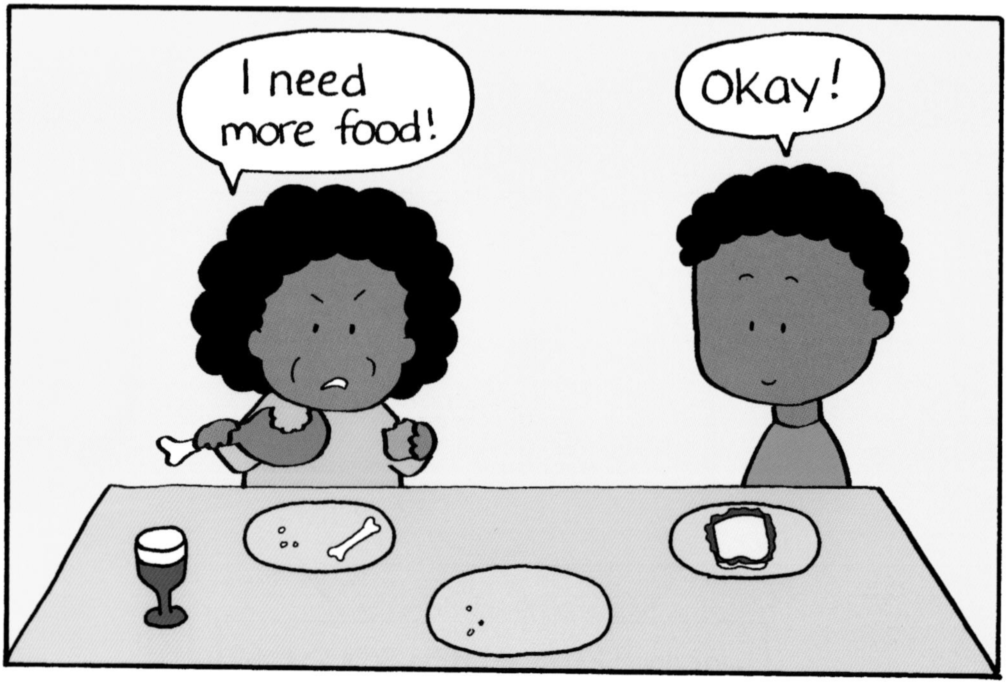
I need more food!
Okay!

As the months passed, the wife craved and demanded weird foods.

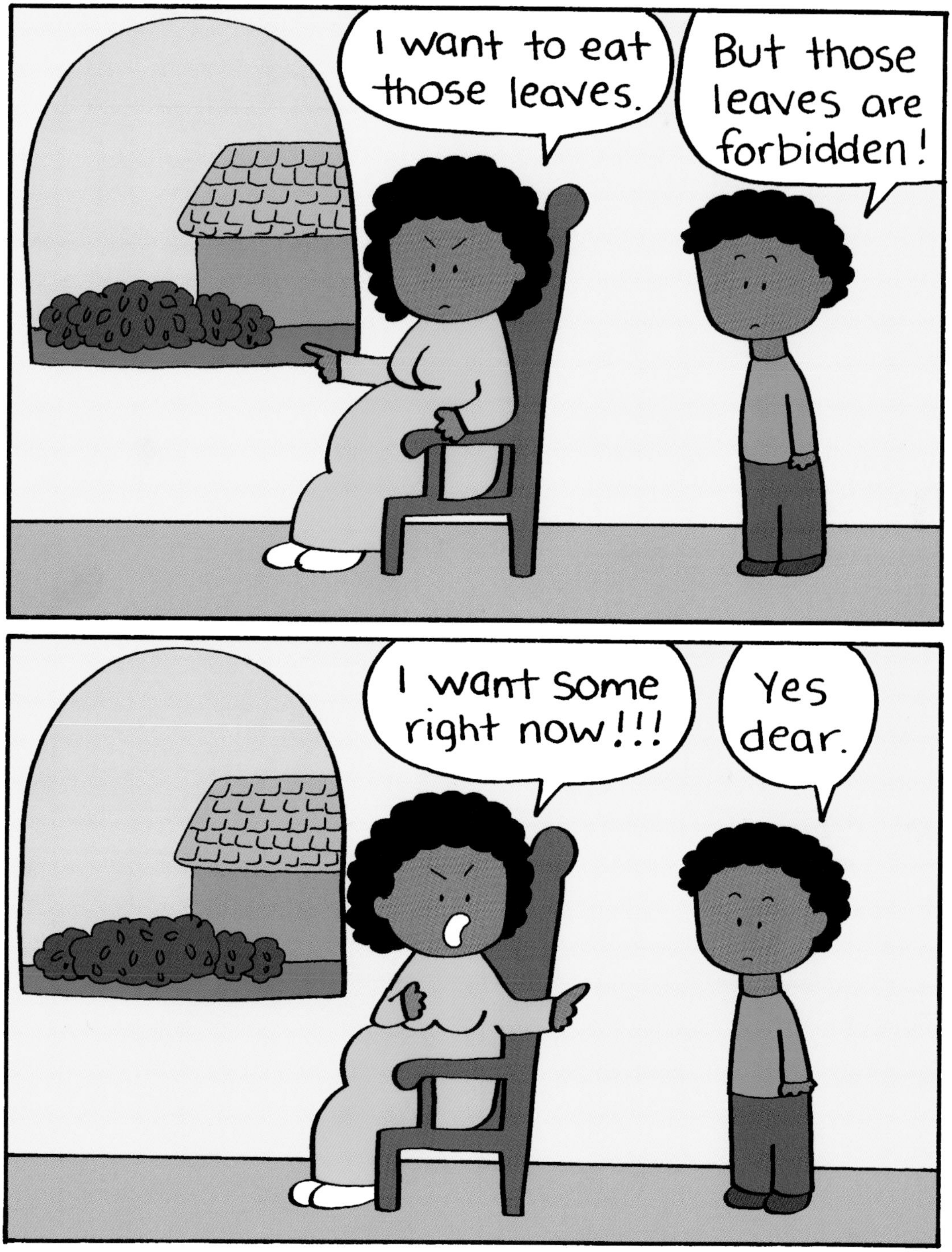
I want to eat those leaves.
But those leaves are forbidden!
I want some right now!!!
Yes dear.

The husband stole the leaves from the yard of their evil neighbor.

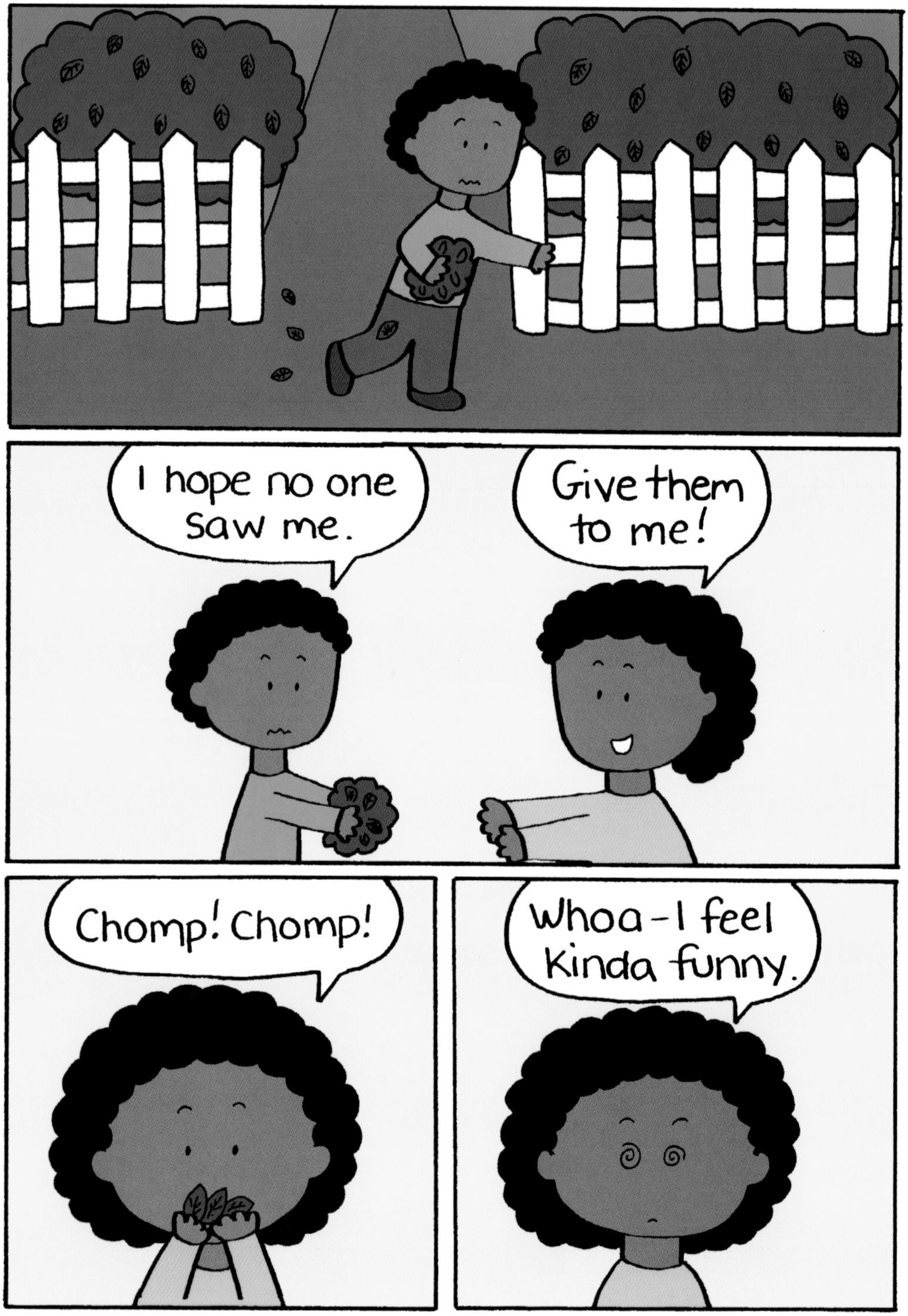
I hope no one saw me.
Give them to me!
Chomp! Chomp!
Whoa-I feel kinda funny.

She fell asleep and slept for days.

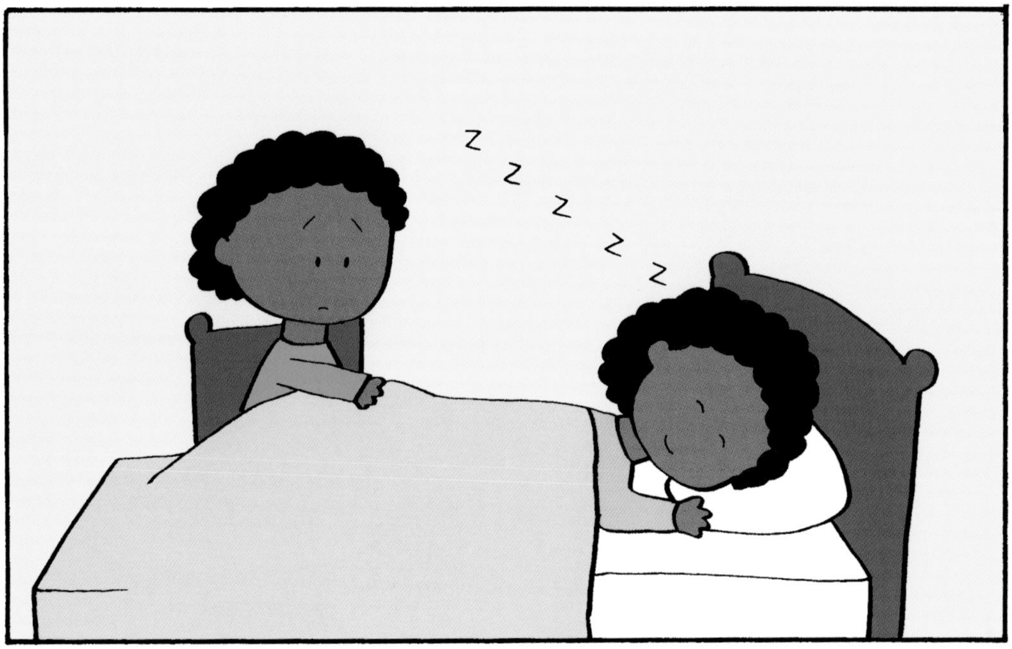

After some time, she finally awoke.

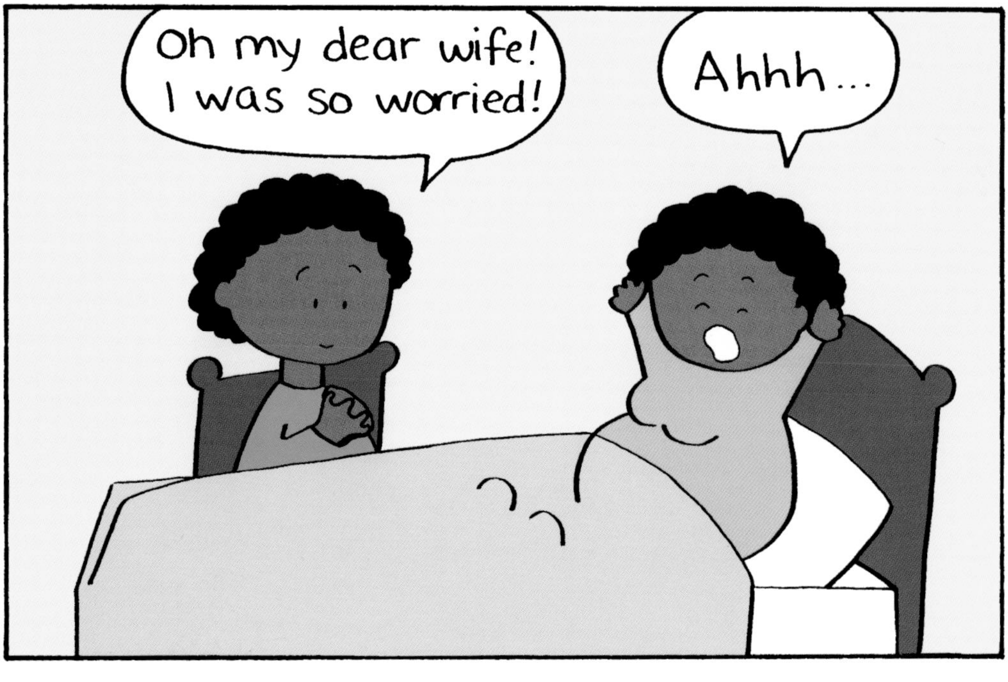
Oh my dear wife! I was so worried!
Ahhh...

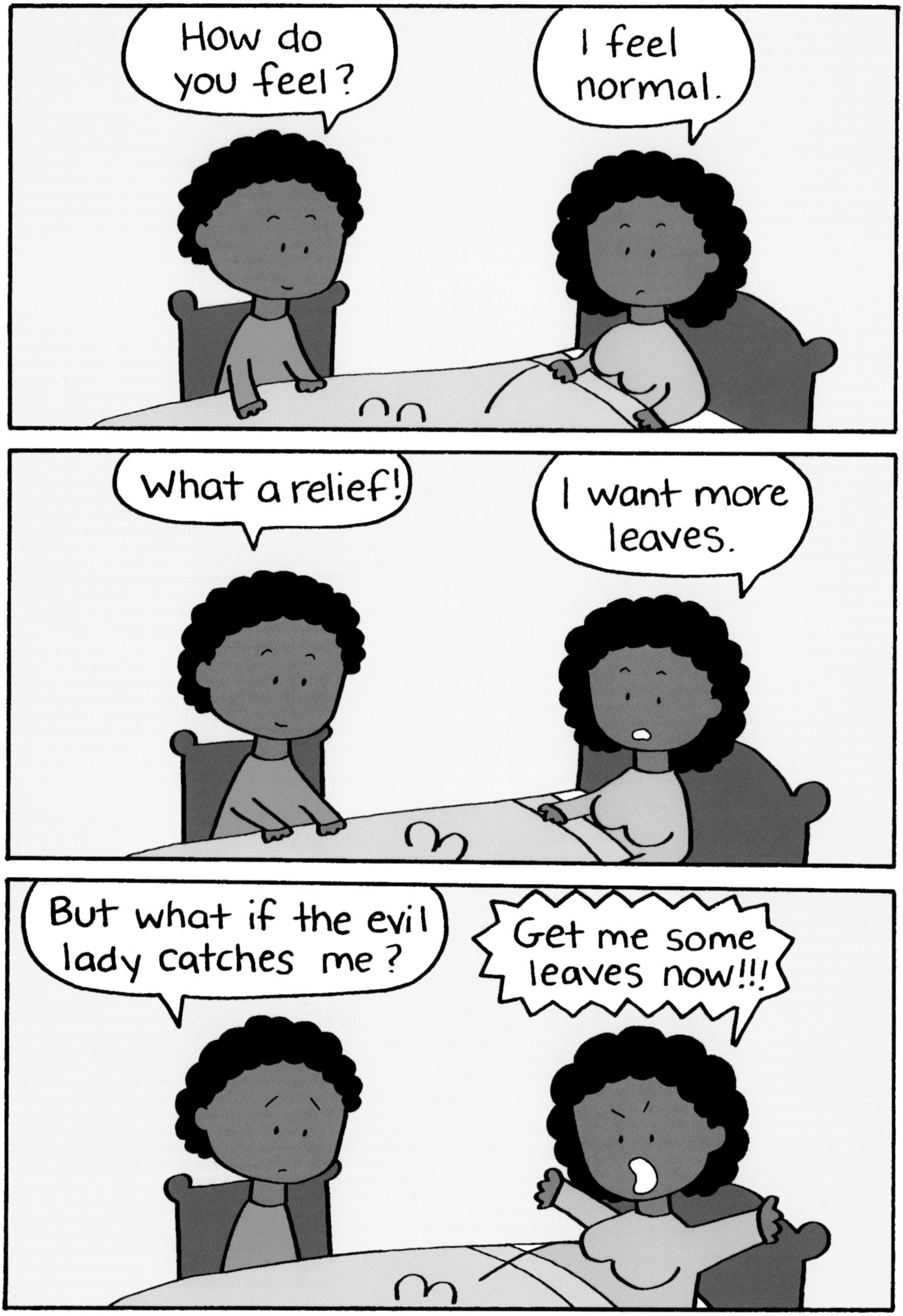
How do you feel?
I feel normal.
What a relief!
I want more leaves.
But what if the evil lady catches me?
Get me some leaves now!!!

He went back to get more leaves.

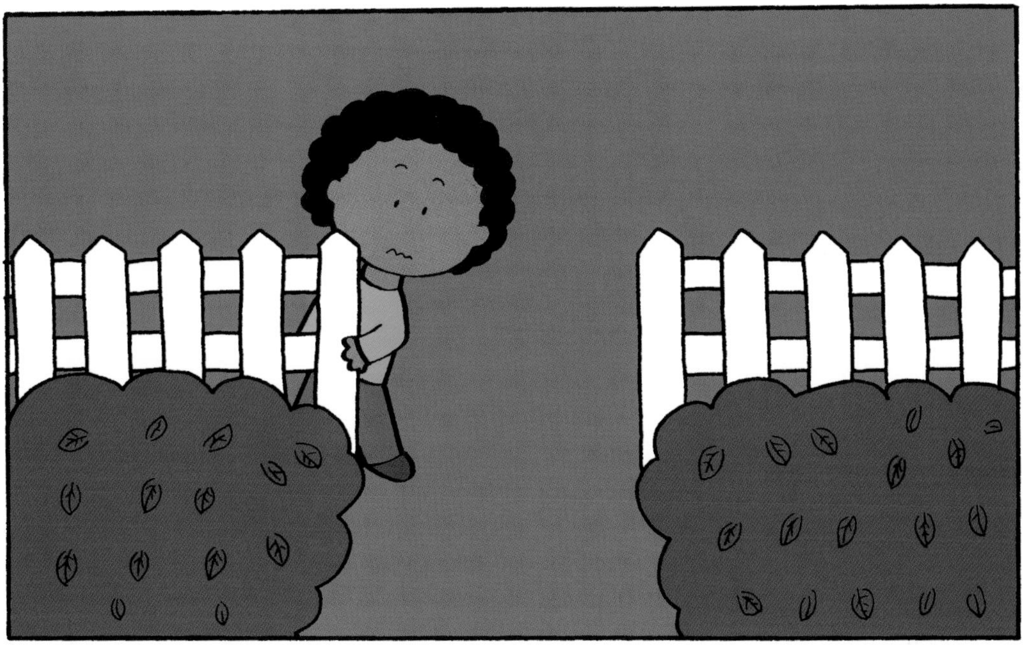

But he was caught by the evil neighbor!

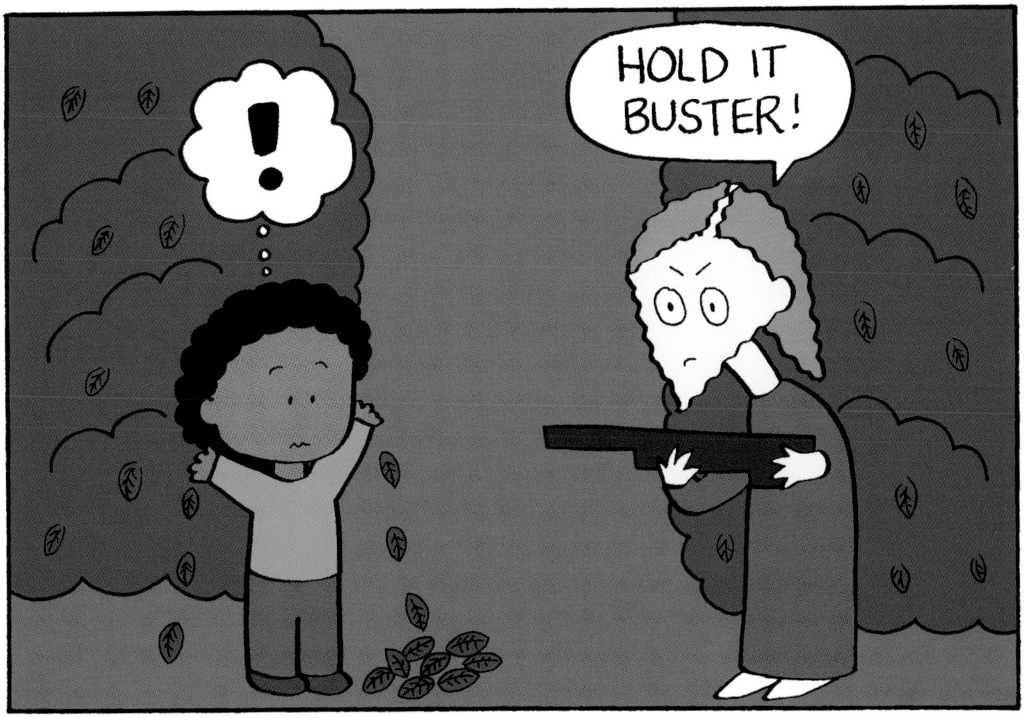
!
HOLD IT BUSTER!

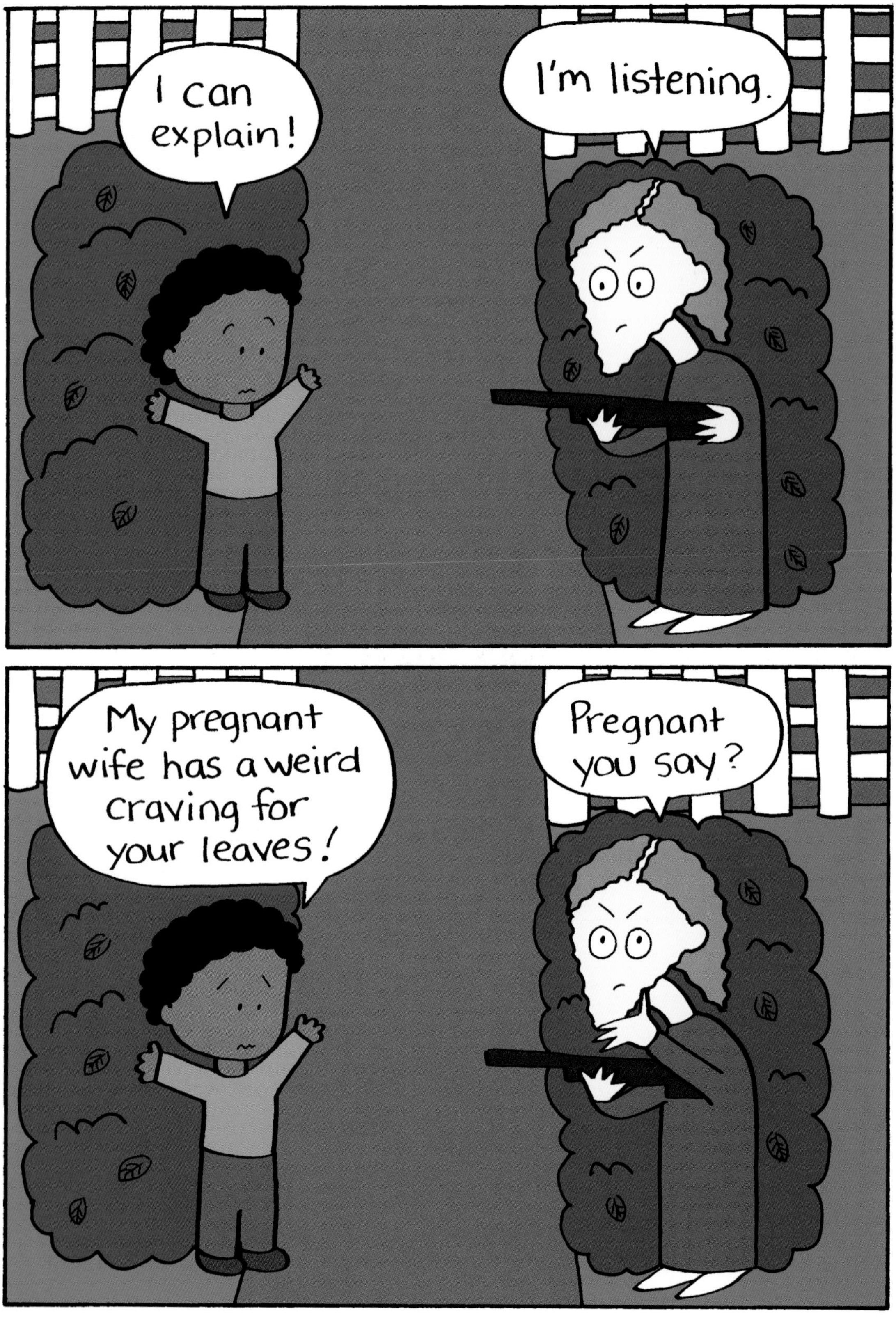
I can explain!
I'm listening.
My pregnant wife has a weird craving for your leaves!
Pregnant you say?

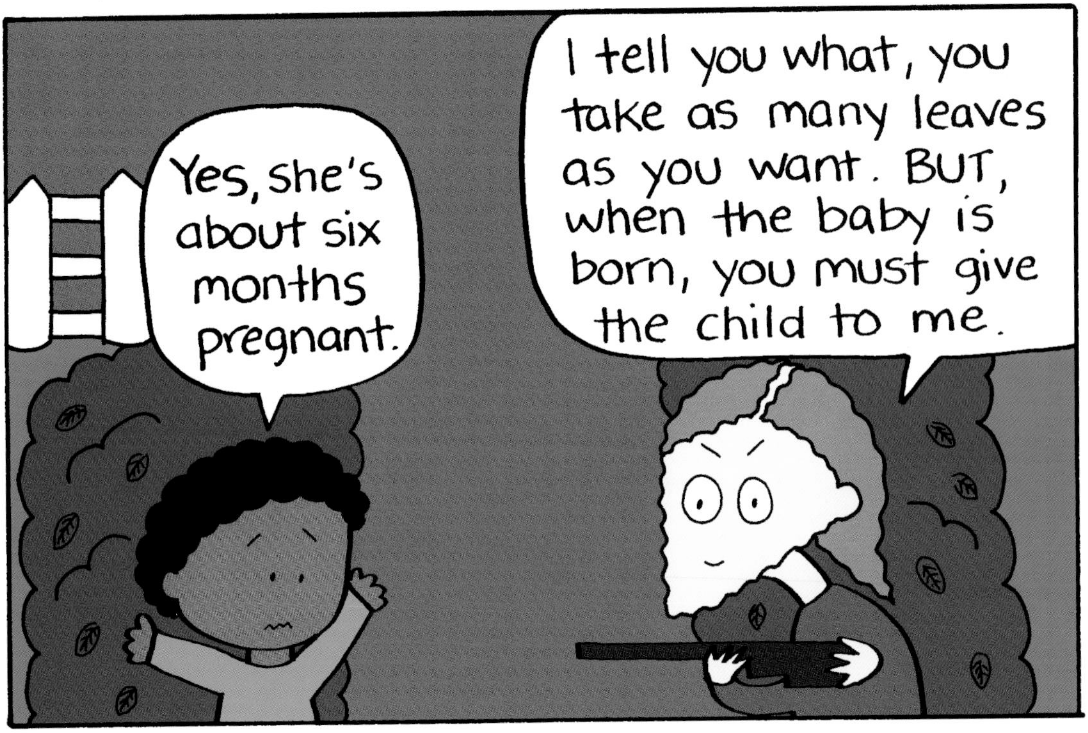
Yes, she's about six months pregnant.
I tell you what, you take as many leaves as you want. BUT, when the baby is born, you must give the child to me.

The man did not believe the old lady.

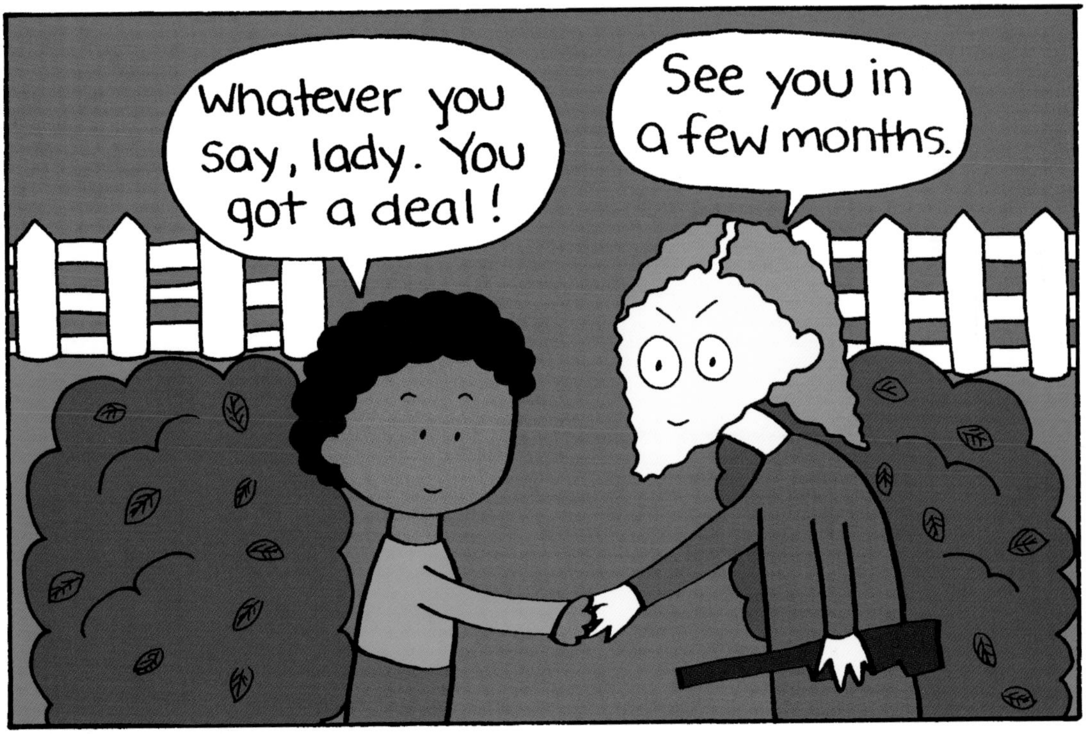
Whatever you say, lady. You got a deal!
See you in a few months.

When the baby was born, the evil lady came to claim the child.

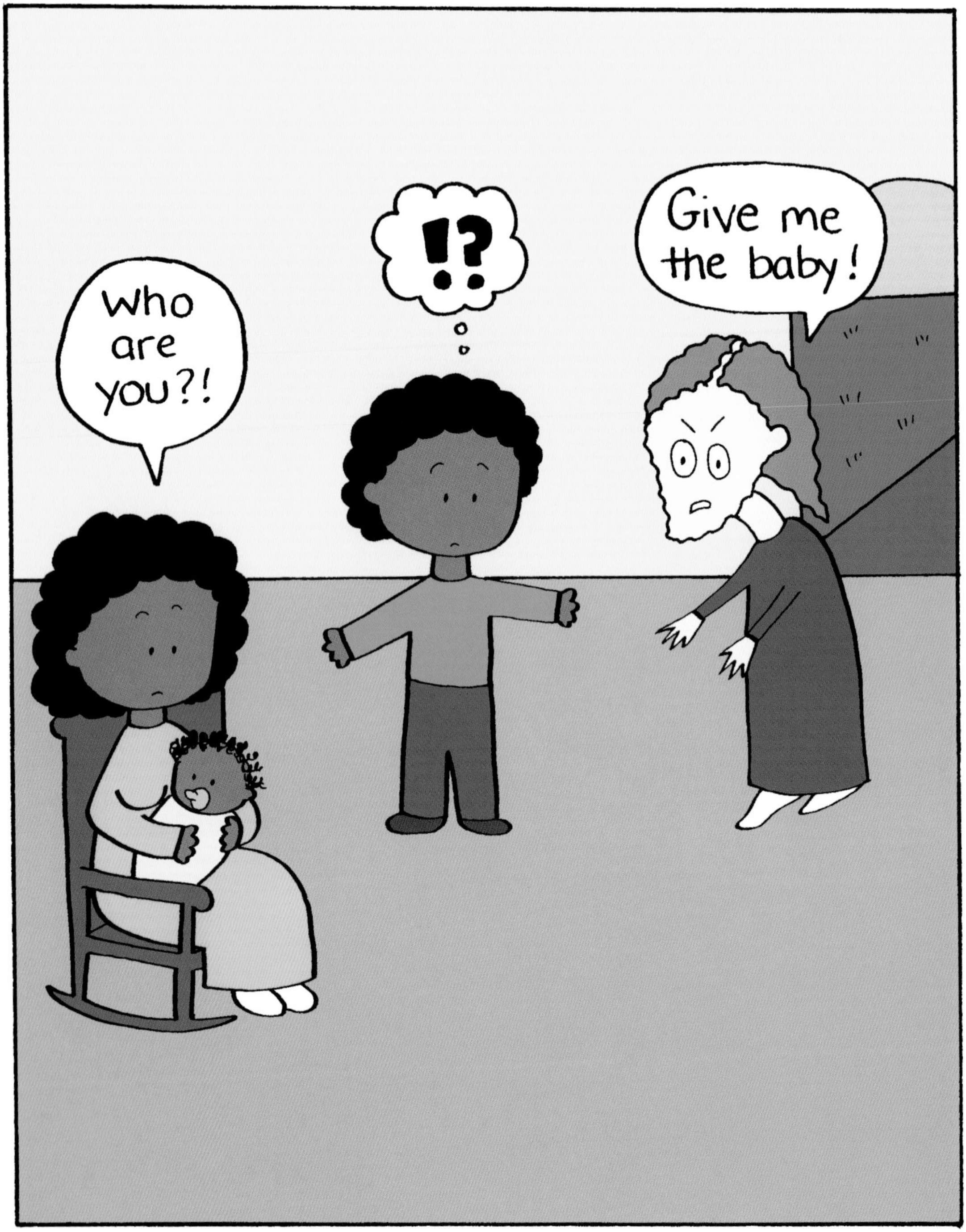
Who are you?!
!?
Give me the baby!

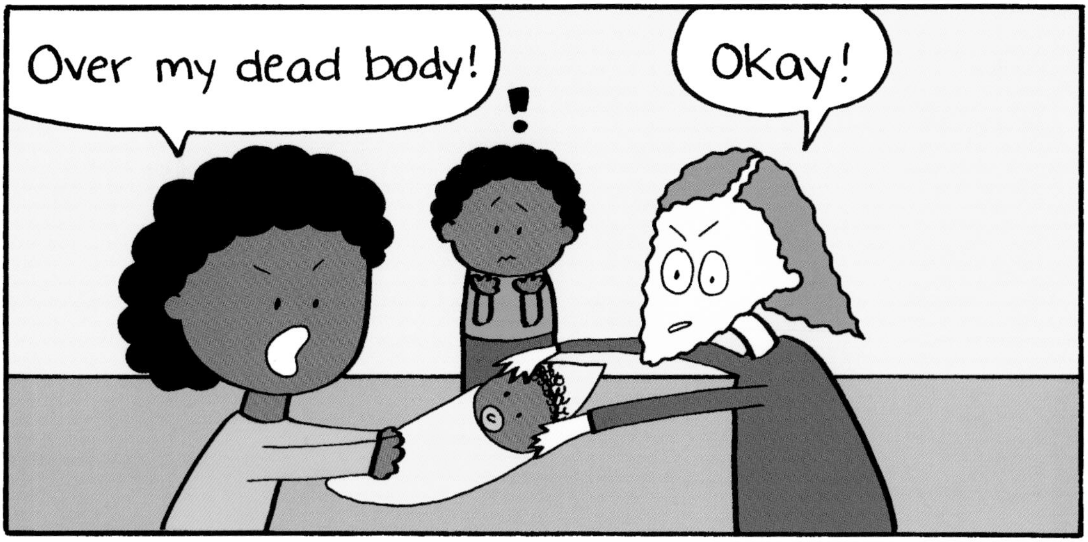
Over my dead body!
Okay!

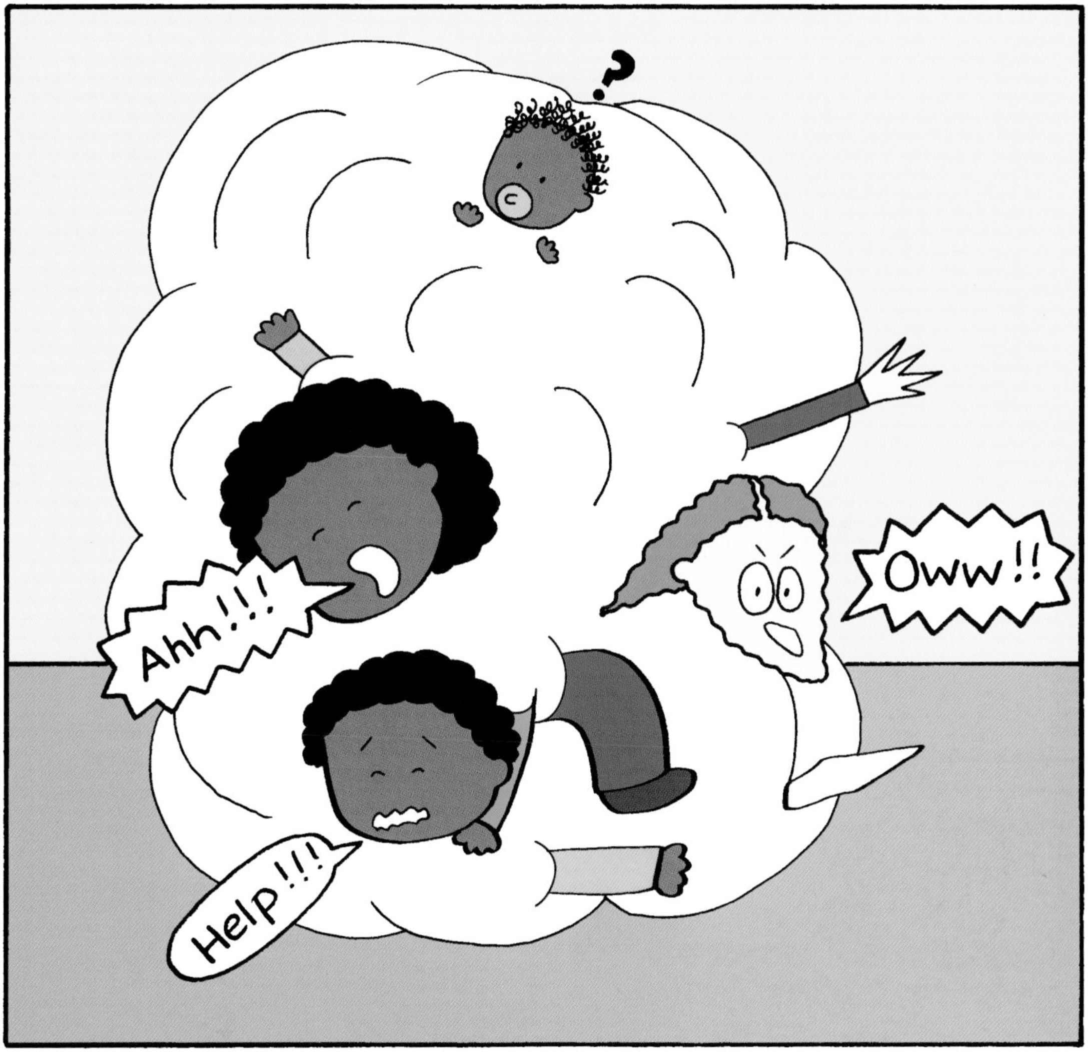
Ahh!!!
Oww!!
Help!!!

The old lady took the baby home.

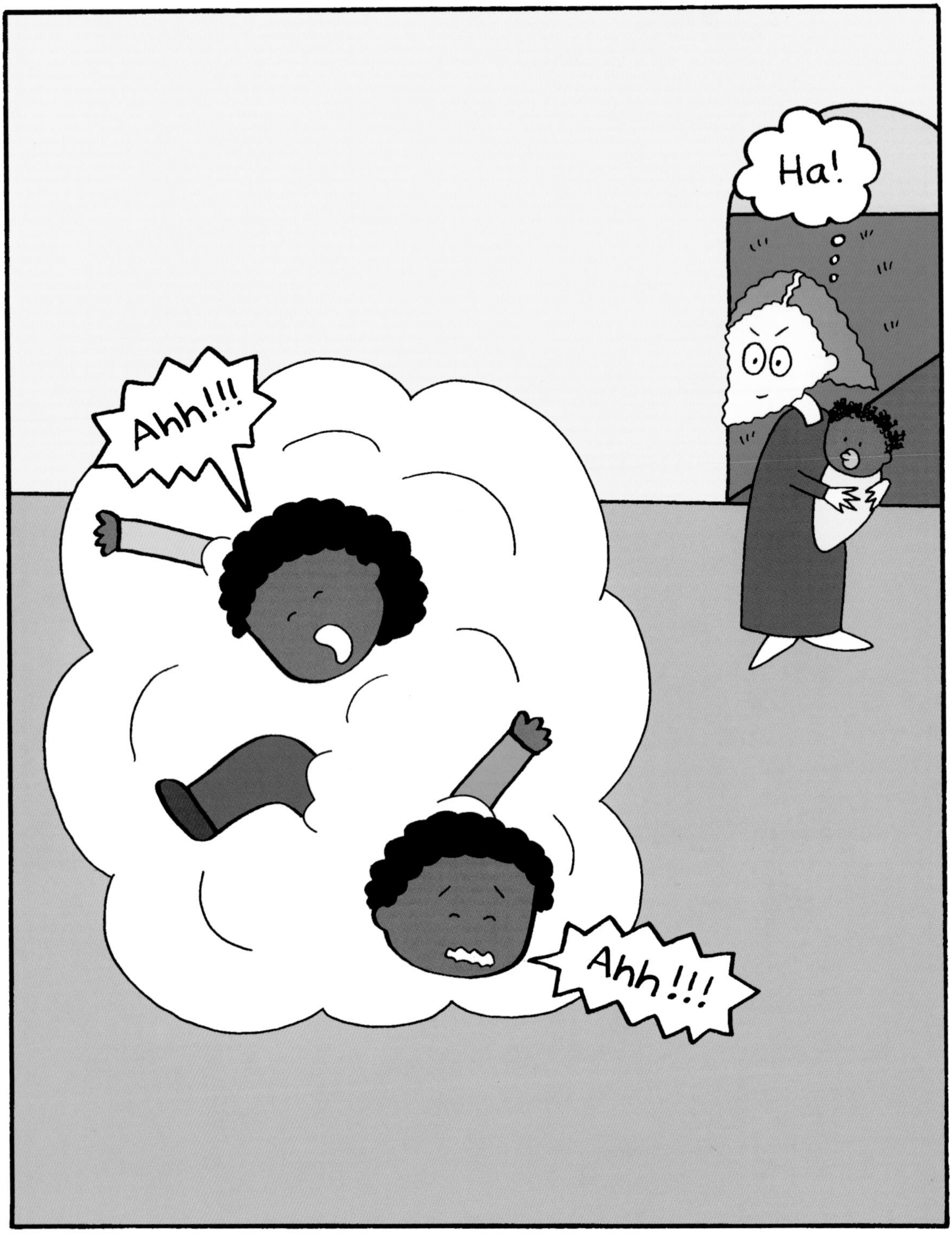
Ha!
Ahh!!!
Ahh!!!

The old lady loved the child as if she were her very own.

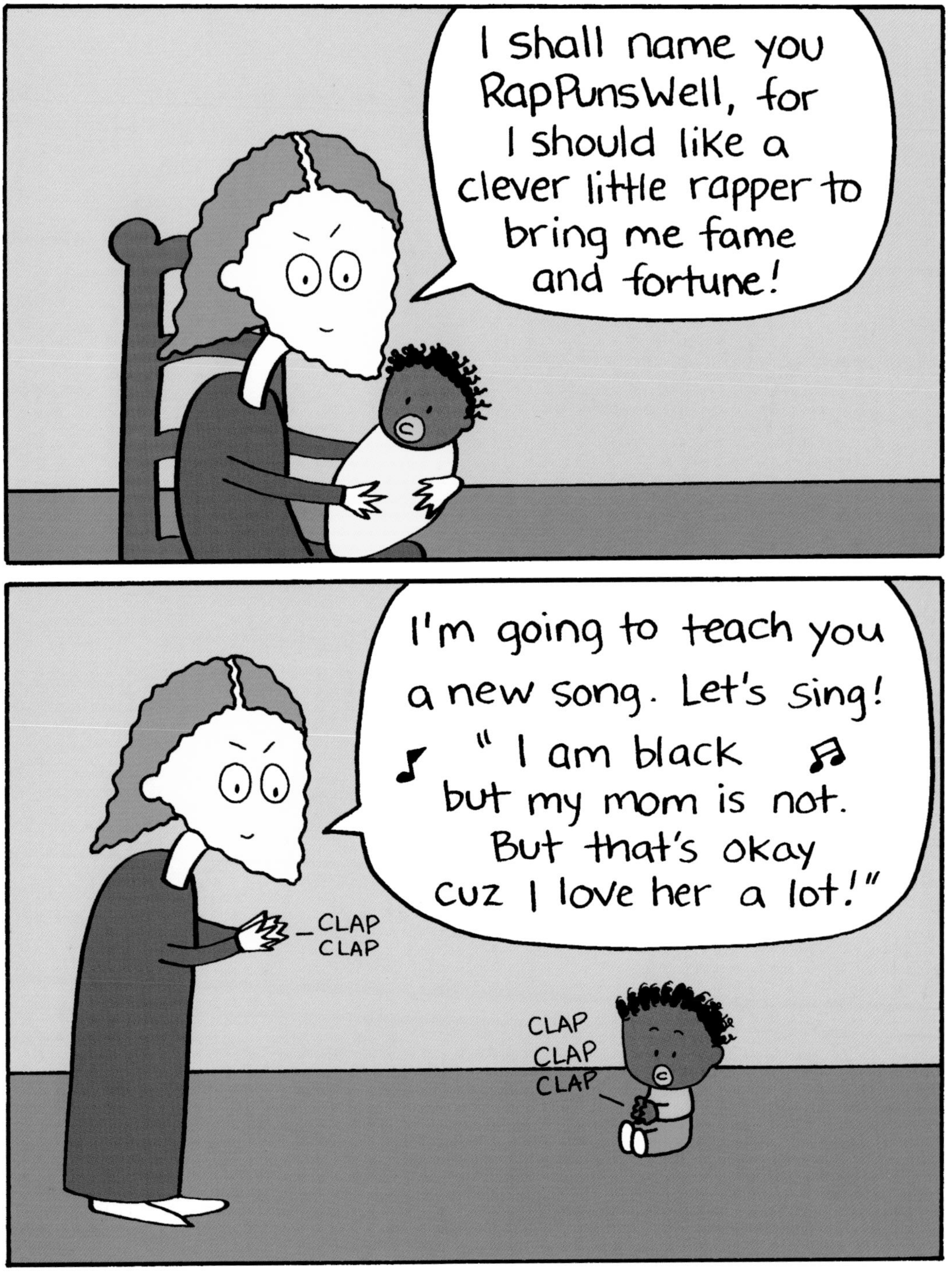
I shall name you RapPunsWell, for I should like a clever little rapper to bring me fame and fortune!
I'm going to teach you a new song. Let's sing! "I am black but my mom is not. But that's okay cuz I love her a lot!"
CLAP CLAP
CLAP CLAP CLAP

RapPunsWell was very talented.
She became very rich and famous.

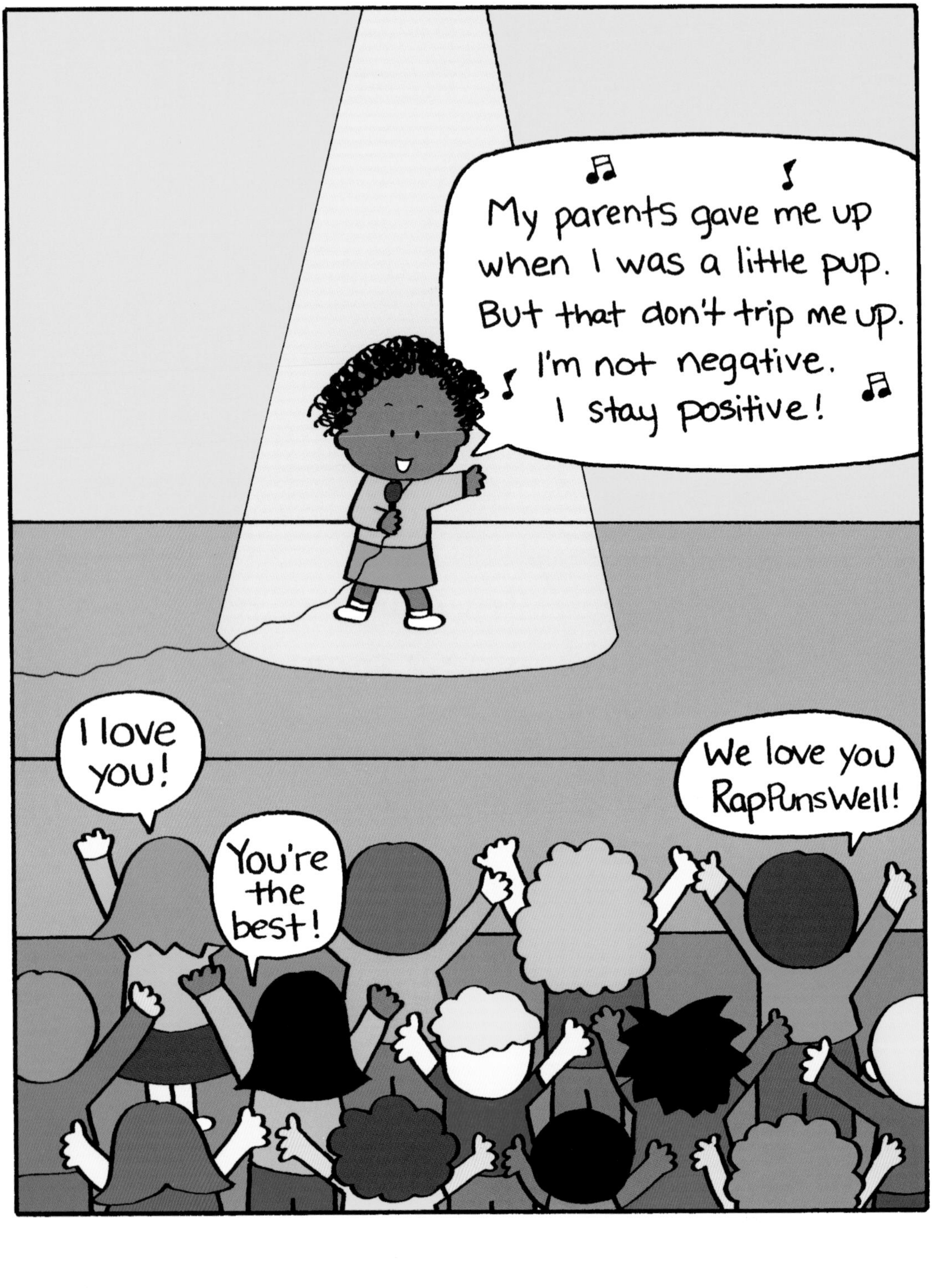
My parents gave me up
when I was a little pup.
But that don't trip me up.
I'm not negative.
I stay positive!
I love you!
You're the best!
We love you RapPunsWell!

But the old lady grew very jealous of RapPunsWell's popularity.

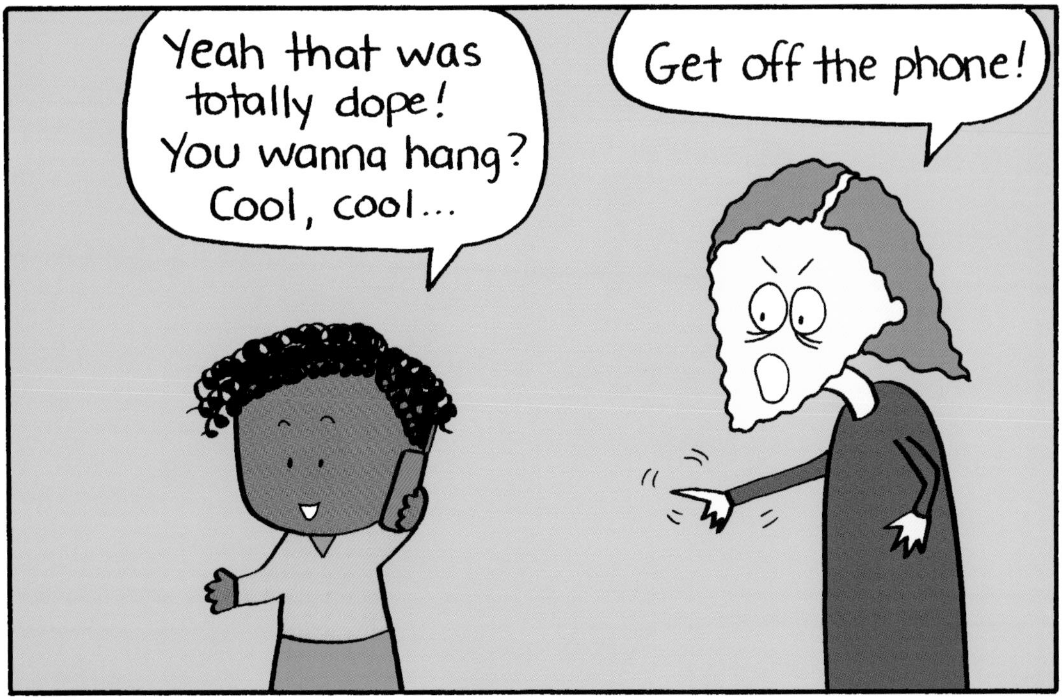

Yeah that was totally dope! You wanna hang? Cool, cool...
Get off the phone!

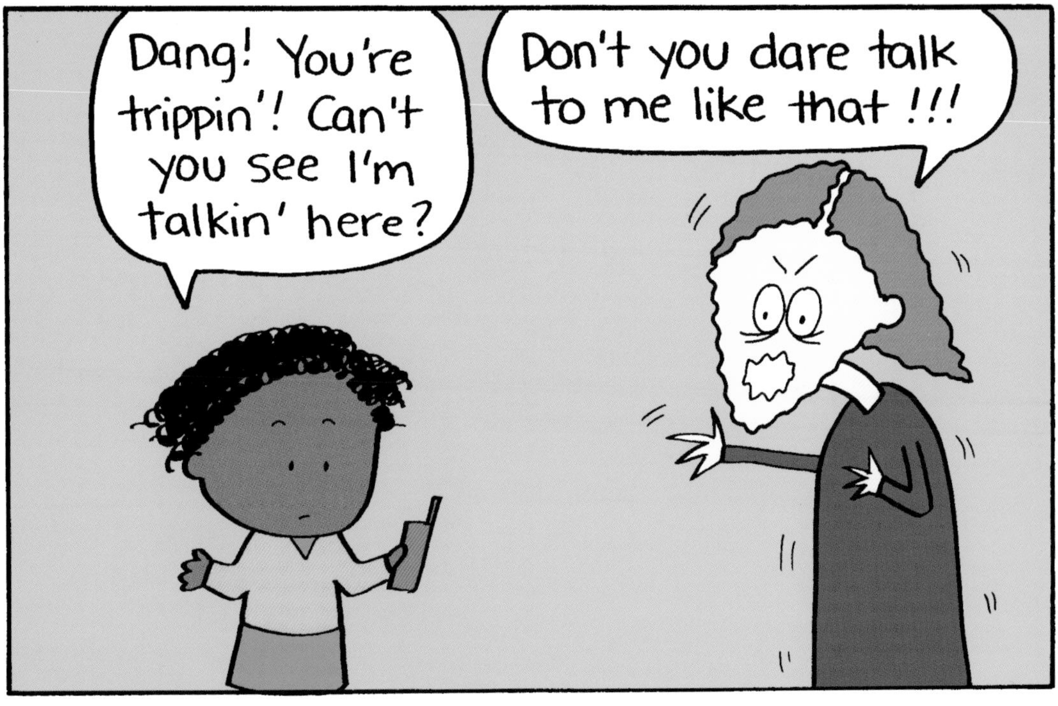

Dang! You're trippin'! Can't you see I'm talkin' here?
Don't you dare talk to me like that !!!

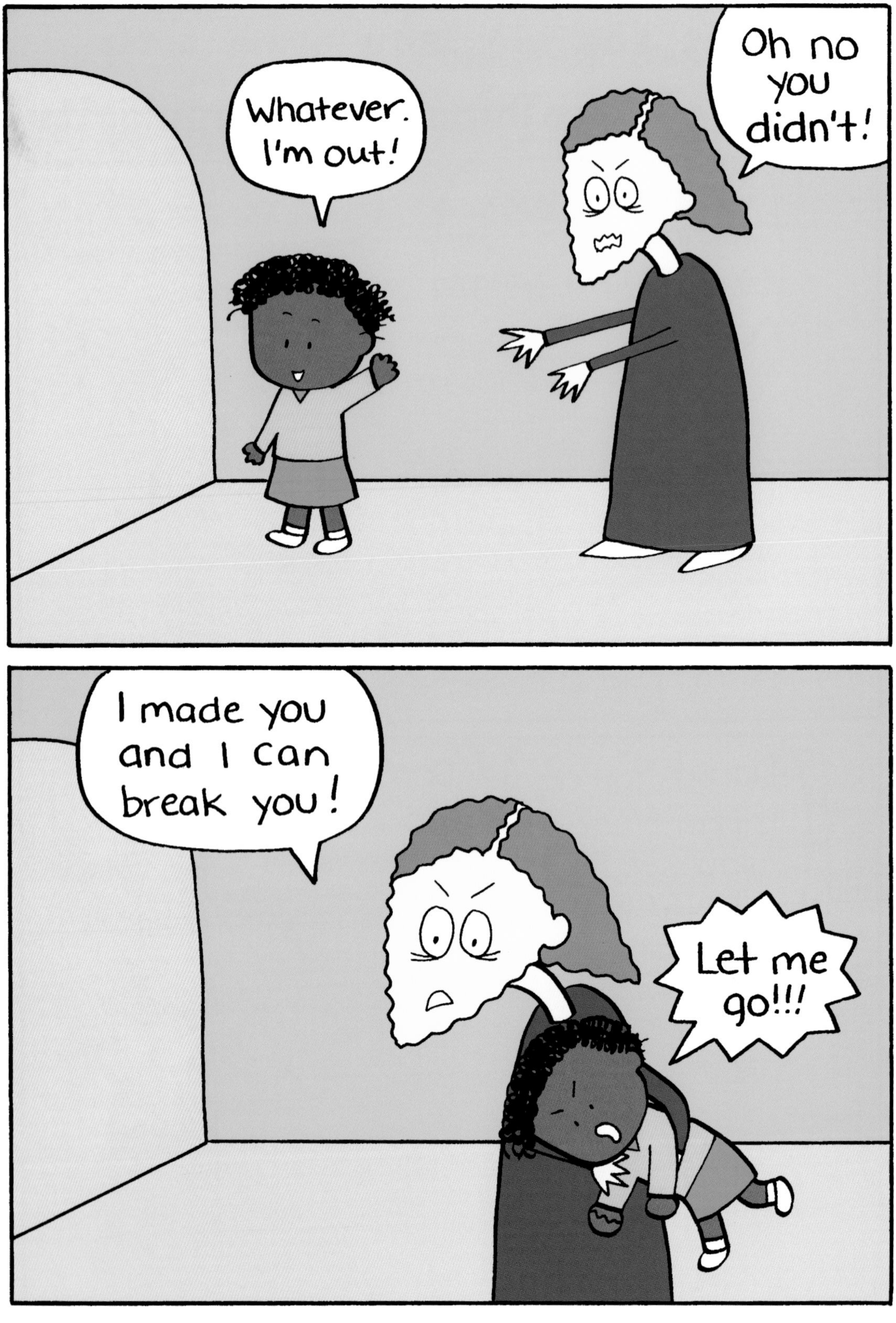
Whatever. I'm out!
Oh no you didn't!
I made you and I can break you!
Let me go!!!

She locked her up in a high tower.

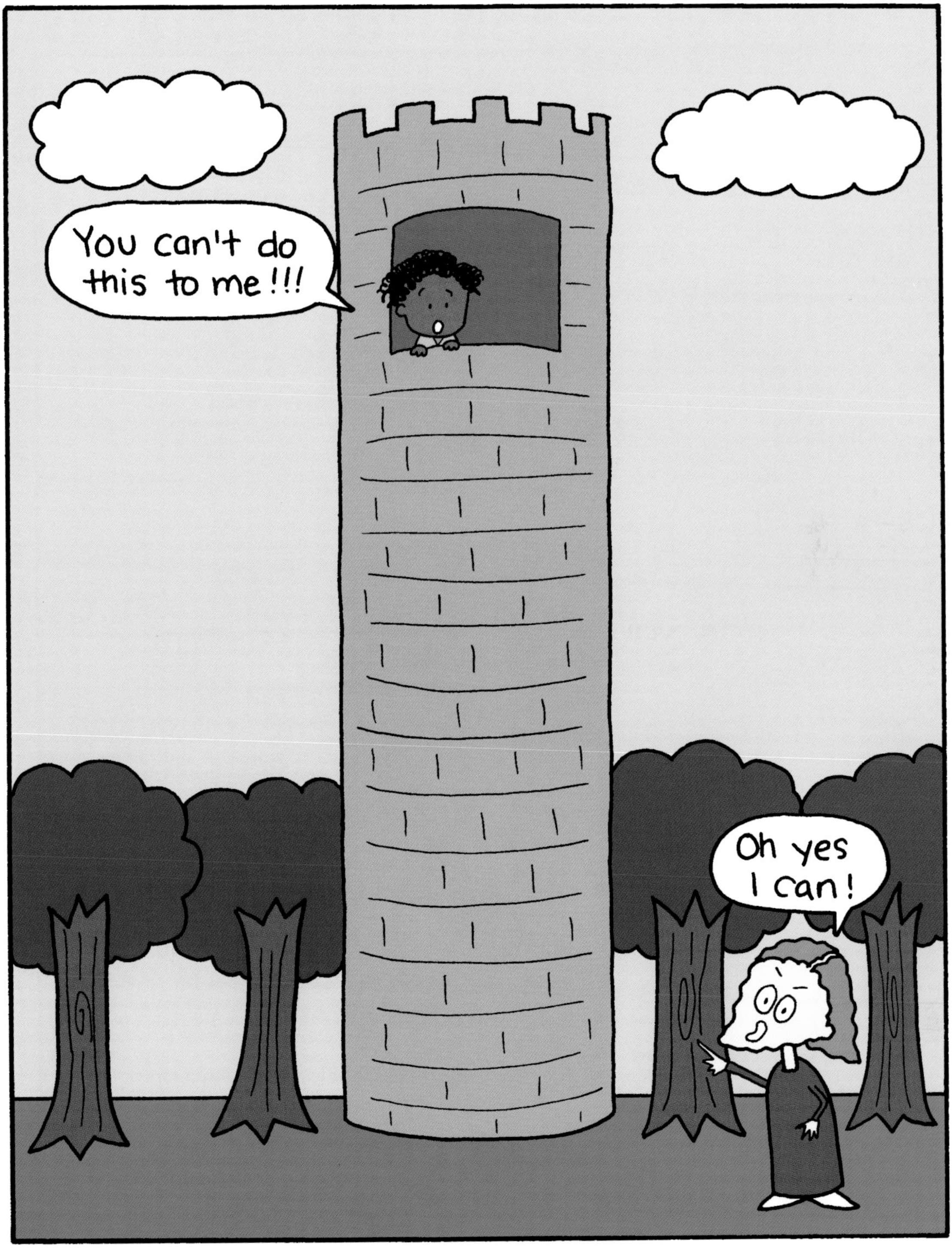

You can't do this to me!!!
Oh yes I can!

Many years passed. To pass the time, RapPunsWell rapped every day.

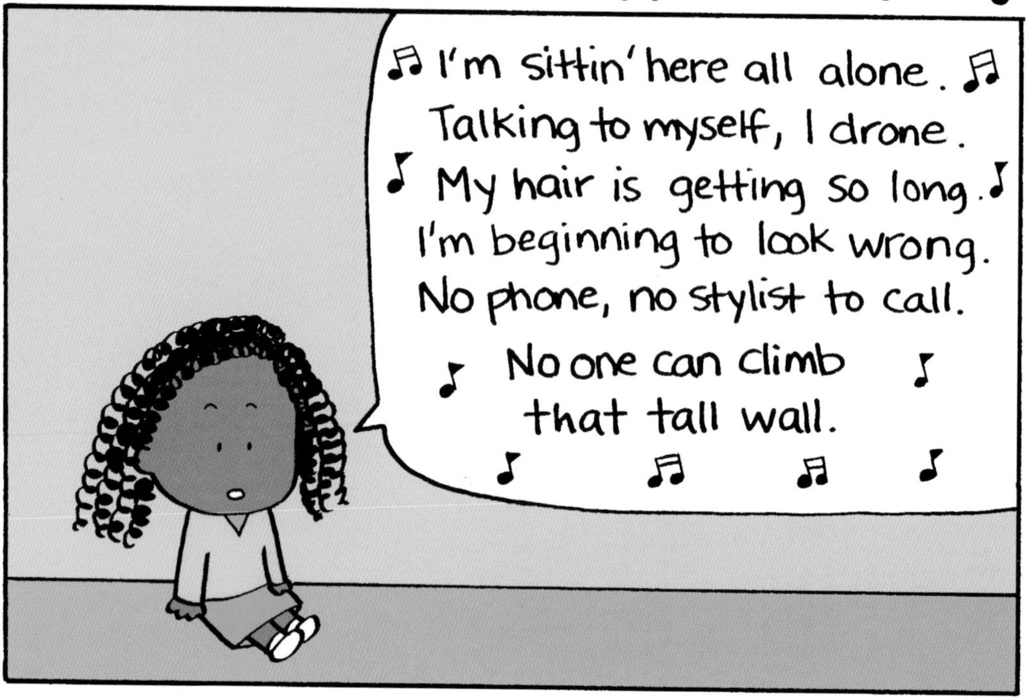
I'm sittin' here all alone.
Talking to myself, I drone.
My hair is getting so long.
I'm beginning to look wrong.
No phone, no stylist to call.
No one can climb that tall wall.

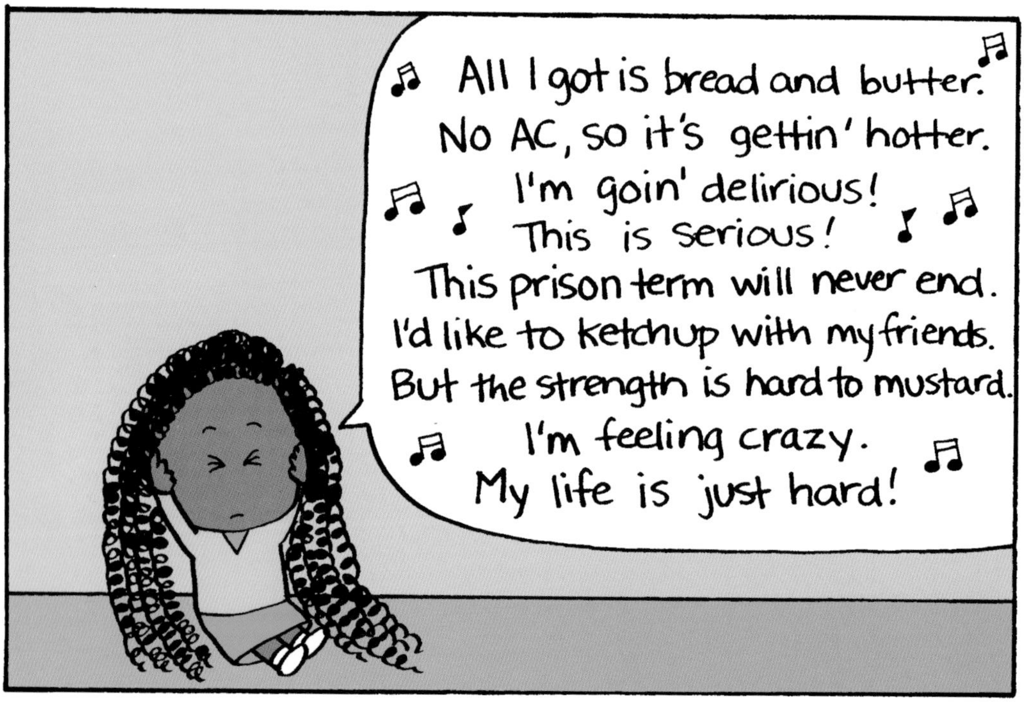
All I got is bread and butter.
No AC, so it's gettin' hotter.
I'm goin' delirious!
This is serious!
This prison term will never end.
I'd like to ketchup with my friends.
But the strength is hard to mustard.
I'm feeling crazy.
My life is just hard!

The old lady visited RapPunsWell.

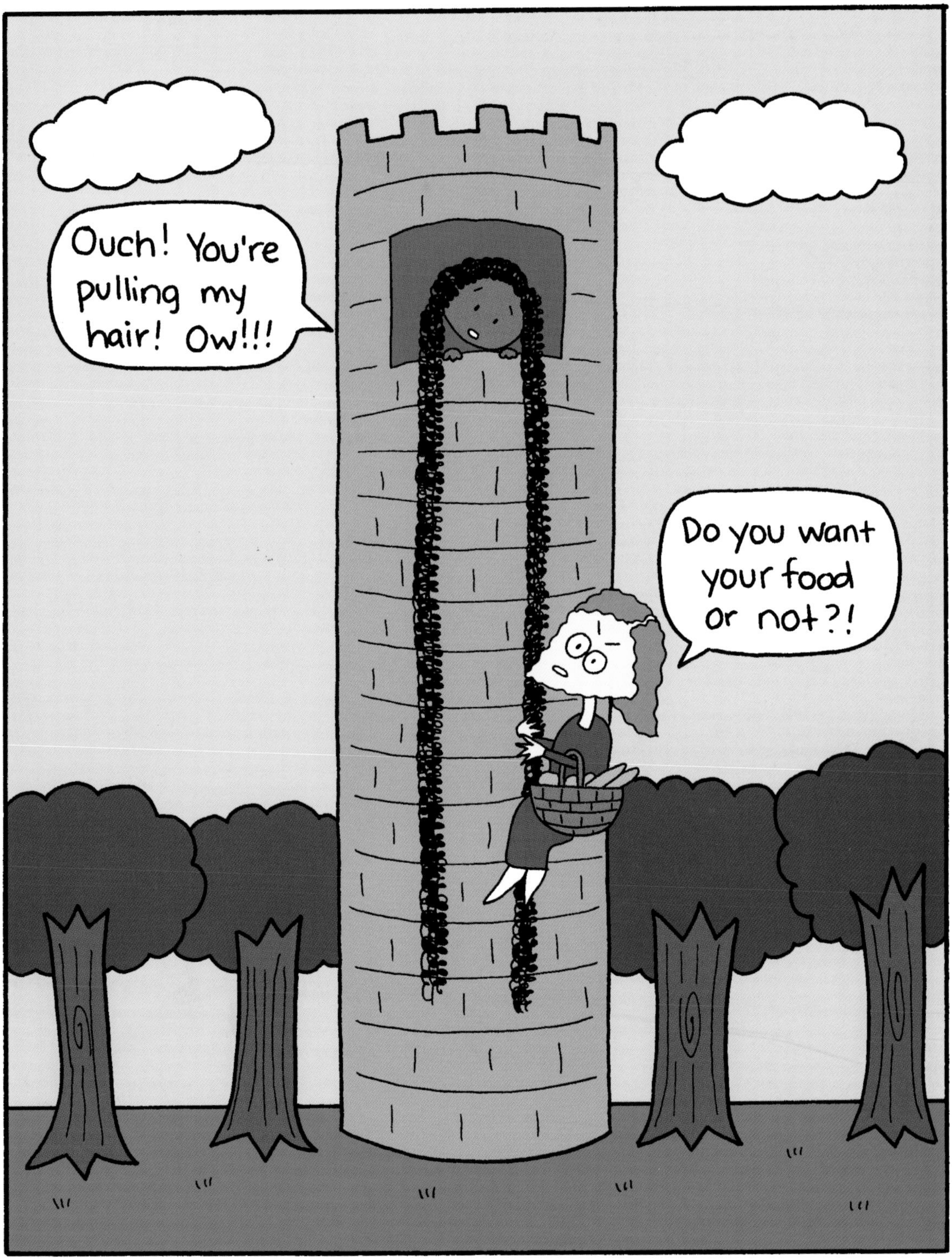
Ouch! You're pulling my hair! Ow!!!
Do you want your food or not?!

One day, a prince heard her rapping.

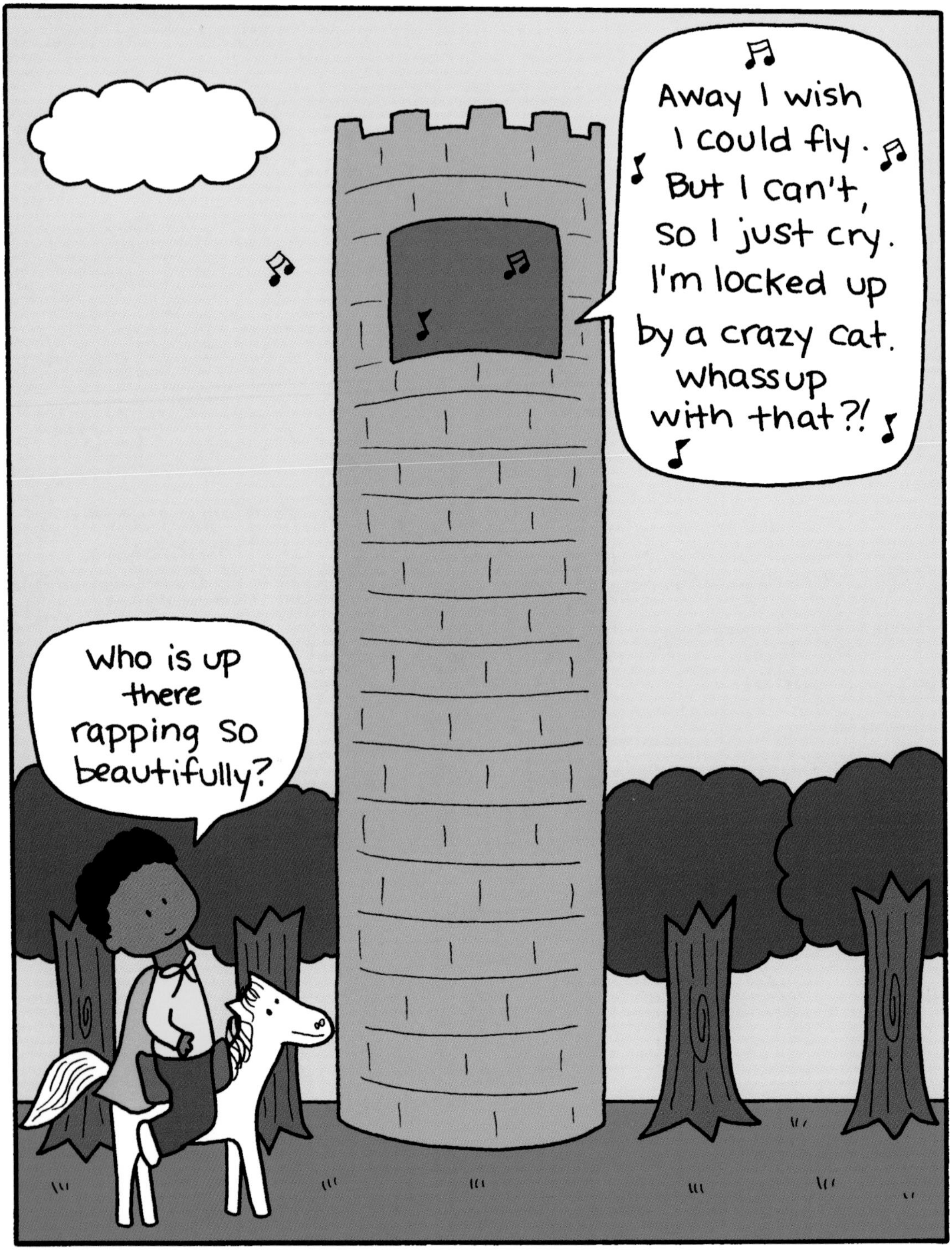
Away I wish I could fly. But I can't, so I just cry. I'm locked up by a crazy cat. Whassup with that?!
Who is up there rapping so beautifully?

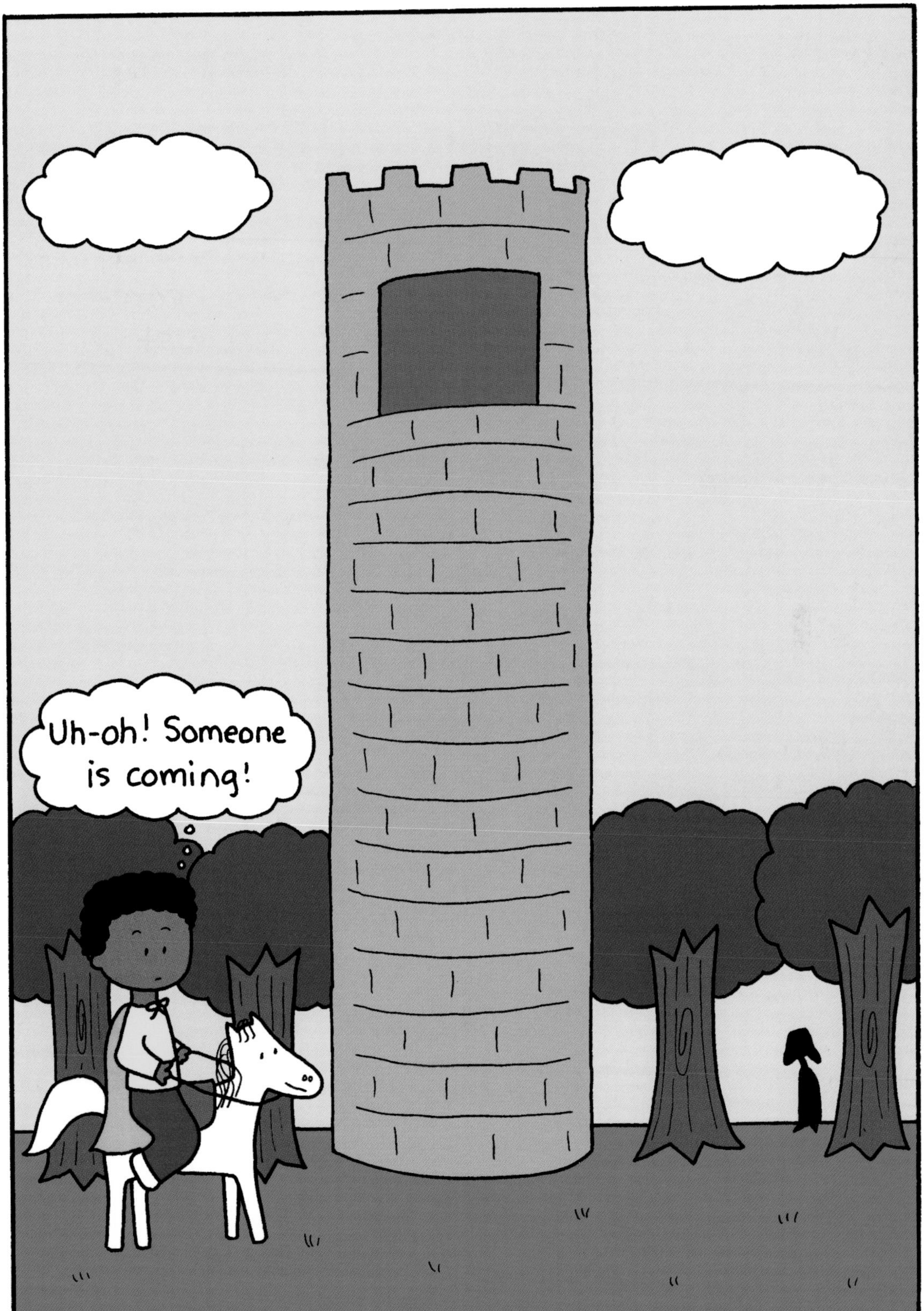
Uh-oh! Someone is coming!

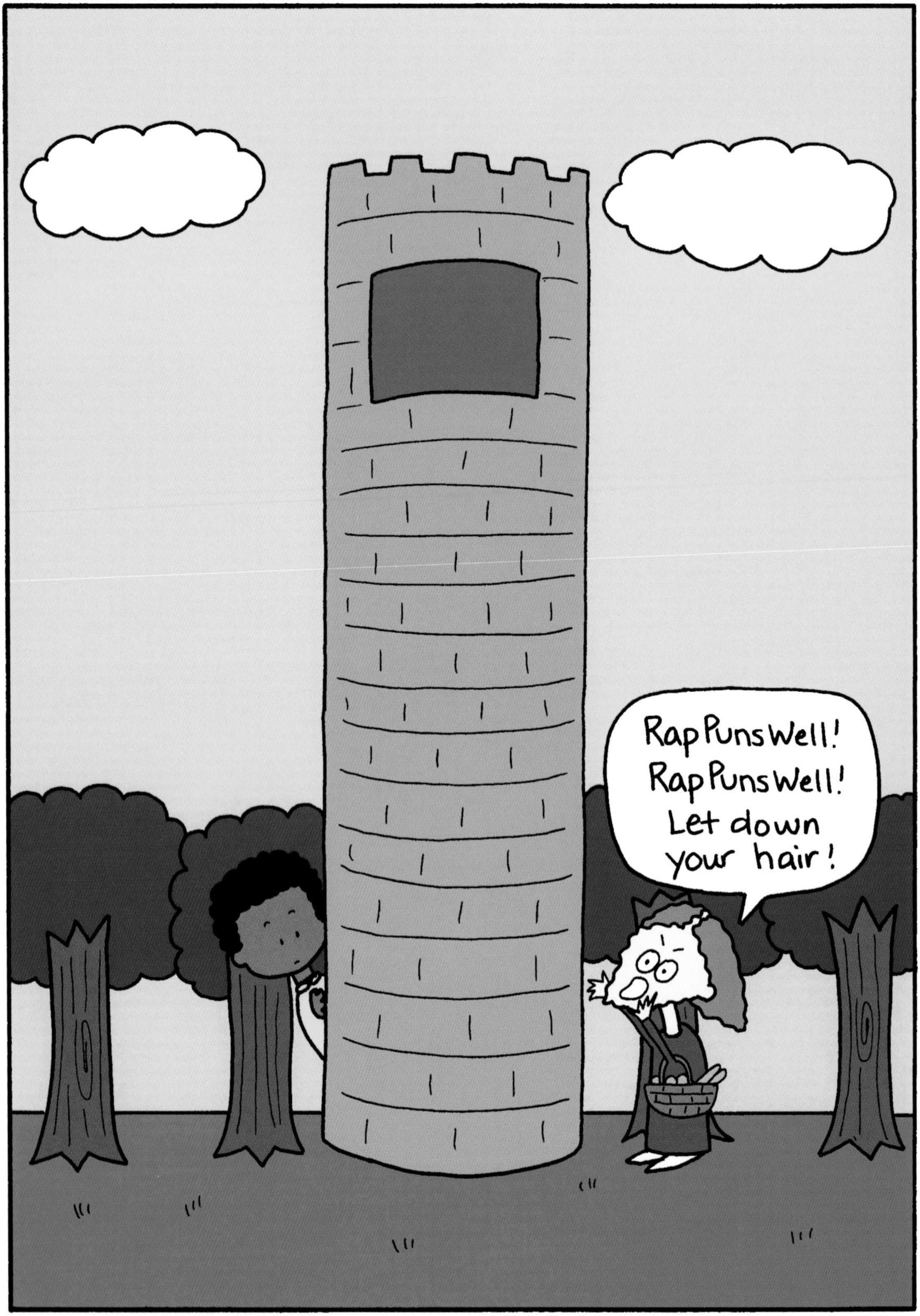
Rap Puns Well! Rap Puns Well! Let down your hair!

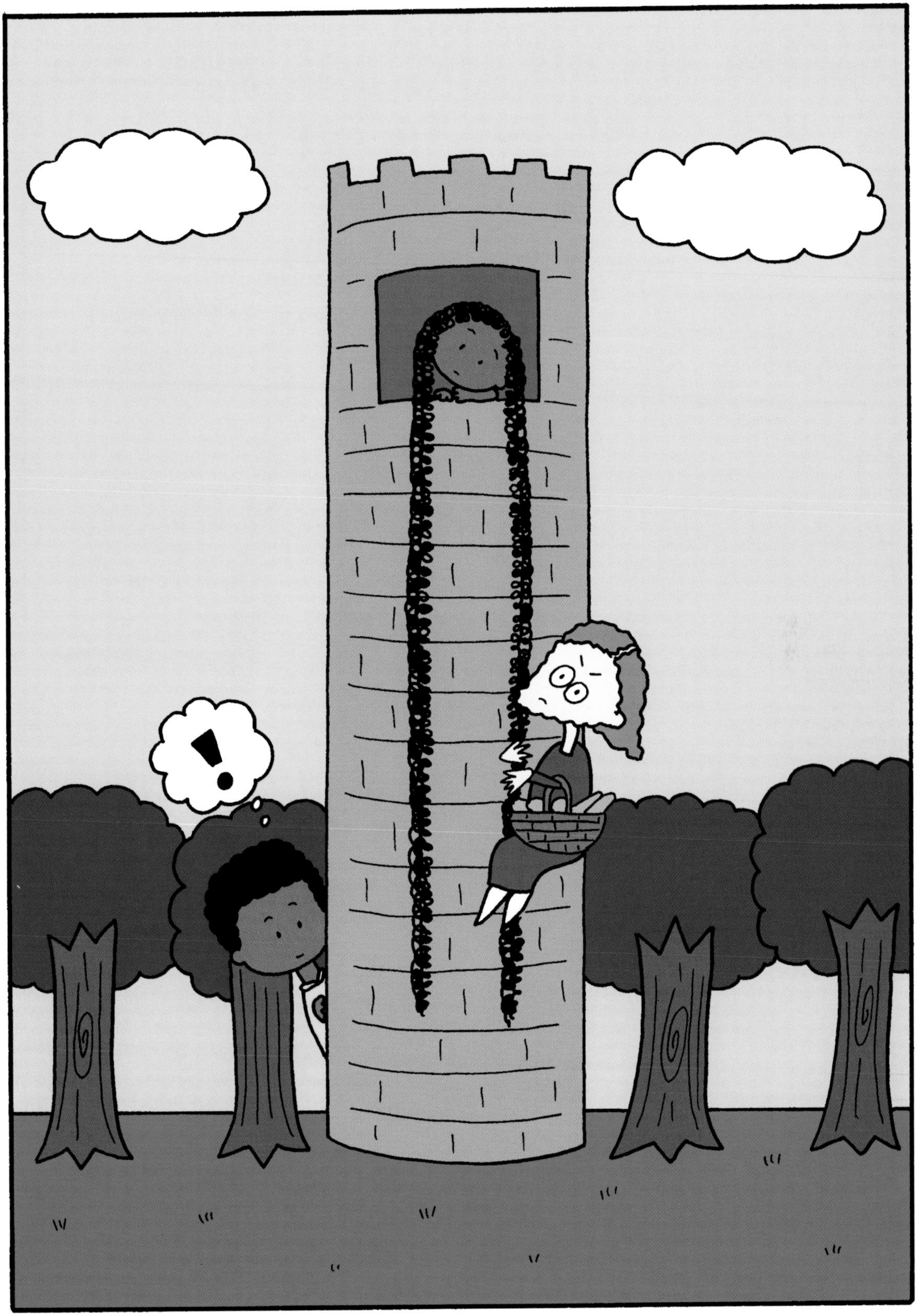
!

When the old lady was gone, the prince called out to RapPunsWell.

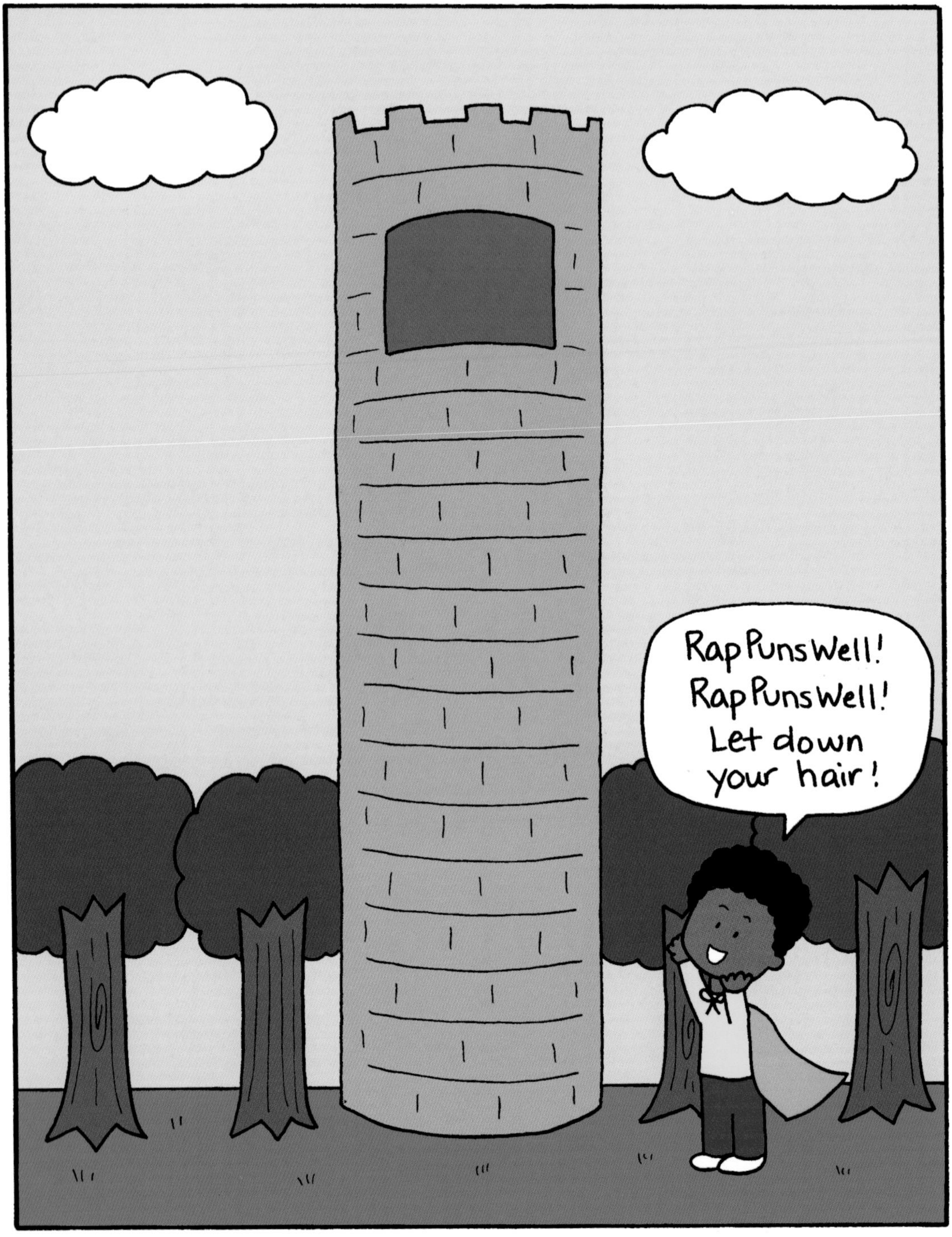
RapPunsWell! RapPunsWell! Let down your hair!

Her hair fell down like a waterfall.

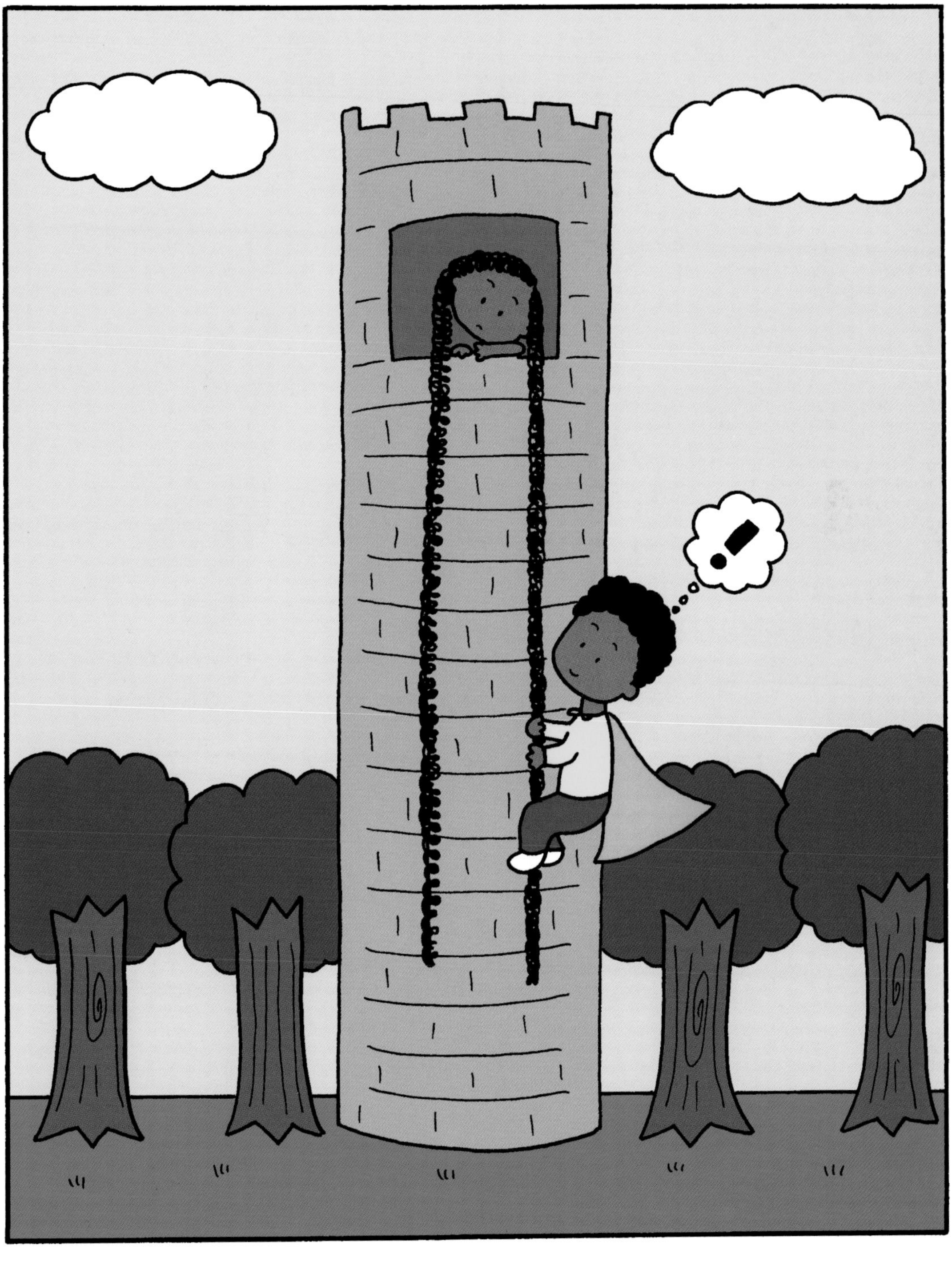
!

When they saw each other, it was love at first sight!

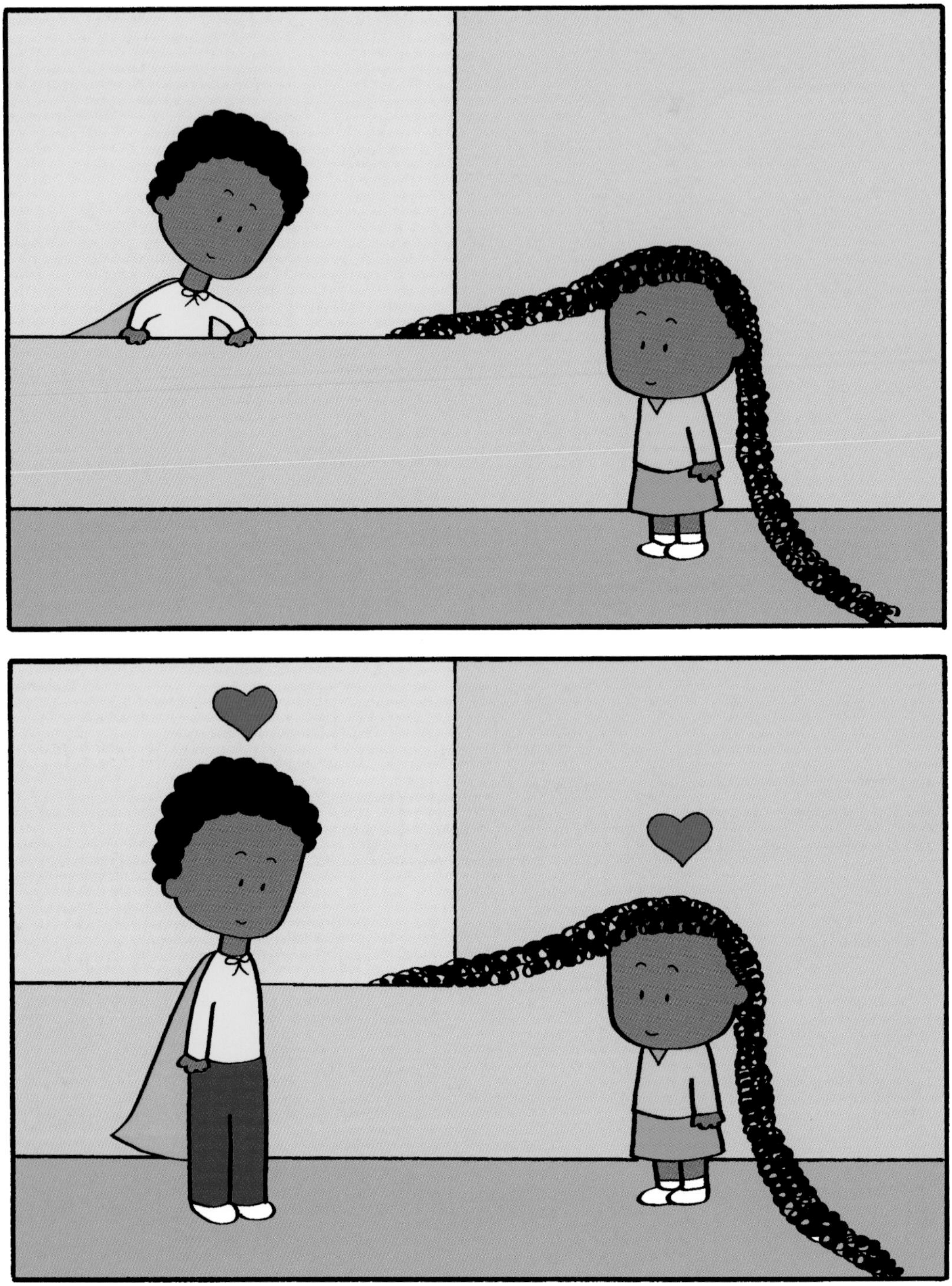

But the old lady discovered her affair.

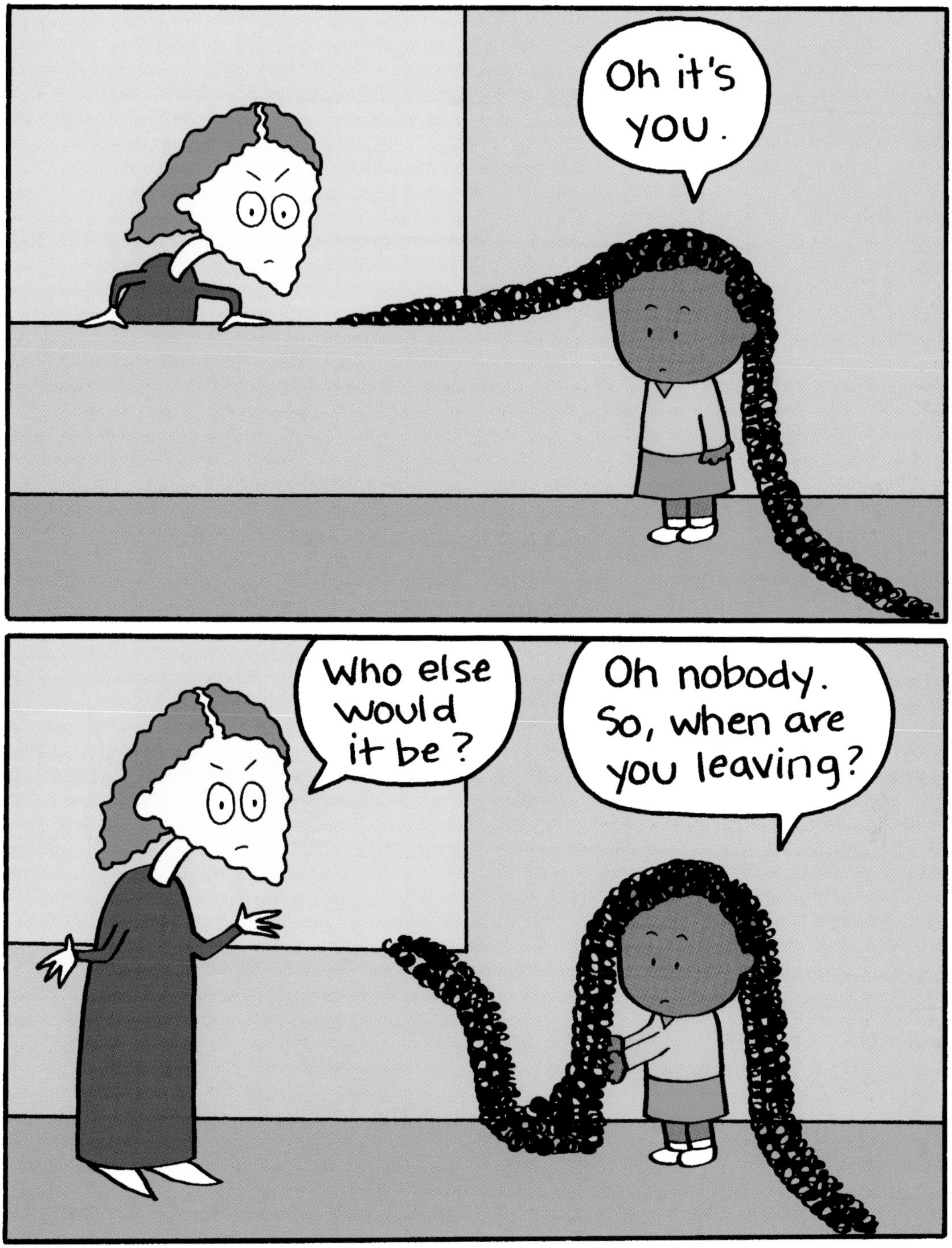
Oh it's you.
Who else would it be?
Oh nobody. So, when are you leaving?

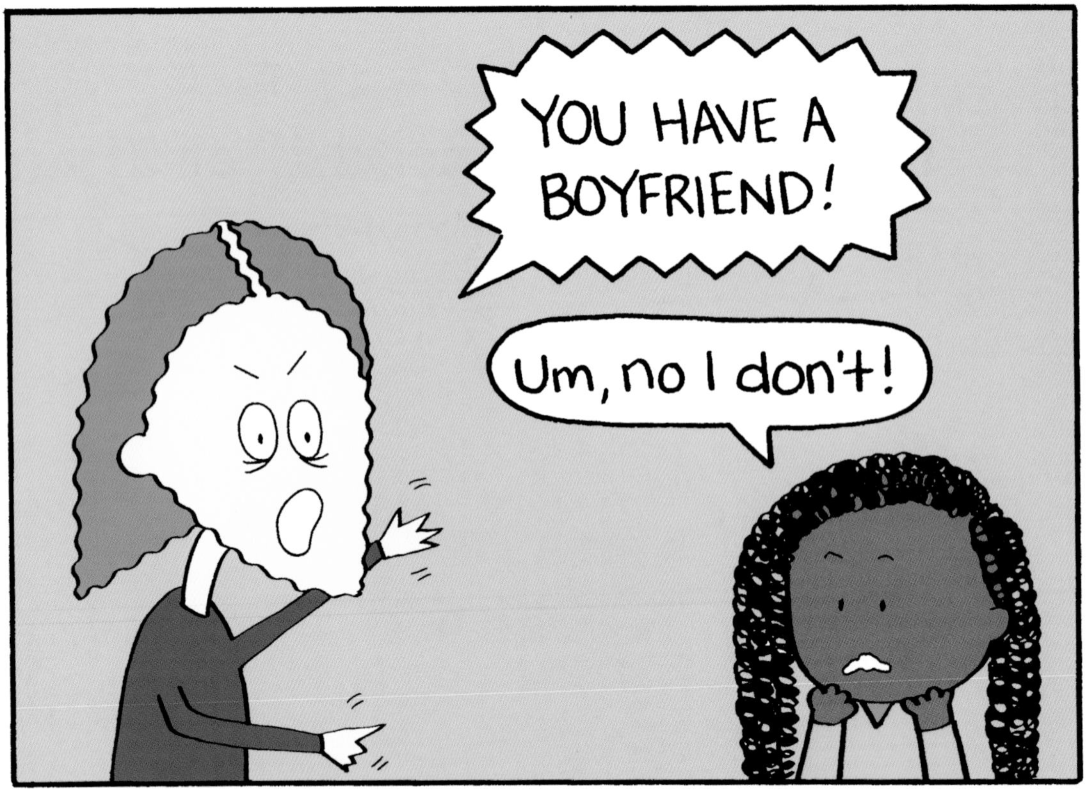
YOU HAVE A BOYFRIEND!
Um, no I don't!

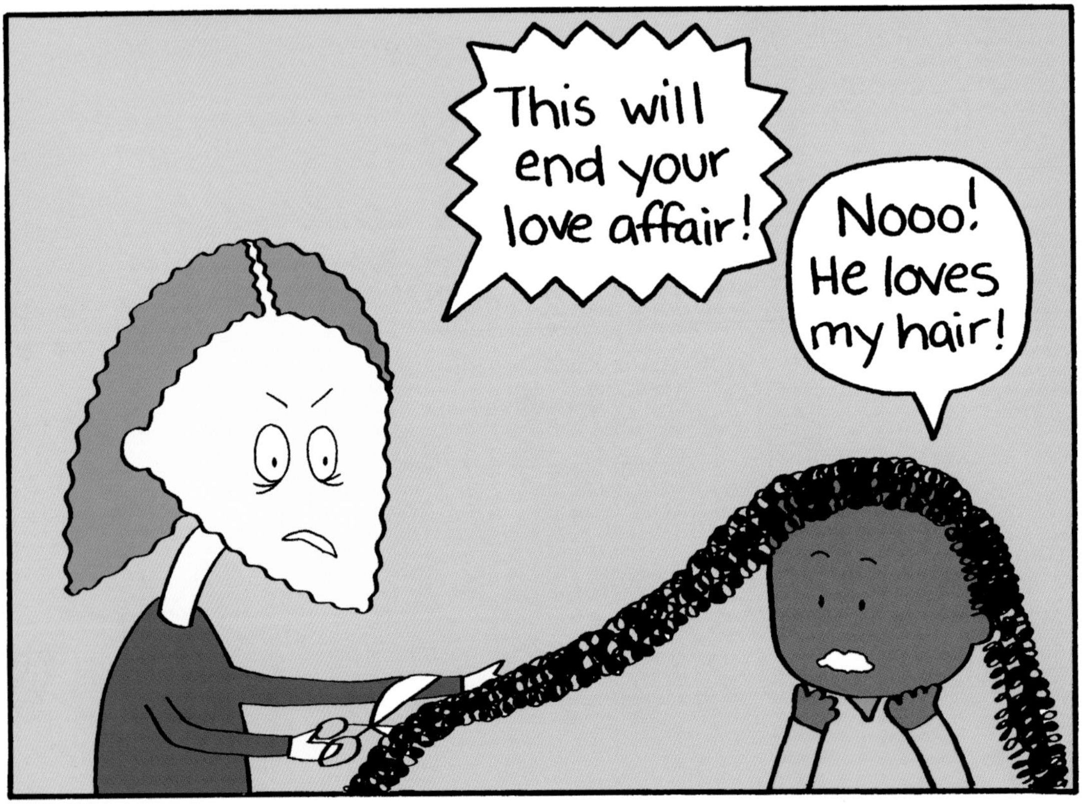
This will end your love affair!
Nooo! He loves my hair!

The old lady was so mad, she threw RapPunsWell out!

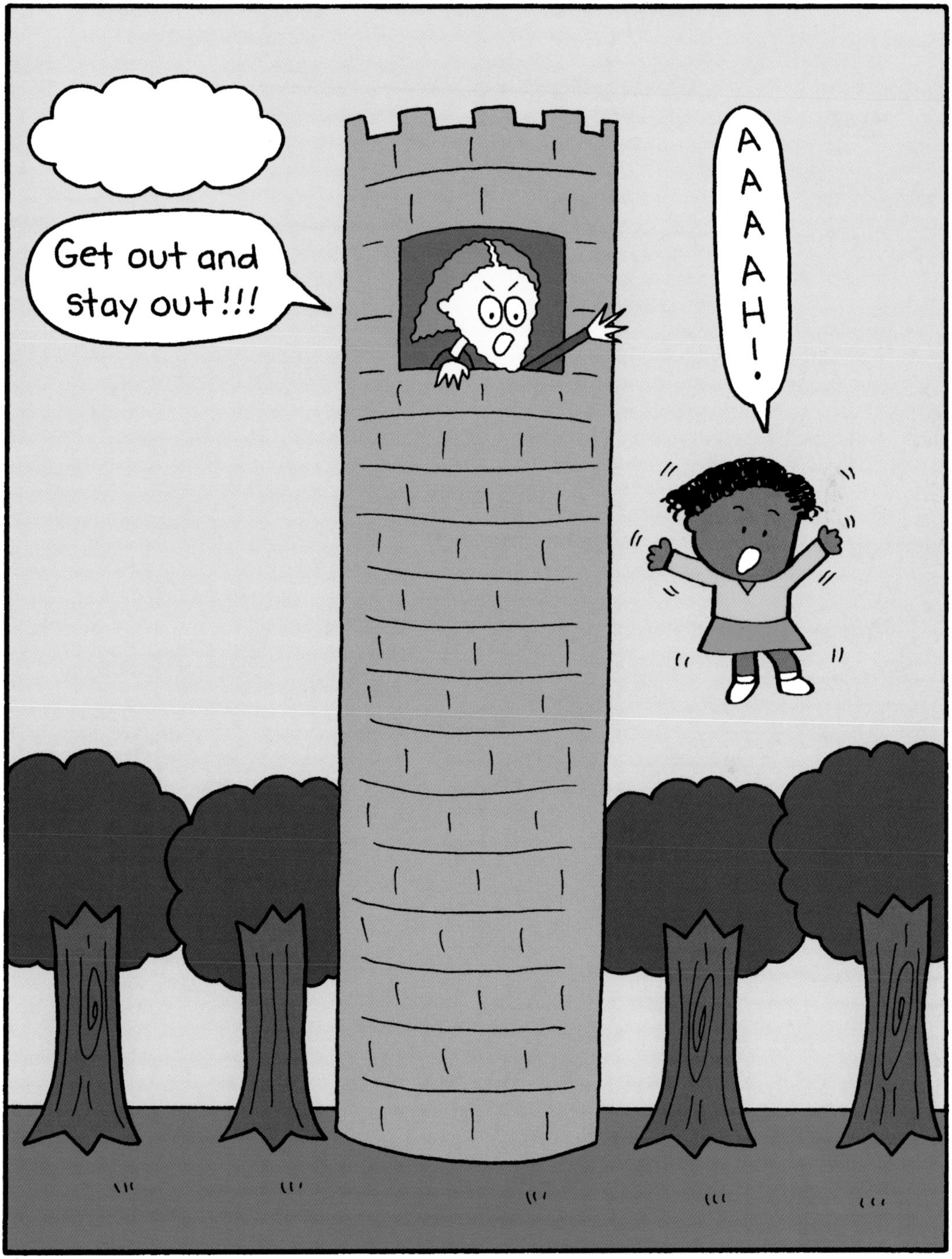
Get out and stay out!!!
AAAAAH!

Later that same day, the prince came to see RapPunsWell.

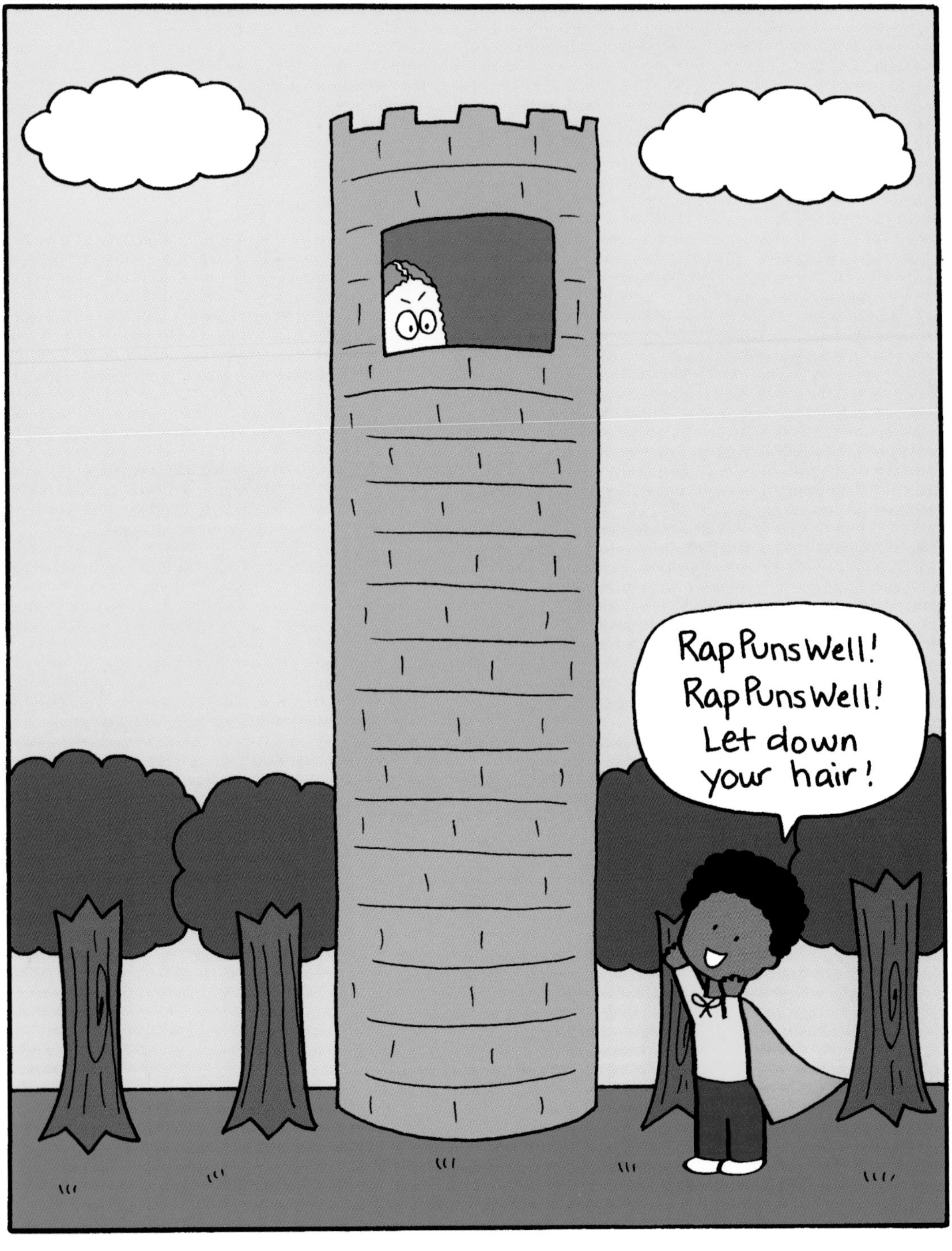
RapPunsWell! RapPunsWell! Let down your hair!

The old lady greeted the prince.

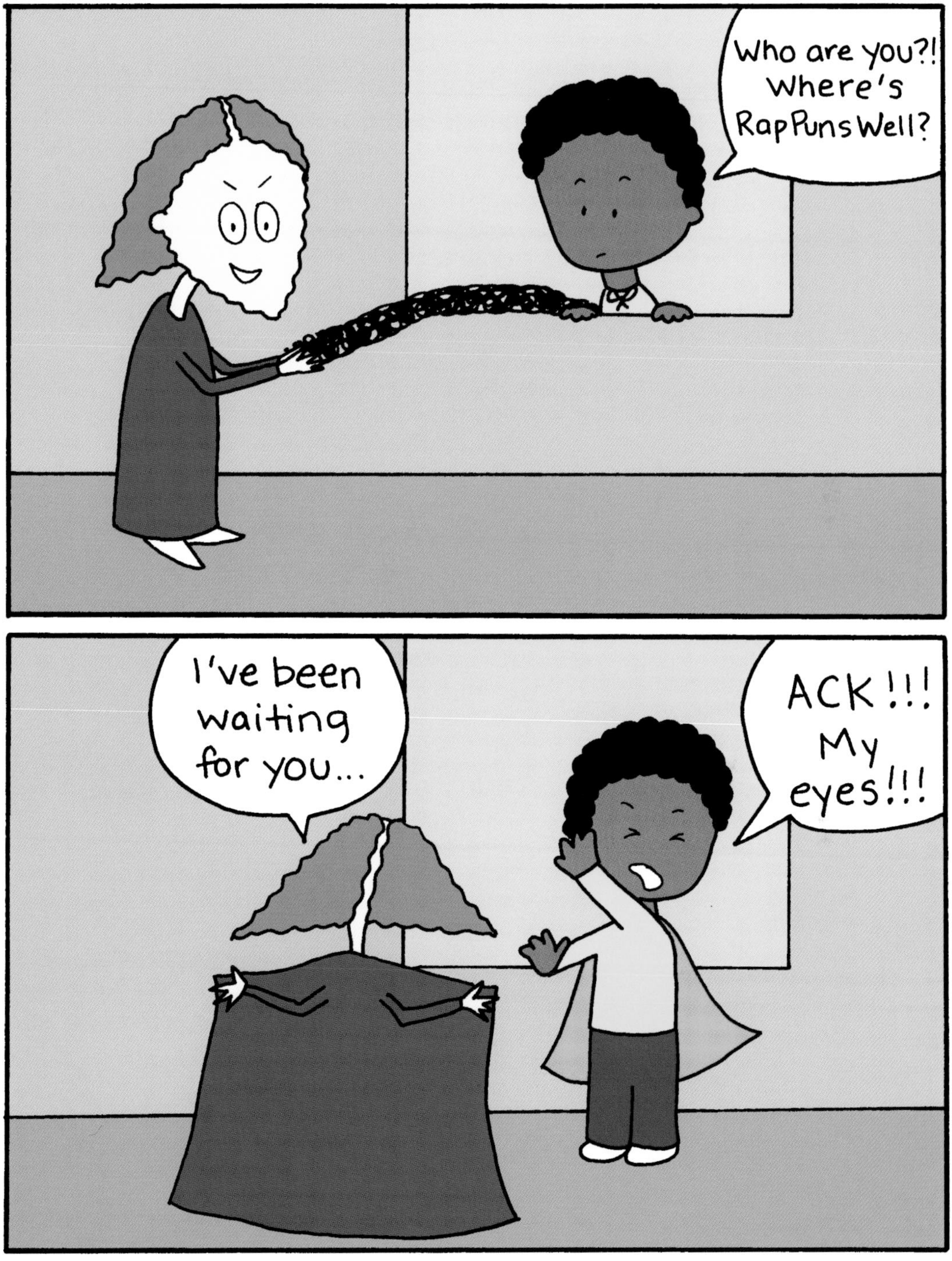
Who are you?! Where's RapPunsWell?
I've been waiting for you...
ACK!!! My eyes!!!

Mad with grief, the prince threw himself from the tower.

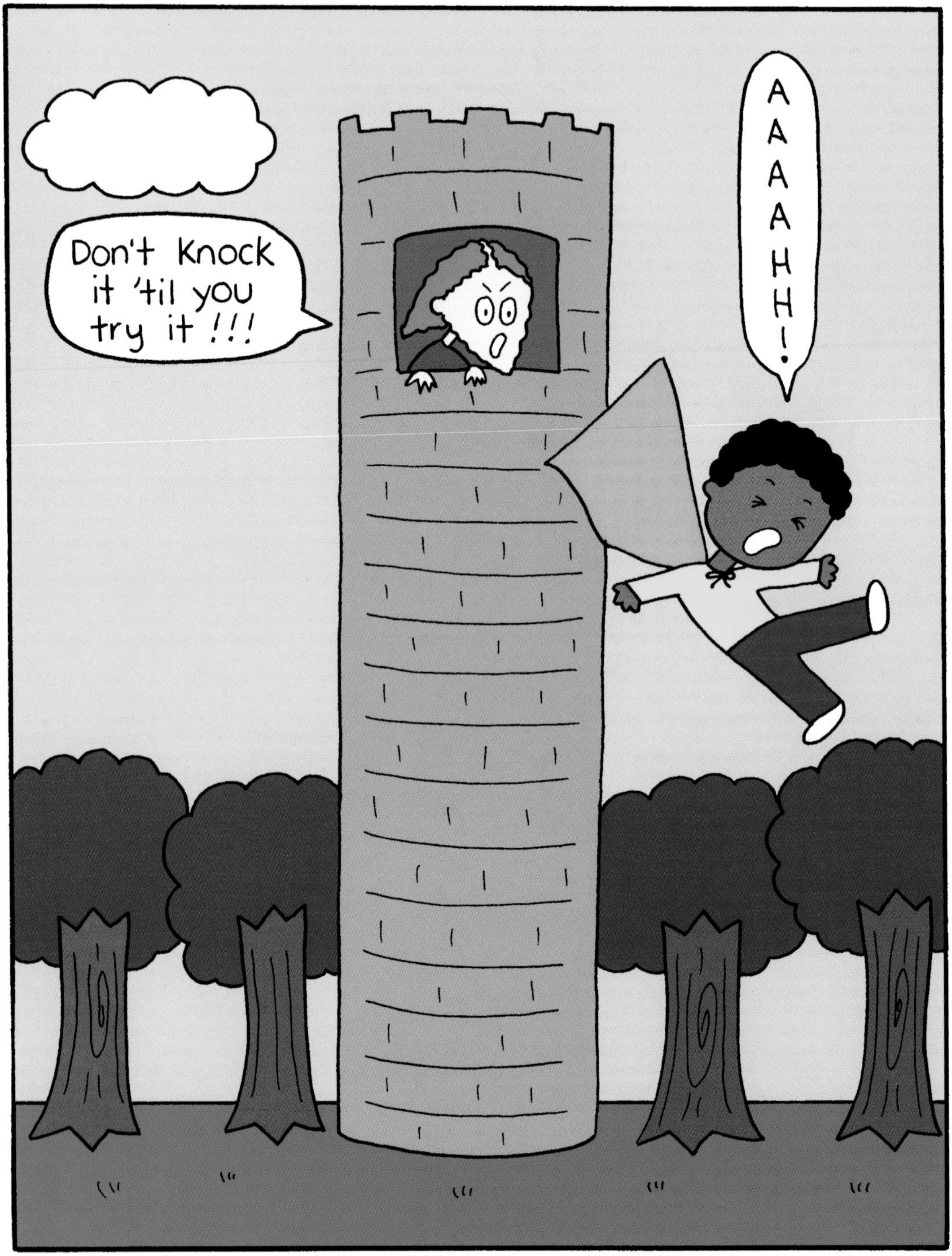
Don't Knock it 'til you try it!!!
AAAAHH!

The trauma left the prince blind.

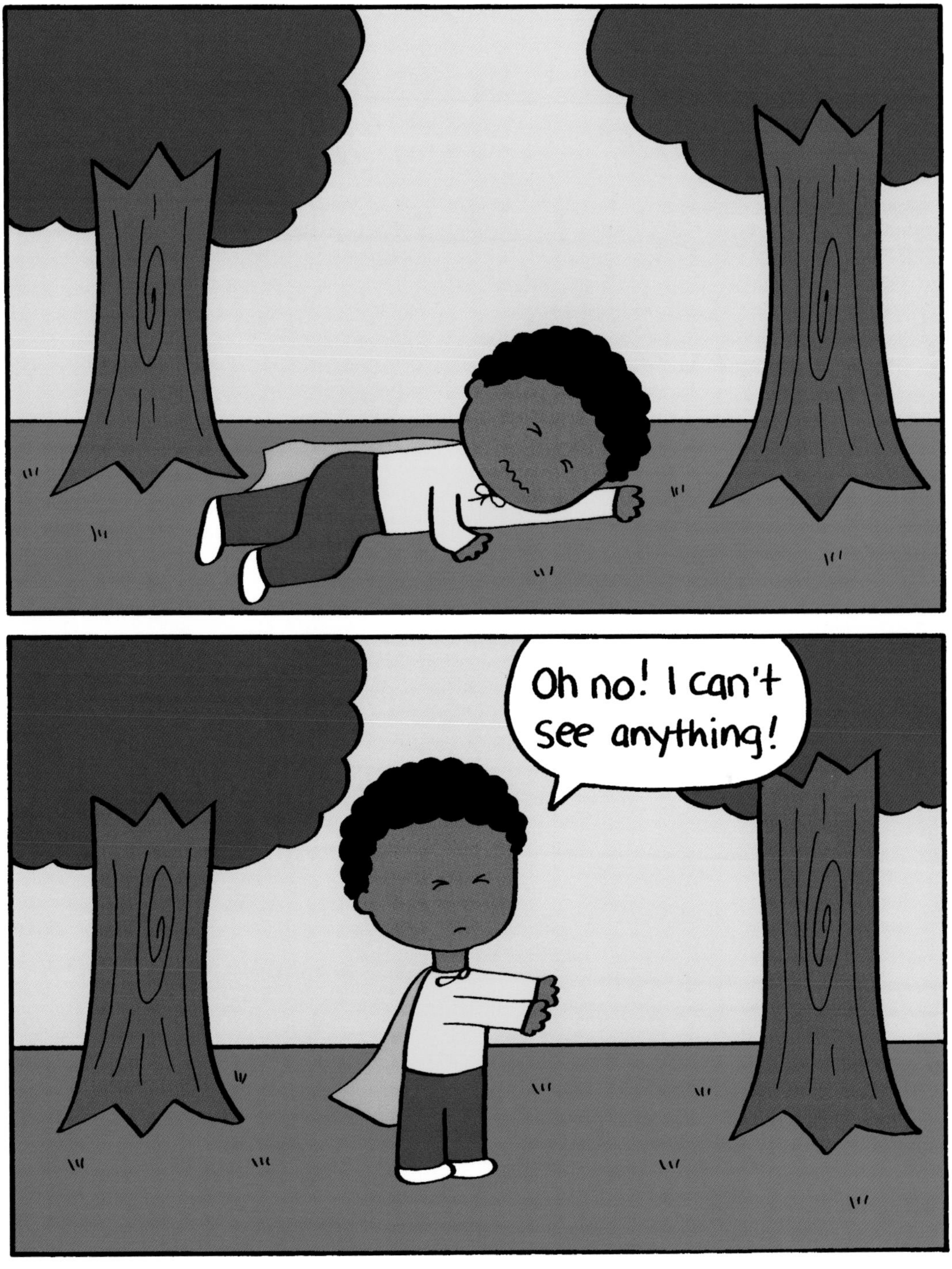
Oh no! I can't see anything!

For many years, the despondent prince wandered through the woods.

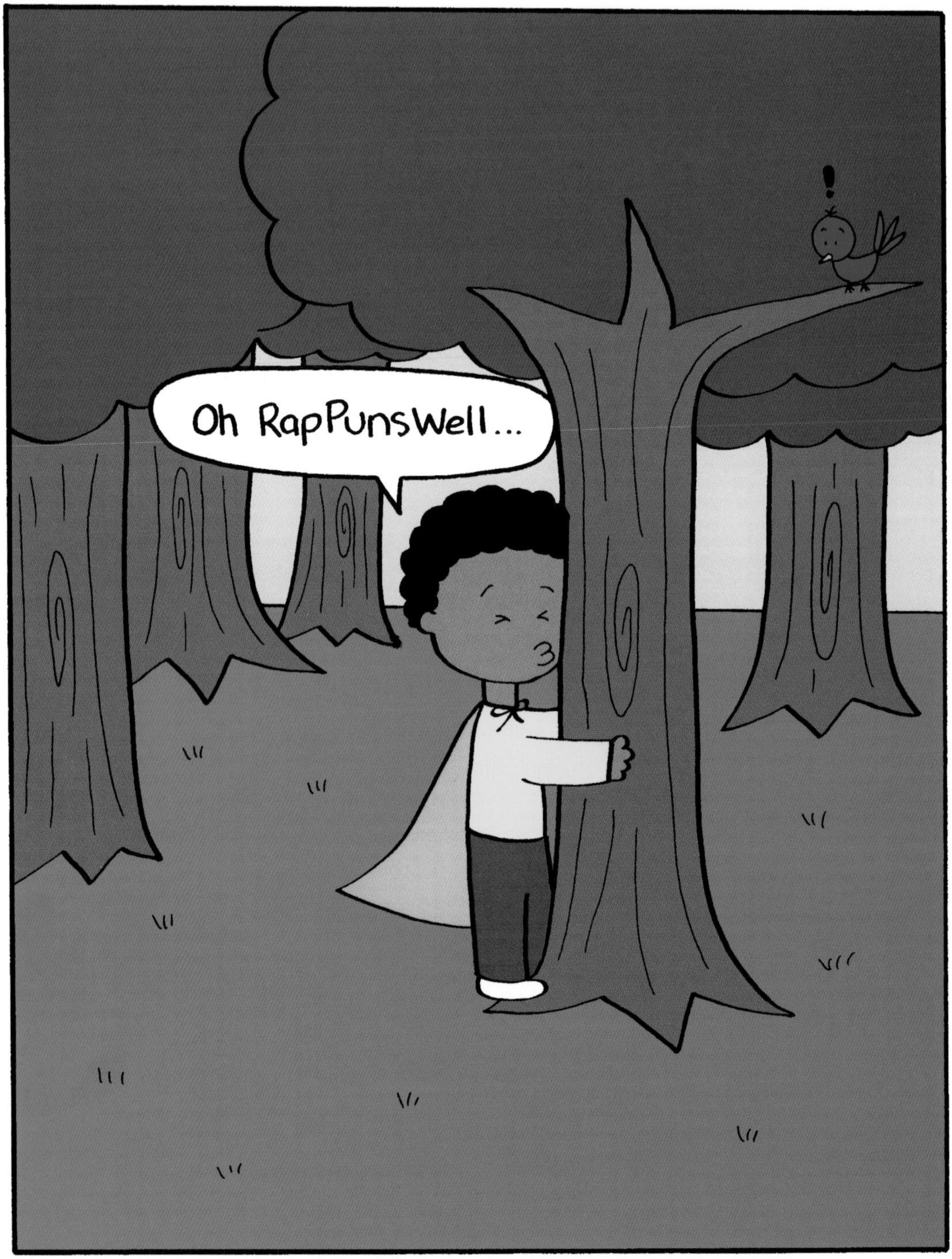
Oh RapPunsWell...
!

Then one day, the prince heard the sweet sound of RapPunsWell's rapping.

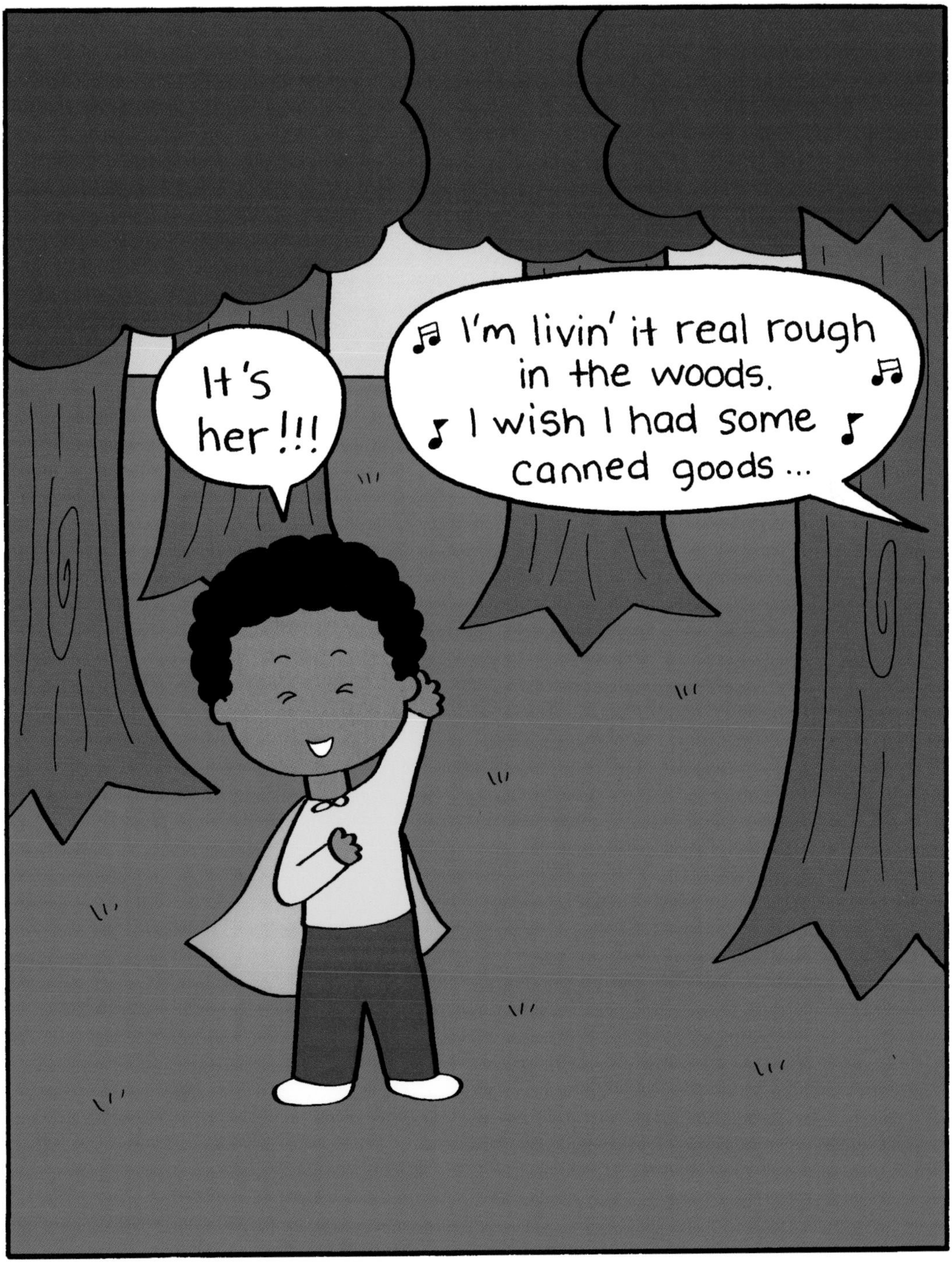
It's her!!!
♫ I'm livin' it real rough in the woods. ♫ ♪ I wish I had some ♪ canned goods ...

The prince and RapPunsWell were overjoyed to be reunited.

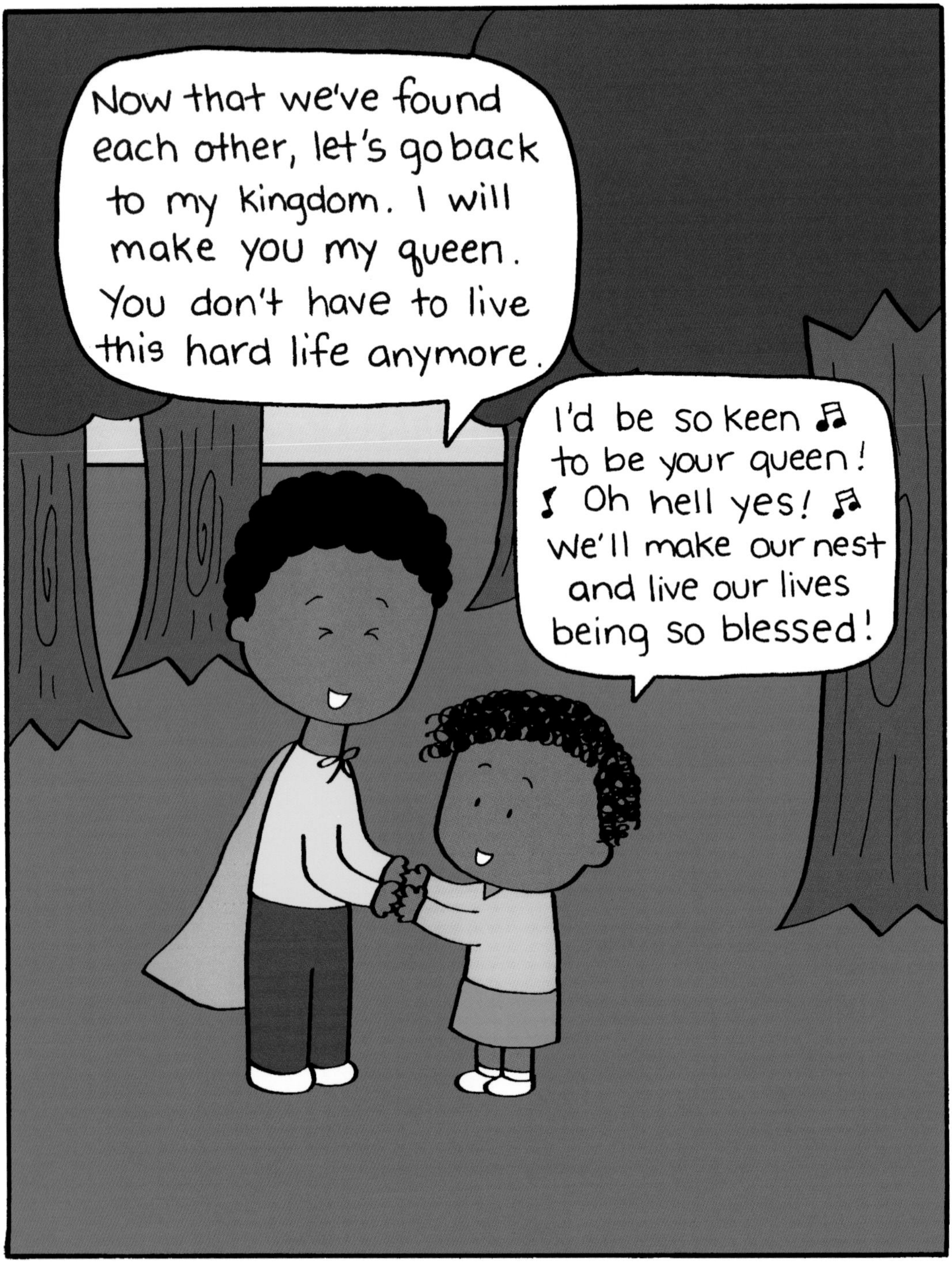

Now that we've found each other, let's go back to my Kingdom. I will make you my queen. You don't have to live this hard life anymore.
I'd be so keen ♫ to be your queen! ♪ Oh hell yes! ♫ We'll make our nest and live our lives being so blessed!

And they lived happily ever after.

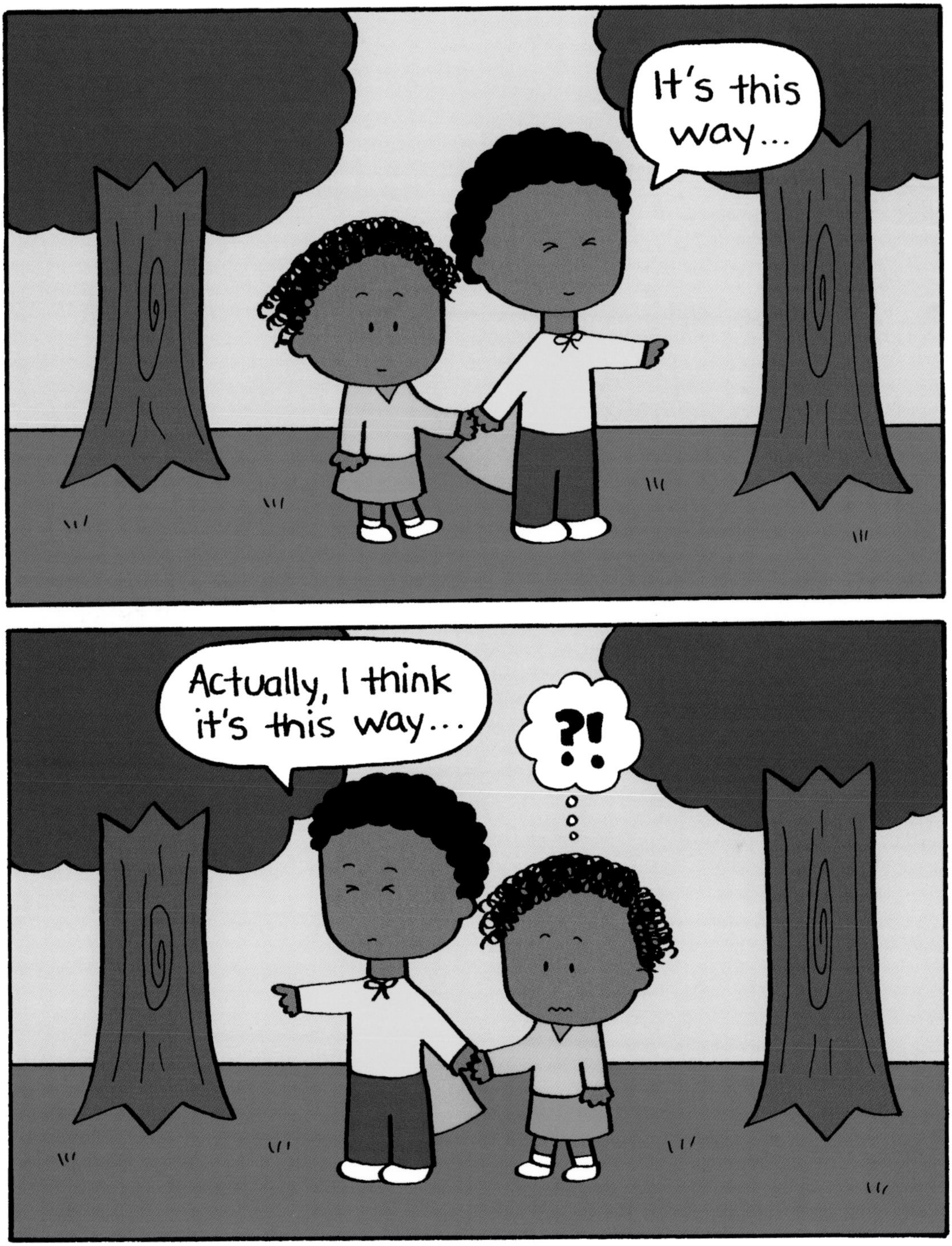
It's this way...
Actually, I think it's this way...
?!

(Well, at least they tried to...)

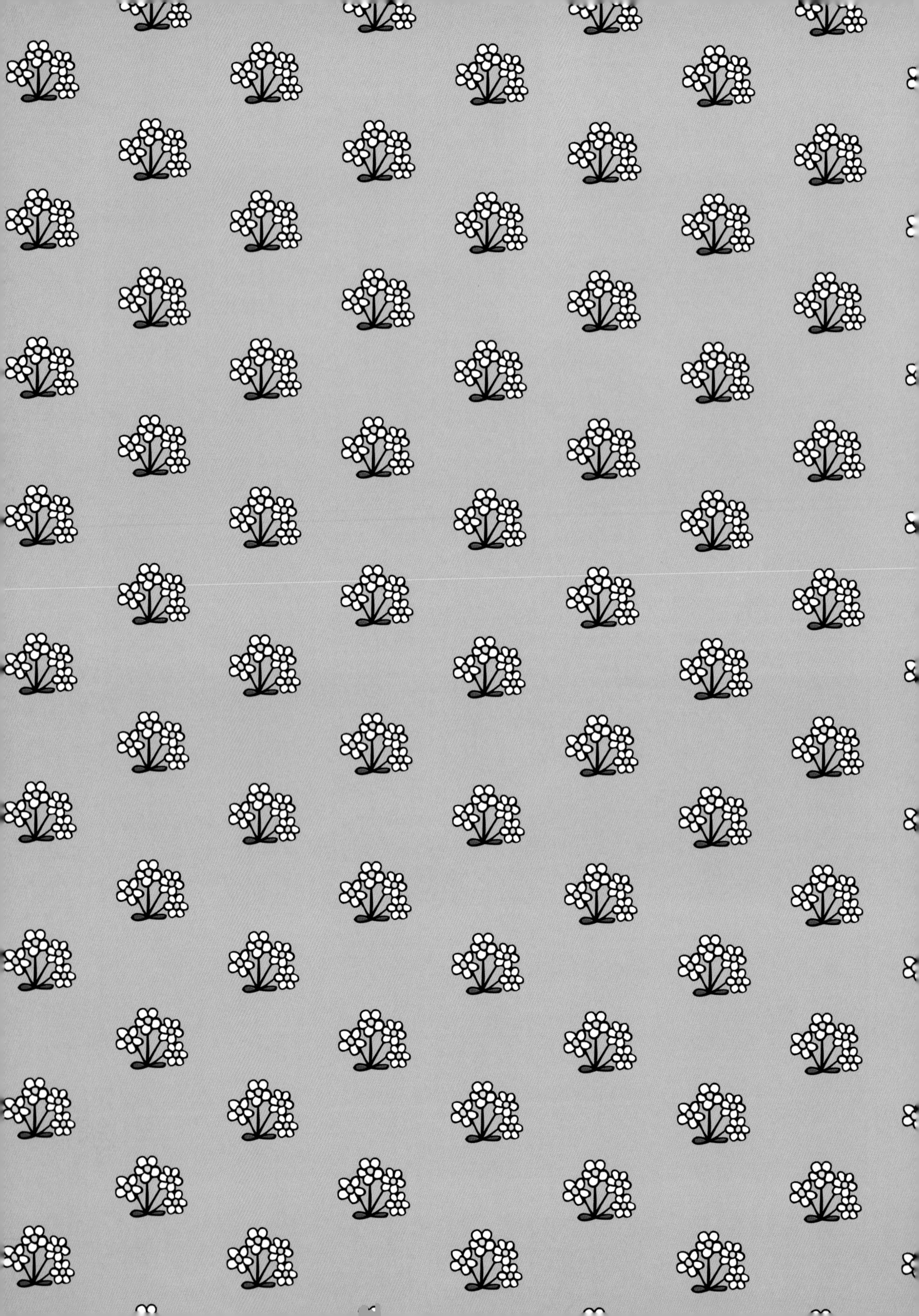

an ANGRY LITTLE GIRL'S FAIRY TALE

Little Miss Wears-a-Hood

Starring
?!
Xyla the "Gloomy Girl"

Once upon a time, in a faraway village, a mother baked some bread.

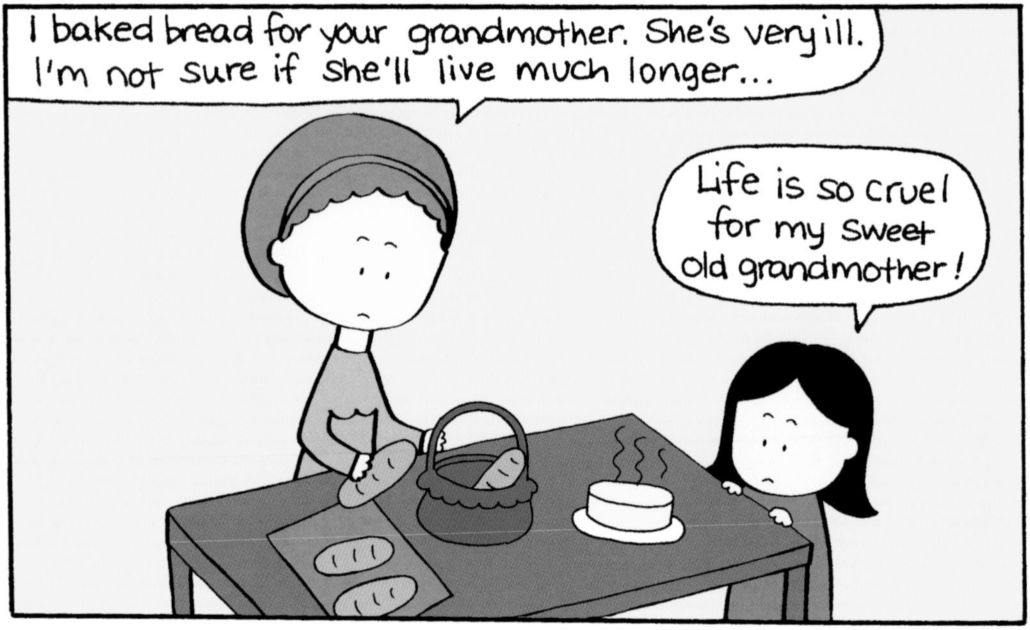
I baked bread for your grandmother. She's very ill. I'm not sure if she'll live much longer...
Life is so cruel for my sweet old grandmother!

The mother asked her daughter to take the bread to her grandmother.

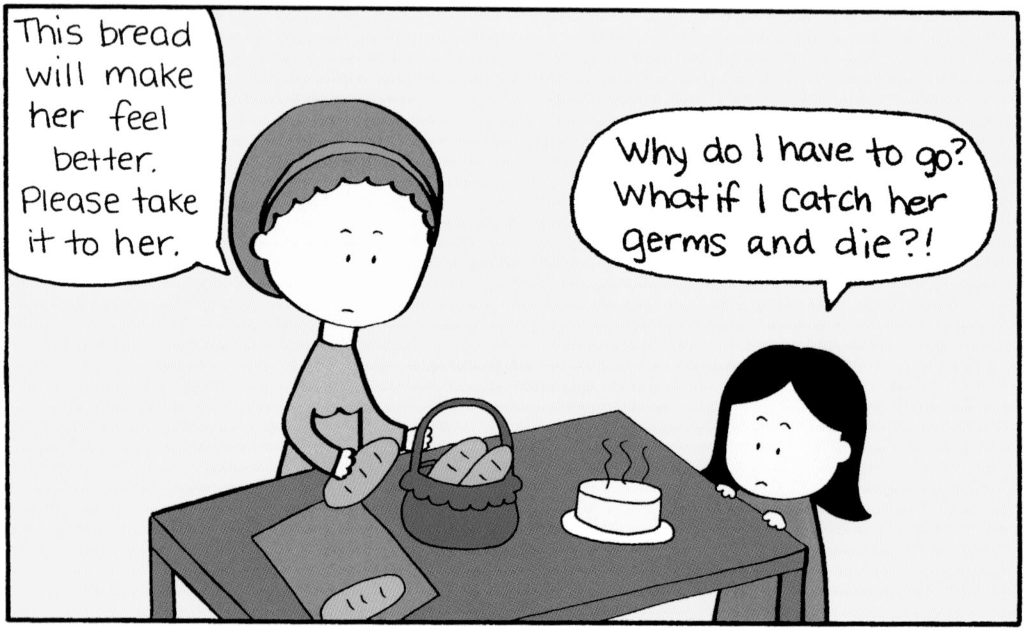
This bread will make her feel better. Please take it to her.
Why do I have to go? What if I catch her germs and die?!

The girl set off to deliver the bread.

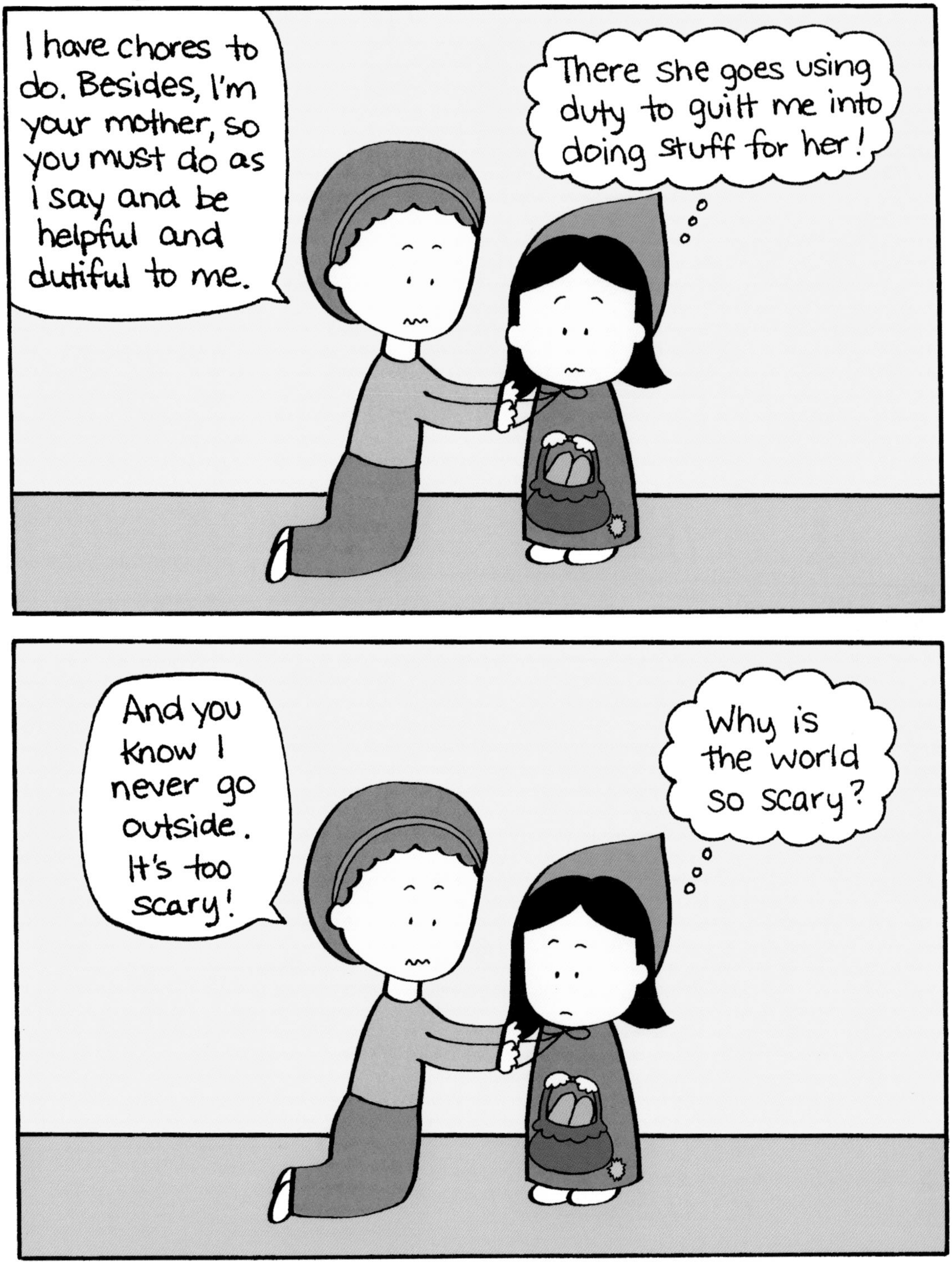
I have chores to do. Besides, I'm your mother, so you must do as I say and be helpful and dutiful to me.
There she goes using duty to guilt me into doing stuff for her!
And you know I never go outside. It's too scary!
Why is the world so scary?

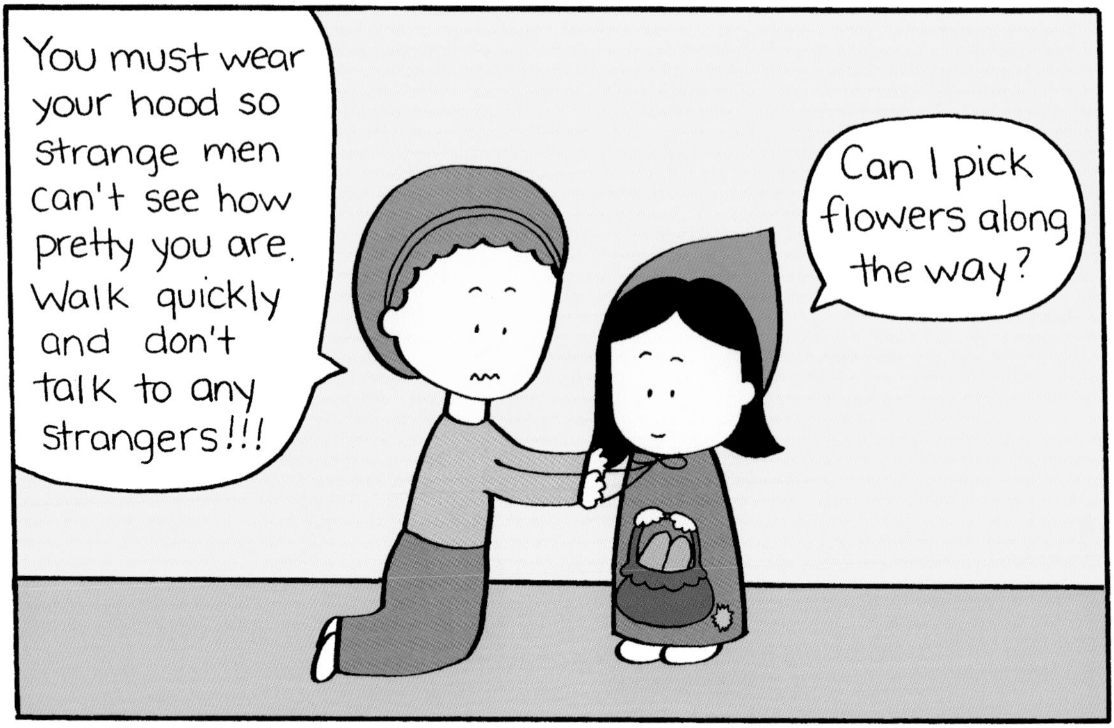
You must wear your hood so strange men can't see how pretty you are. Walk quickly and don't talk to any strangers!!!
Can I pick flowers along the way?

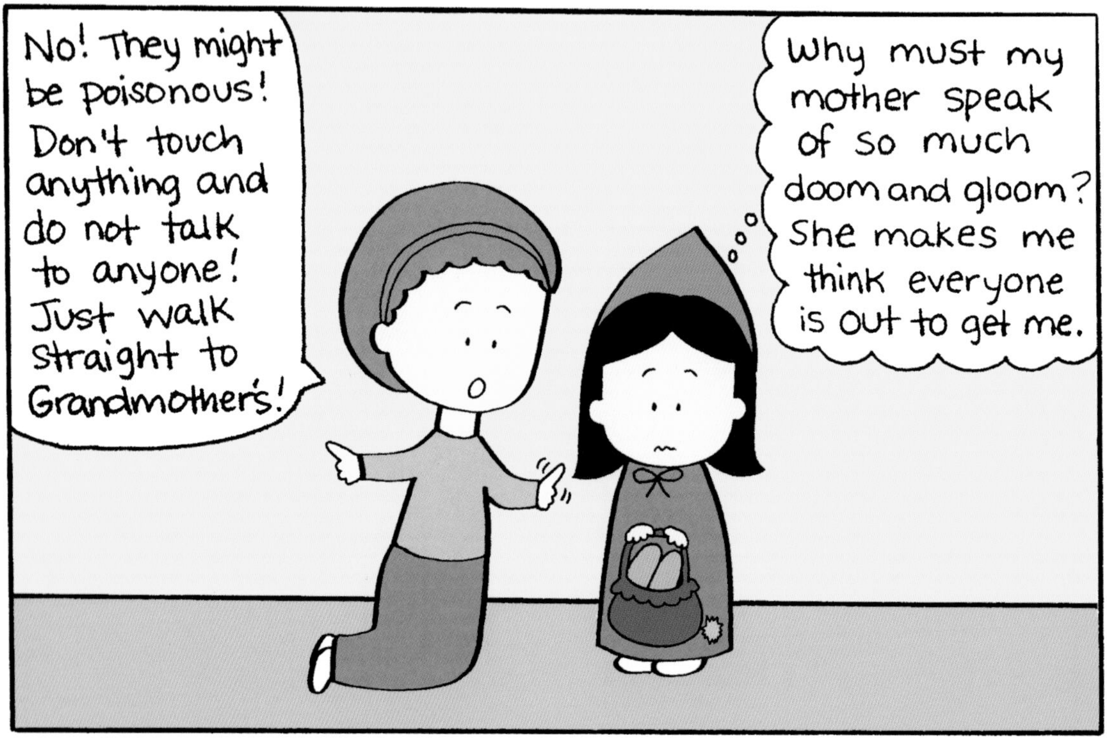
No! They might be poisonous! Don't touch anything and do not talk to anyone! Just walk straight to Grandmother's!
Why must my mother speak of so much doom and gloom? She makes me think everyone is out to get me.

Along the way, she met a woodsman.

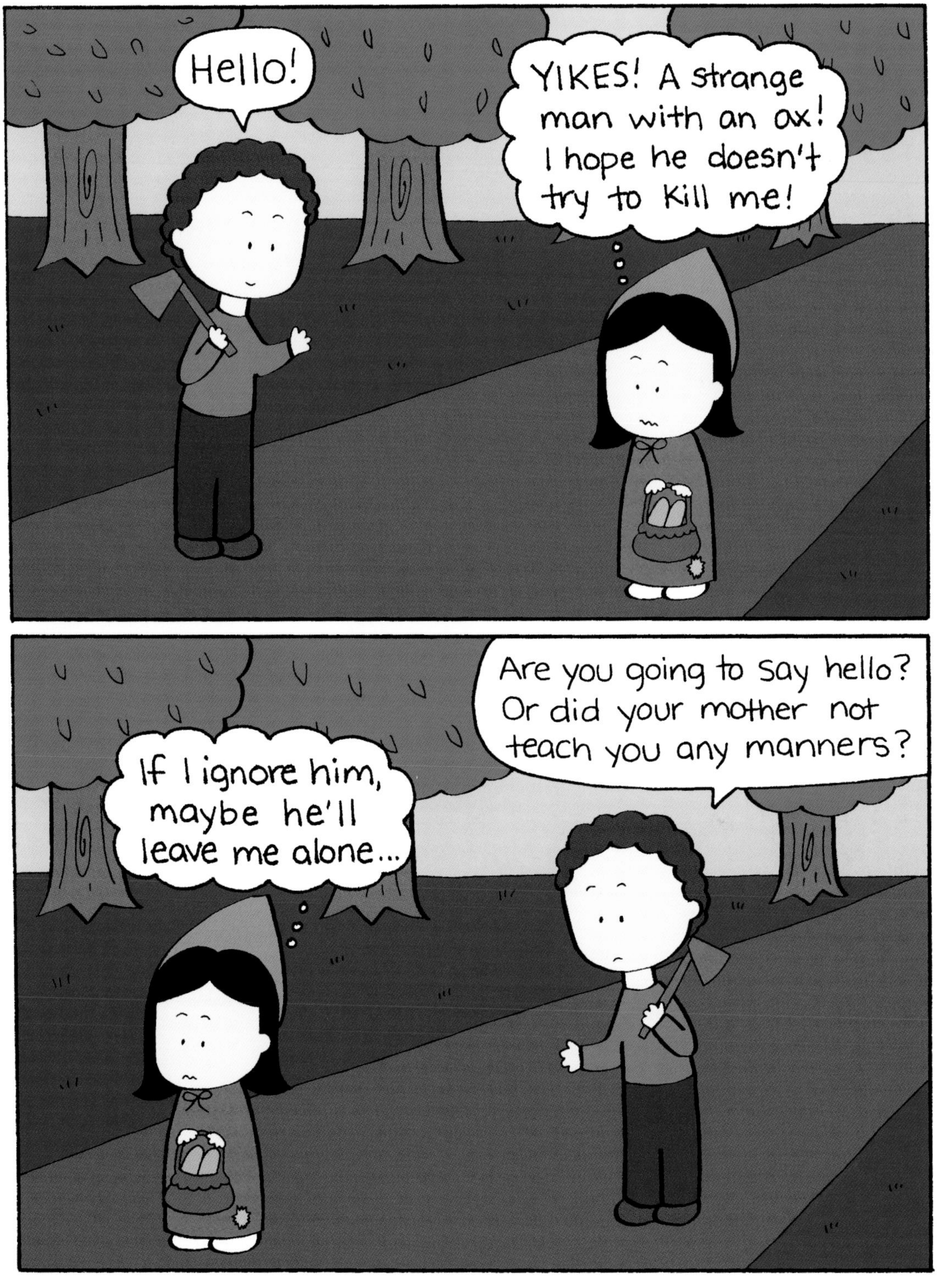
Hello!
YIKES! A strange man with an ax! I hope he doesn't try to kill me!
If I ignore him, maybe he'll leave me alone...
Are you going to say hello? Or did your mother not teach you any manners?

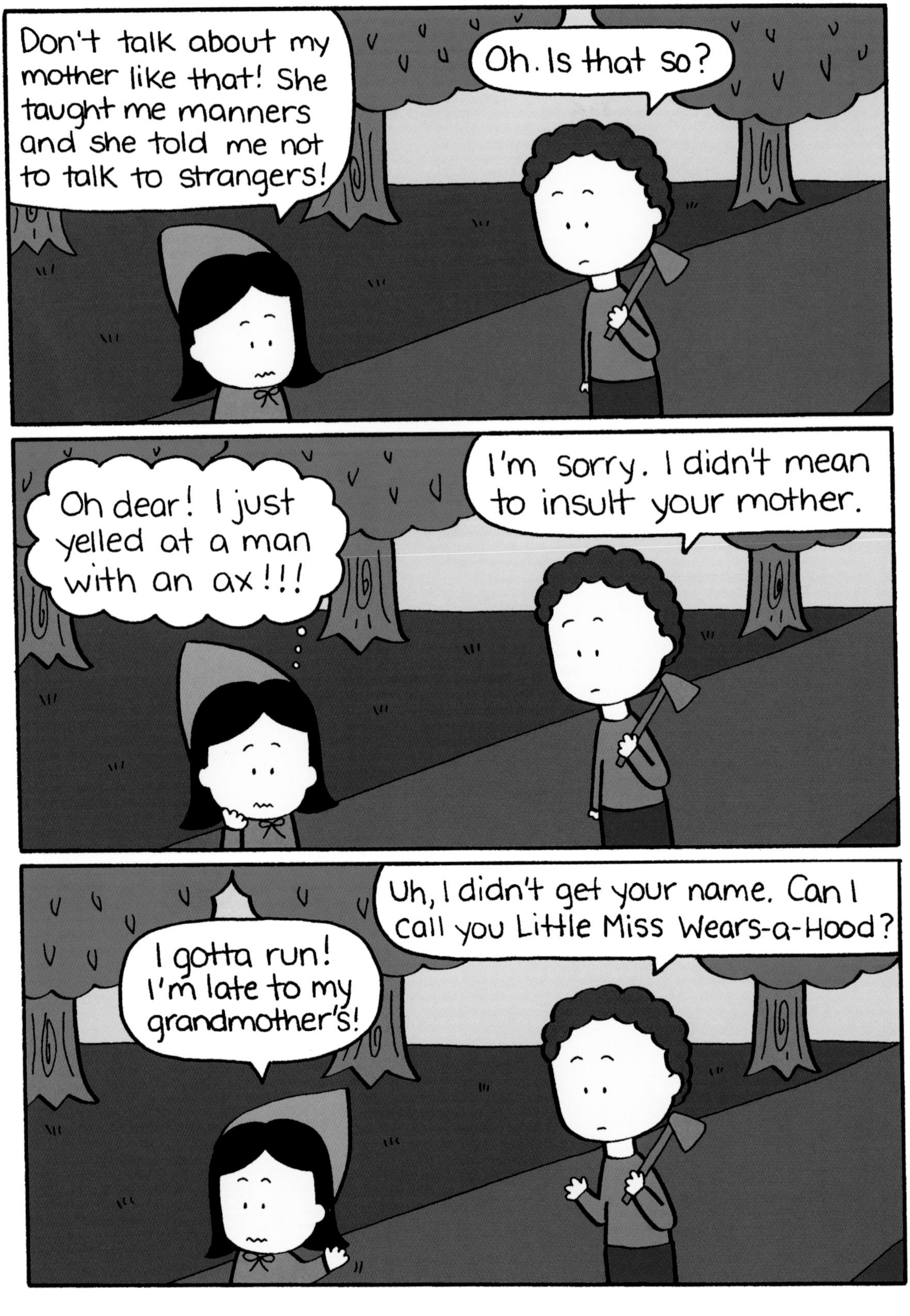
Don't talk about my mother like that! She taught me manners and she told me not to talk to strangers!
Oh. Is that so?
Oh dear! I just yelled at a man with an ax!!!
I'm sorry. I didn't mean to insult your mother.
Uh, I didn't get your name. Can I call you Little Miss Wears-a-Hood?
I gotta run! I'm late to my grandmother's!

Little Miss Wears-a-Hood ran as fast as she could—into a wolf!

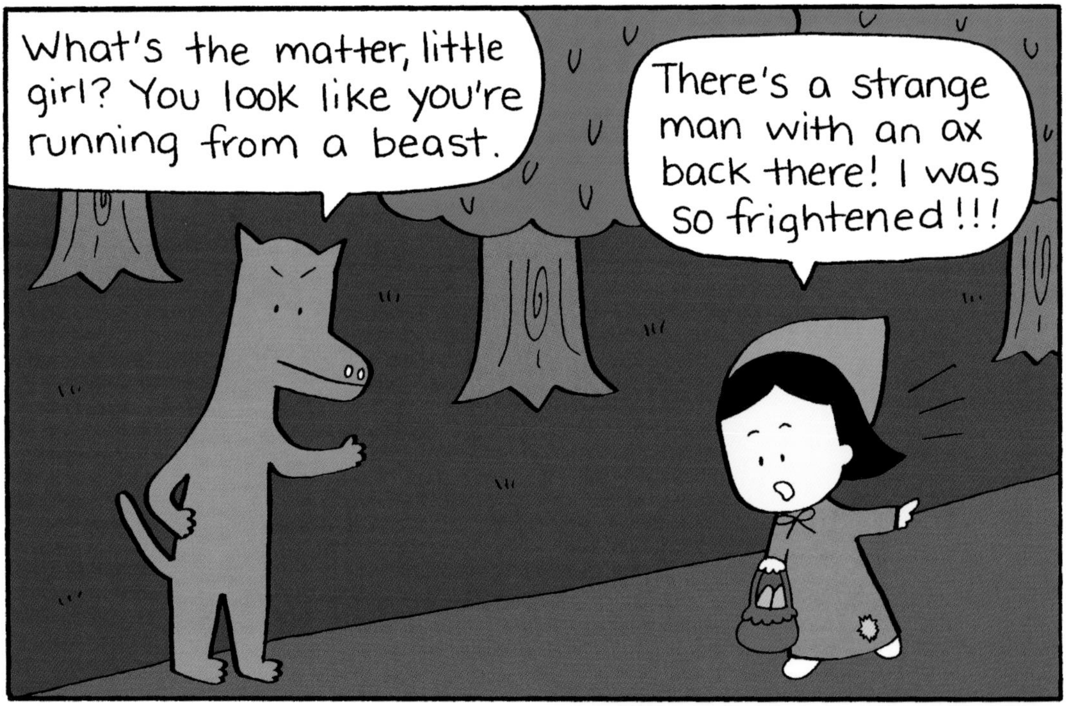
What's the matter, little girl? You look like you're running from a beast.
There's a strange man with an ax back there! I was so frightened!!!

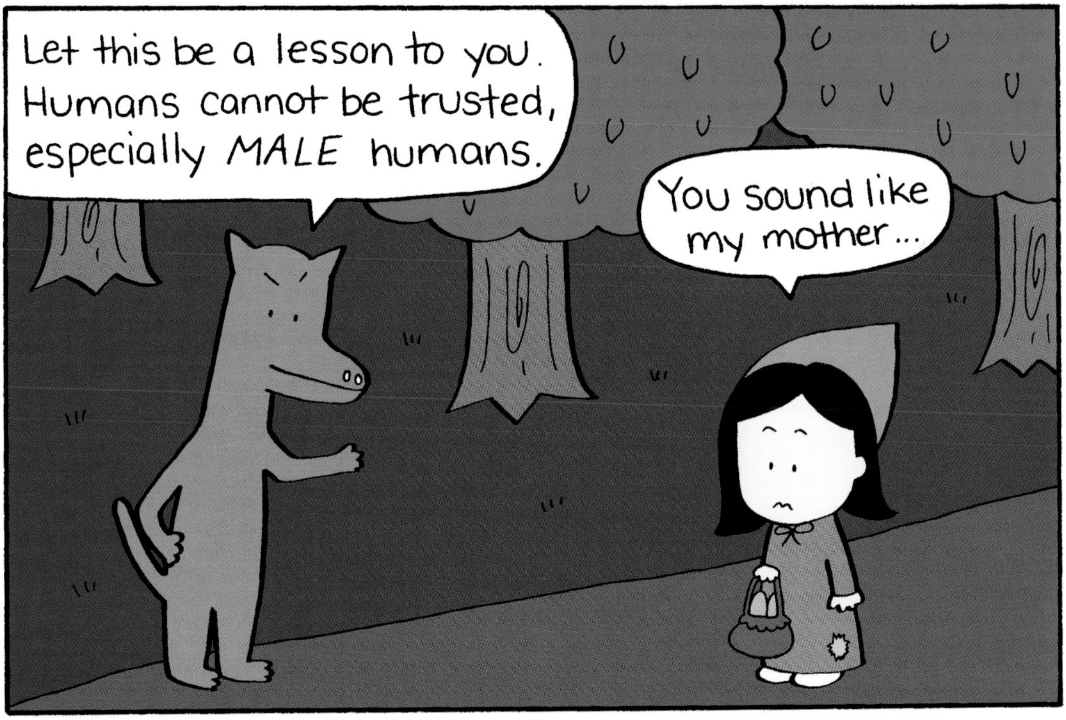
Let this be a lesson to you. Humans cannot be trusted, especially *MALE* humans.
You sound like my mother...

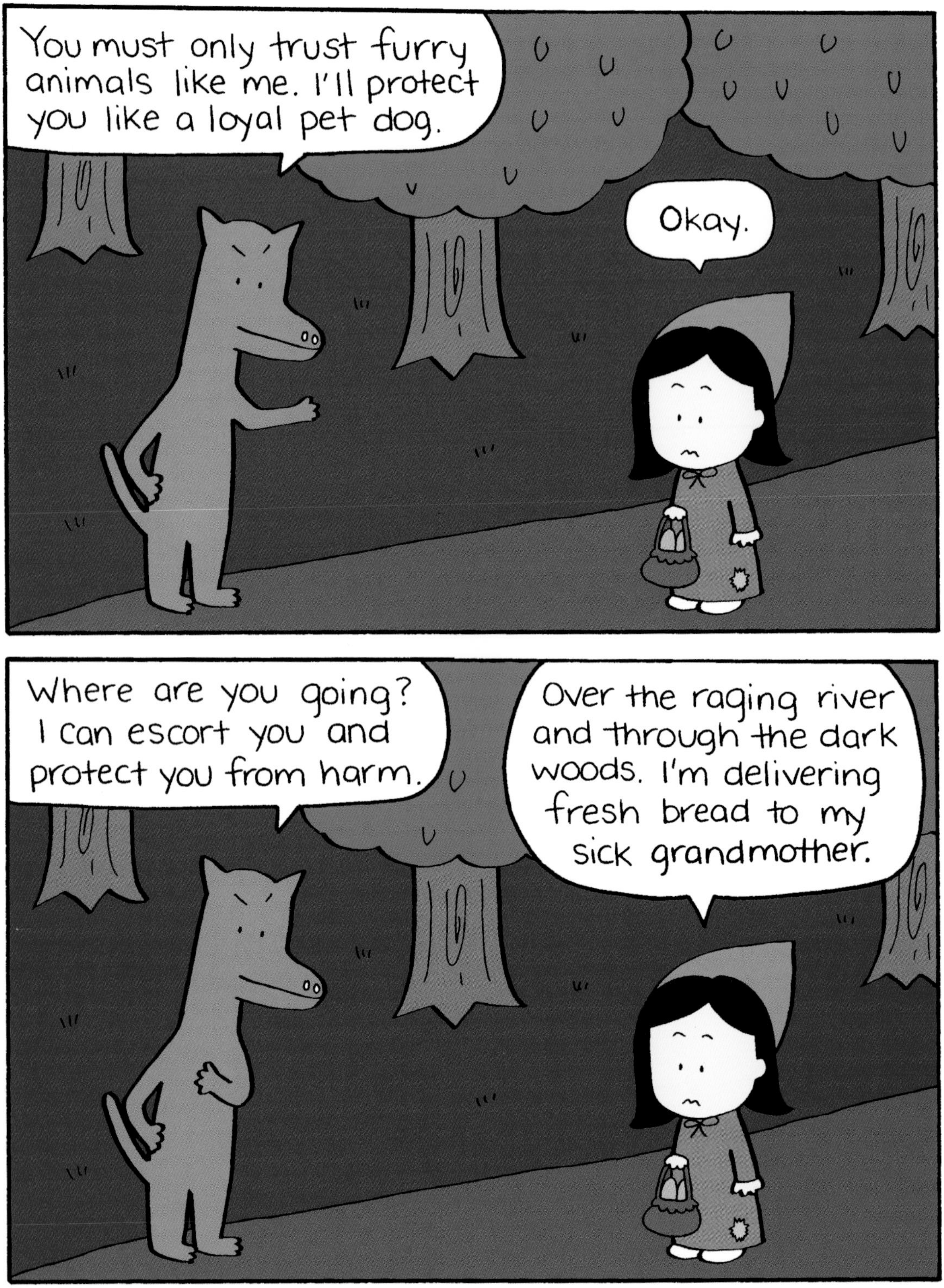
You must only trust furry animals like me. I'll protect you like a loyal pet dog.
Okay.
Where are you going? I can escort you and protect you from harm.
Over the raging river and through the dark woods. I'm delivering fresh bread to my sick grandmother.

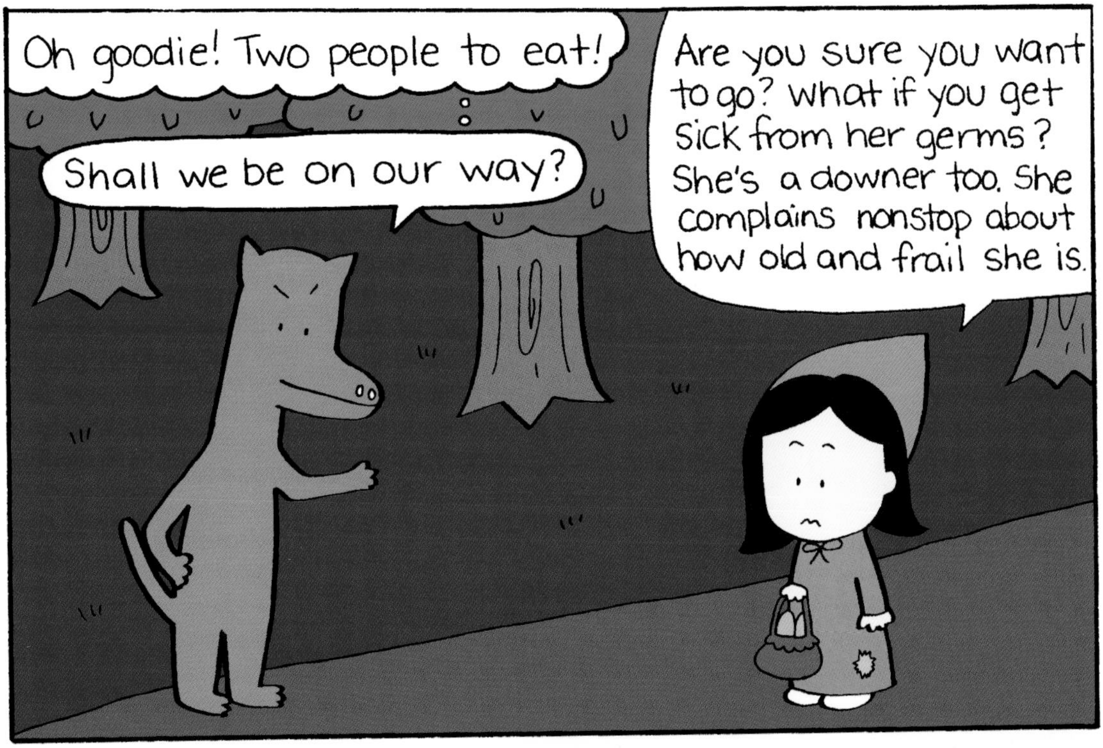
Oh goodie! Two people to eat!
Shall we be on our way?
Are you sure you want to go? what if you get sick from her germs? She's a downer too. She complains nonstop about how old and frail she is.

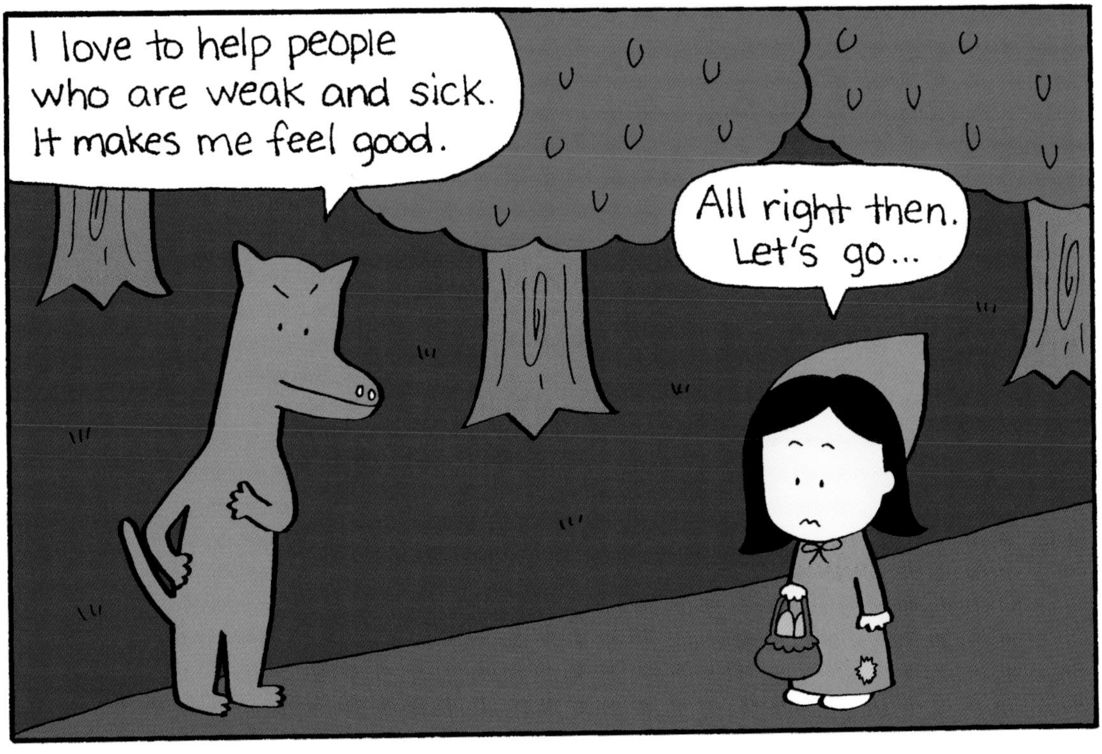
I love to help people who are weak and sick. It makes me feel good.
All right then. Let's go...

The wolf escorted Little Miss Wears-a-Hood through the woods.

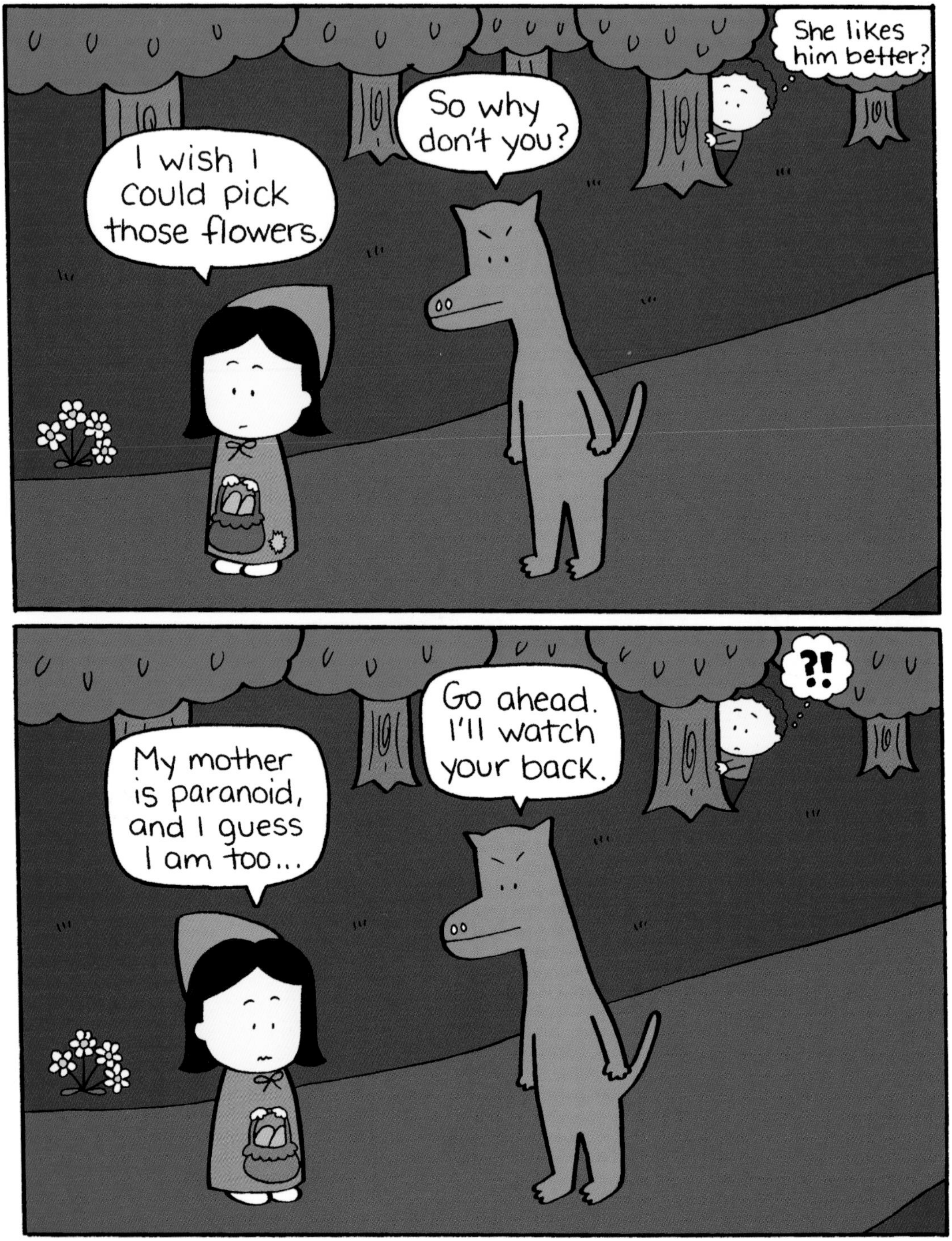
I wish I could pick those flowers.
So why don't you?
She likes him better?
My mother is paranoid, and I guess I am too...
Go ahead. I'll watch your back.
?!

The wolf left her and ran ahead to her grandmother's house.

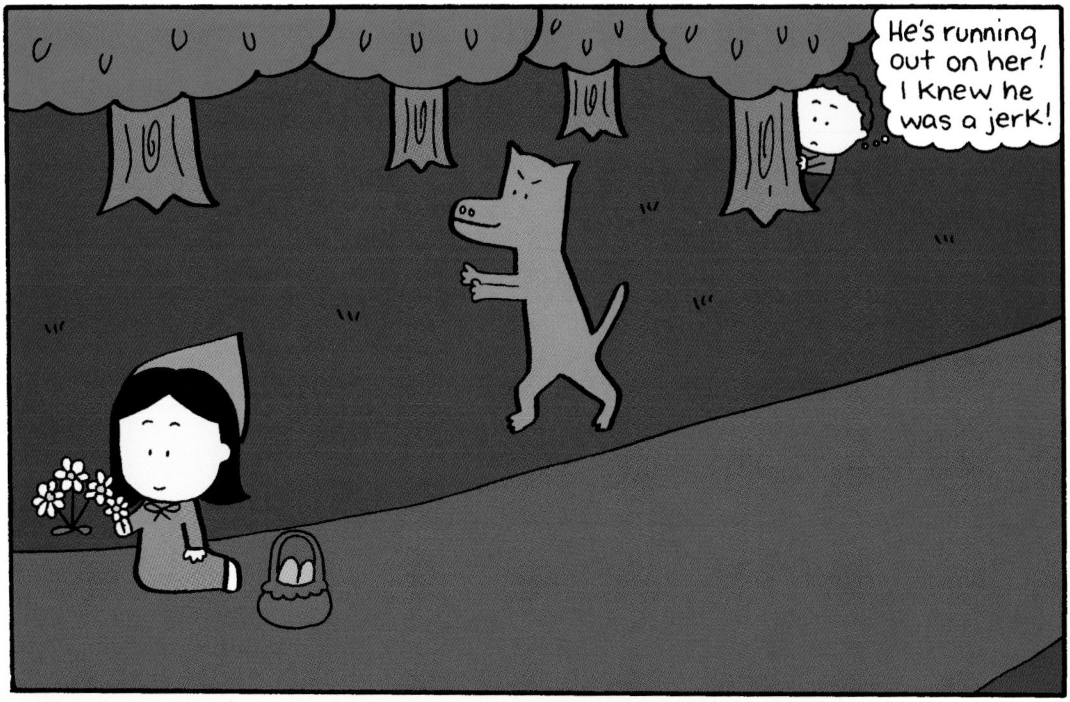
He's running out on her! I knew he was a jerk!

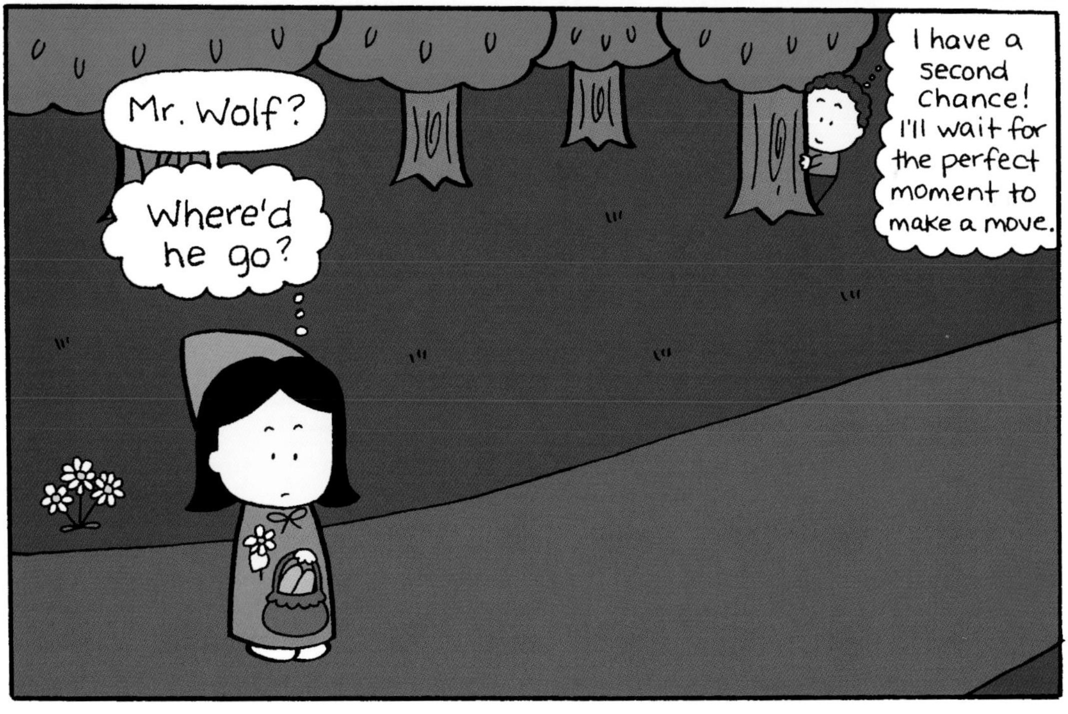
Mr. Wolf?
Where'd he go?
I have a second chance! I'll wait for the perfect moment to make a move.

The wolf finally arrived at the grandmother's house.

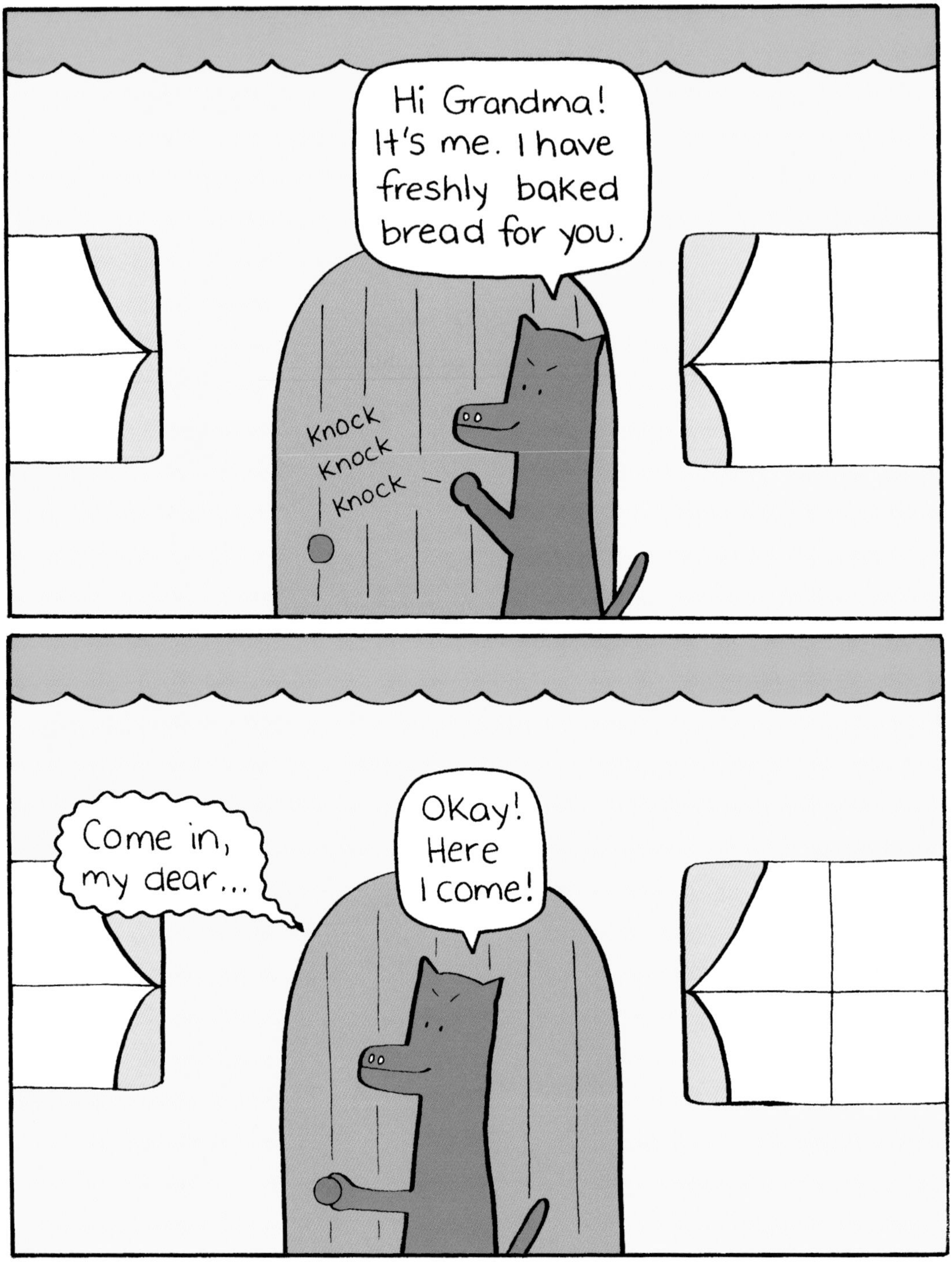
Hi Grandma! It's me. I have freshly baked bread for you.
Knock Knock Knock
Come in, my dear...
Okay! Here I come!

The wolf quickly gobbled her up!

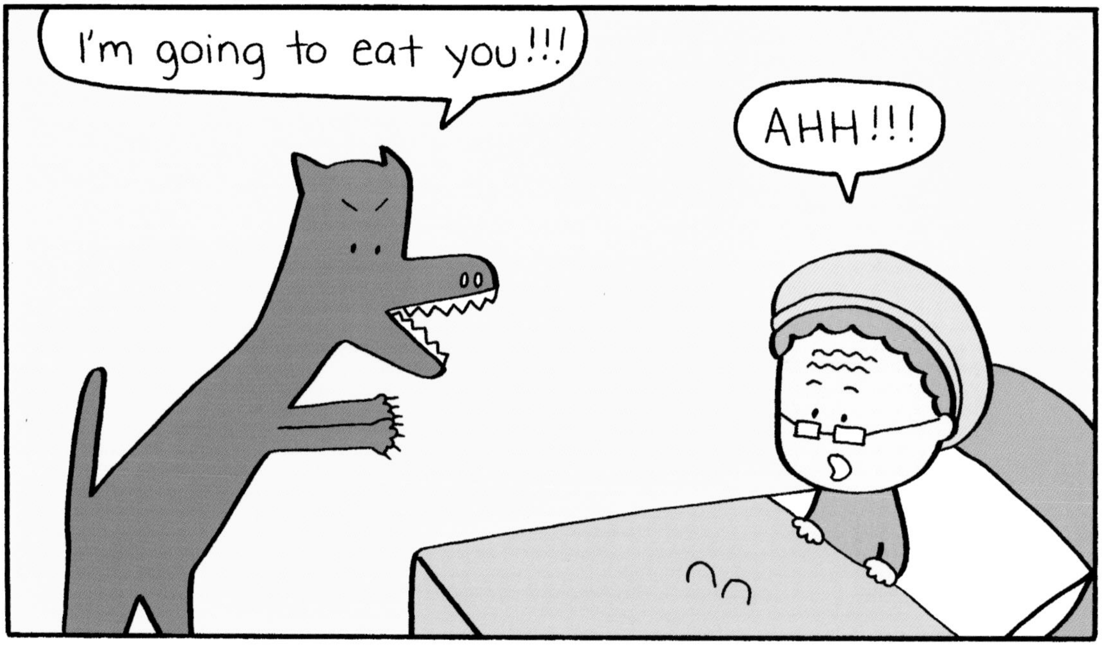
I'm going to eat you!!!
AHH!!!

He put on the grandmother's clothes.

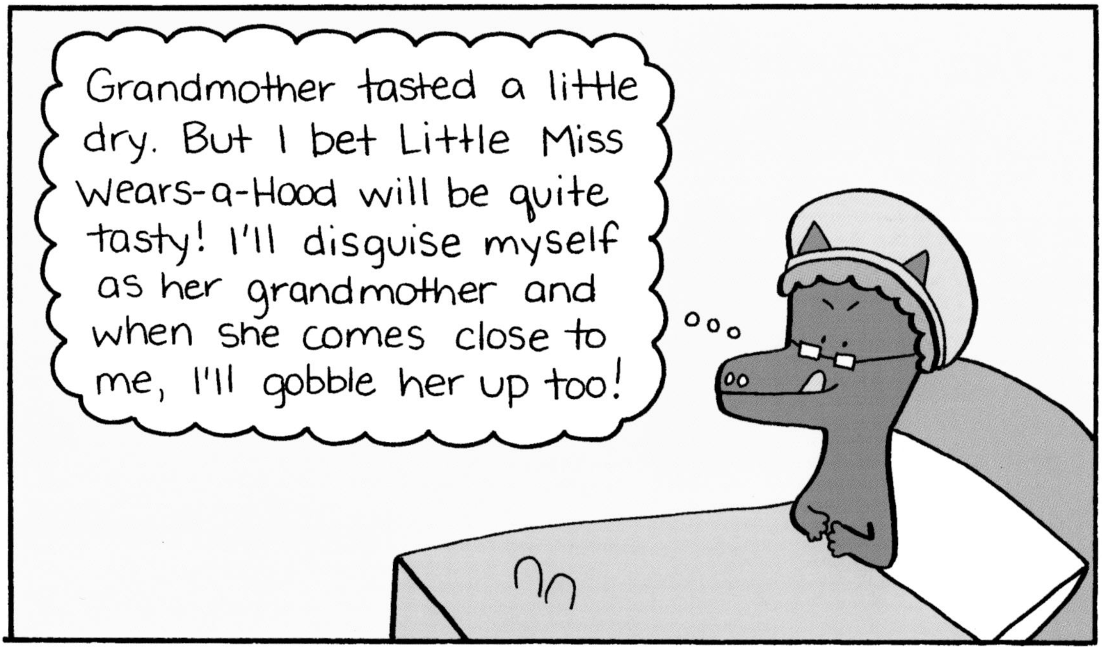
Grandmother tasted a little dry. But I bet Little Miss Wears-a-Hood will be quite tasty! I'll disguise myself as her grandmother and when she comes close to me, I'll gobble her up too!

Meanwhile, Little Miss Wears-a-Hood continued on her journey alone.

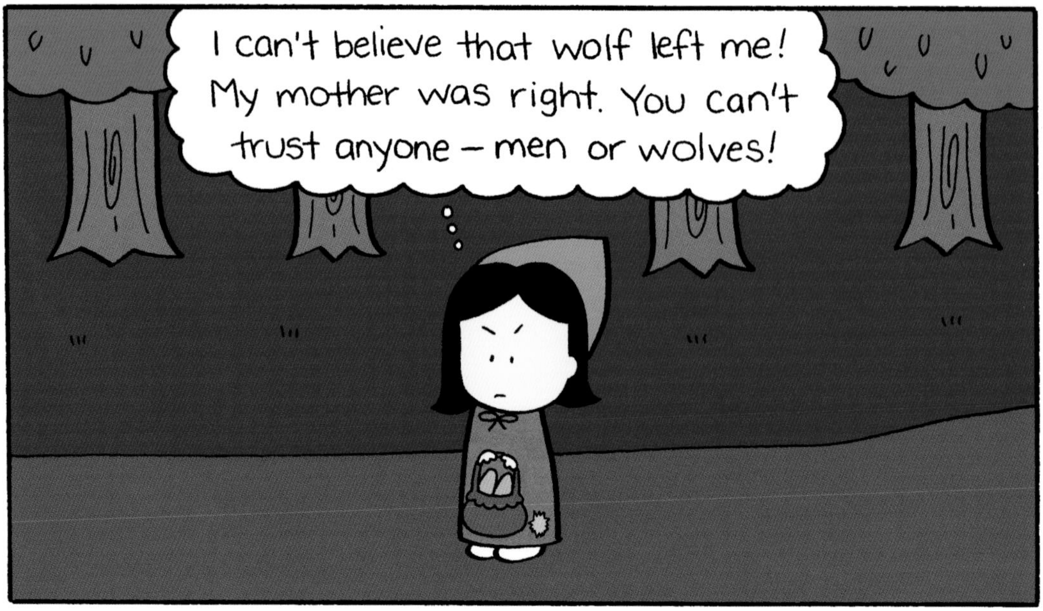
I can't believe that wolf left me! My mother was right. You can't trust anyone – men or wolves!

Little Miss Wears-a-Hood finally reached her grandmother's house.

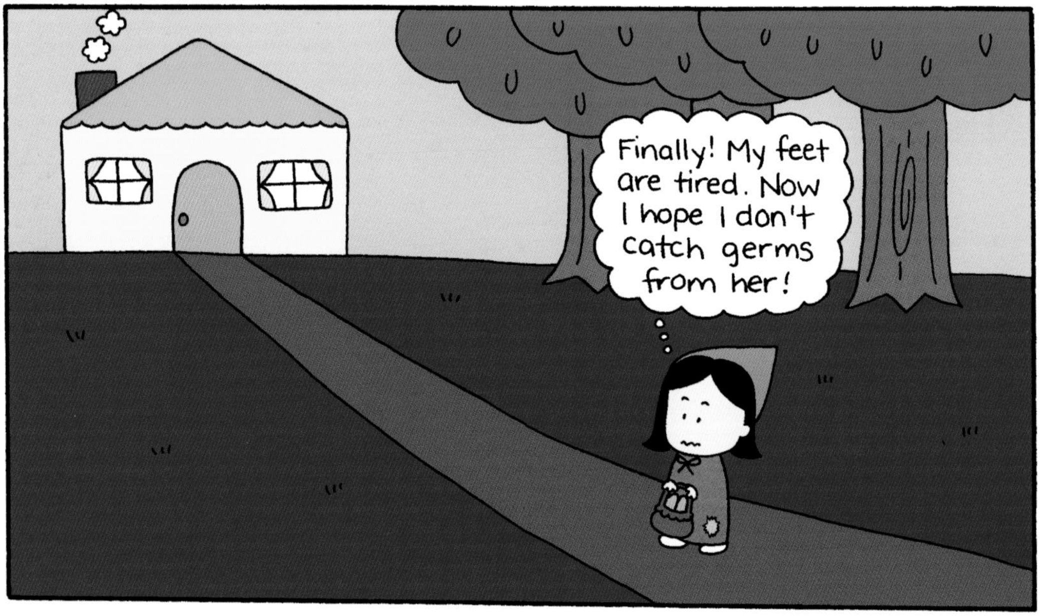
Finally! My feet are tired. Now I hope I don't catch germs from her!

She knocked on her grandmother's door.

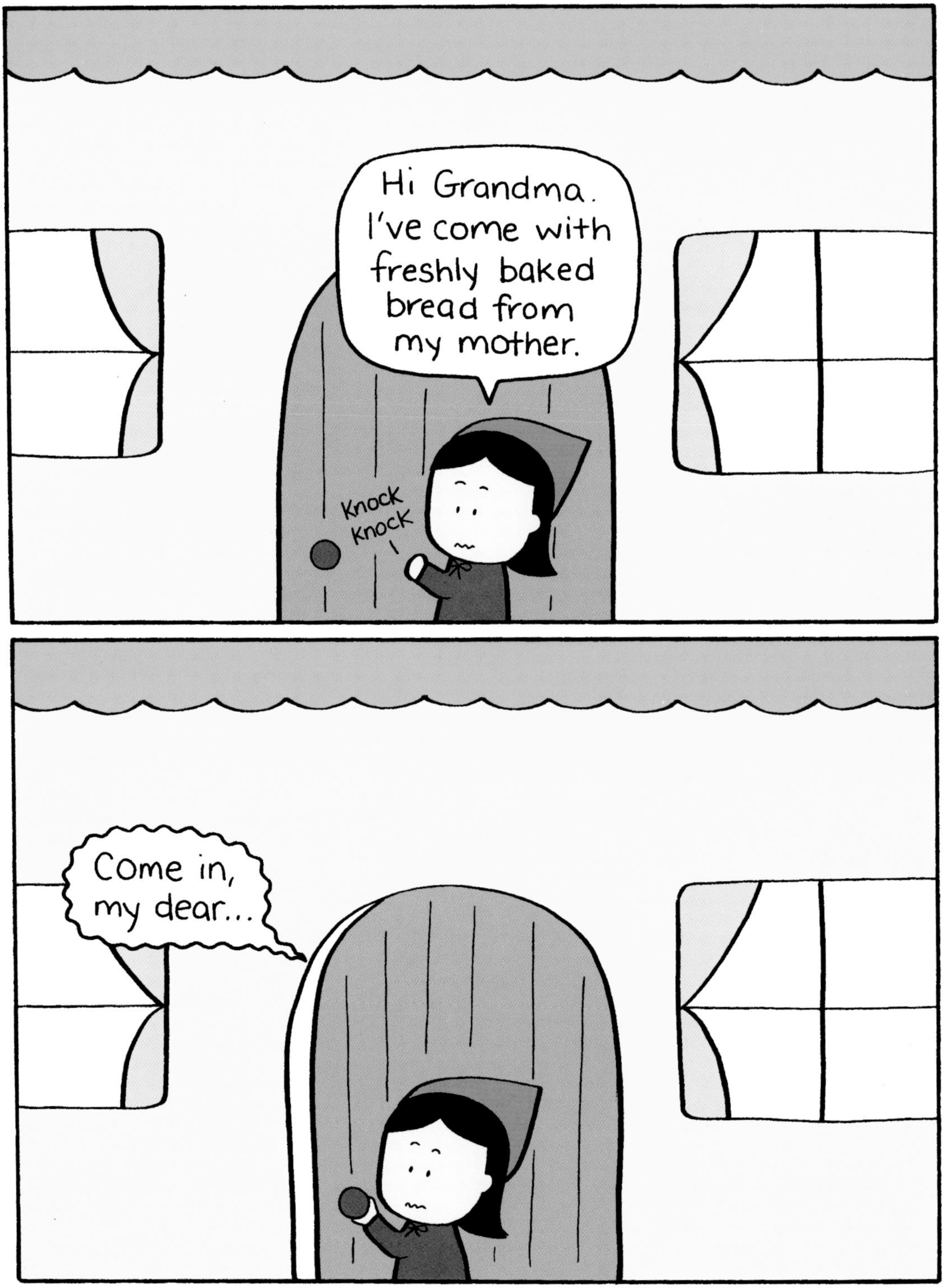
Hi Grandma. I've come with freshly baked bread from my mother.
Knock Knock
Come in, my dear...

Little Miss Wears-a-Hood thought her grandmother looked a bit strange.

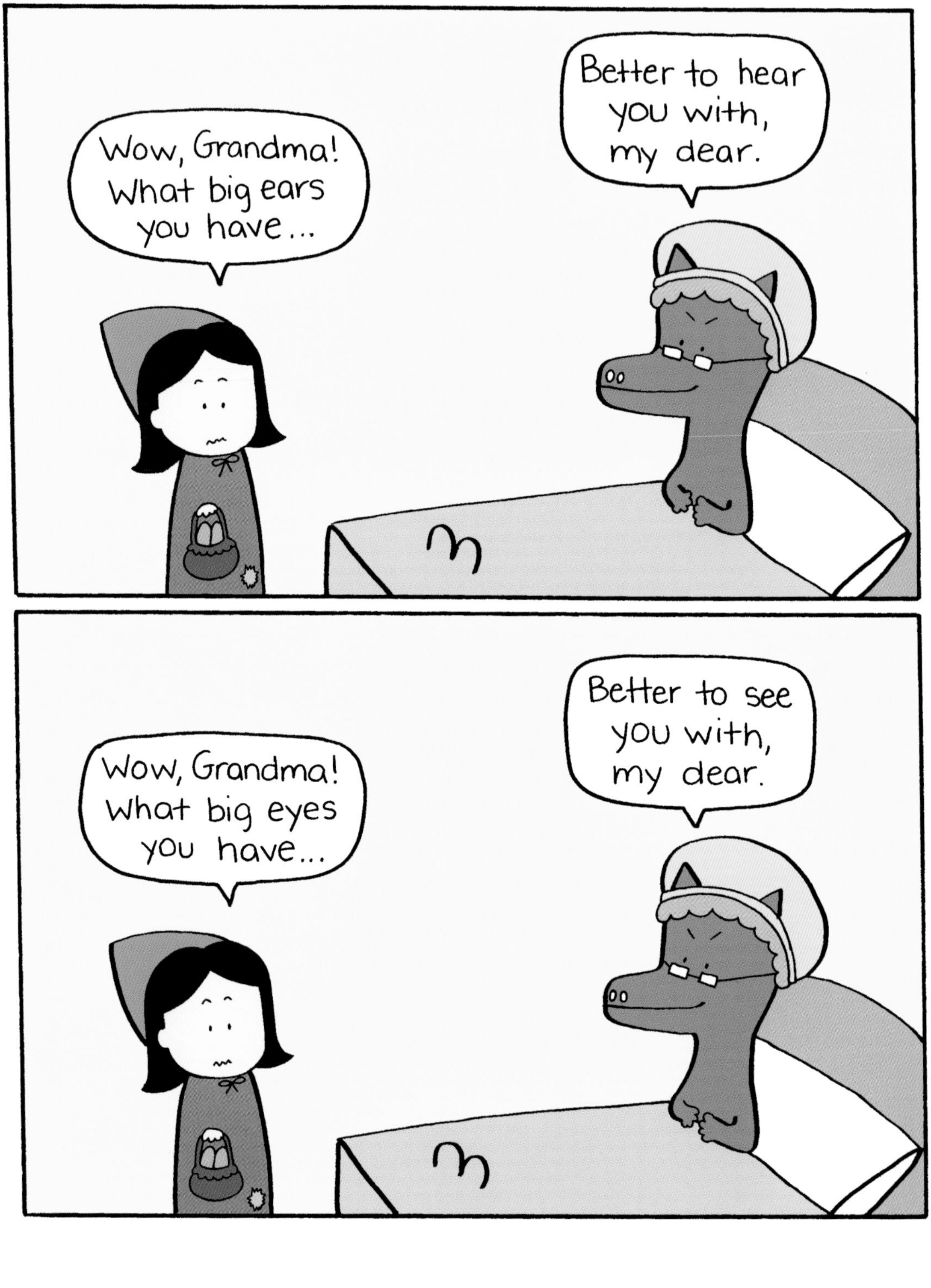
Wow, Grandma! What big ears you have...
Better to hear you with, my dear.
Wow, Grandma! What big eyes you have...
Better to see you with, my dear.

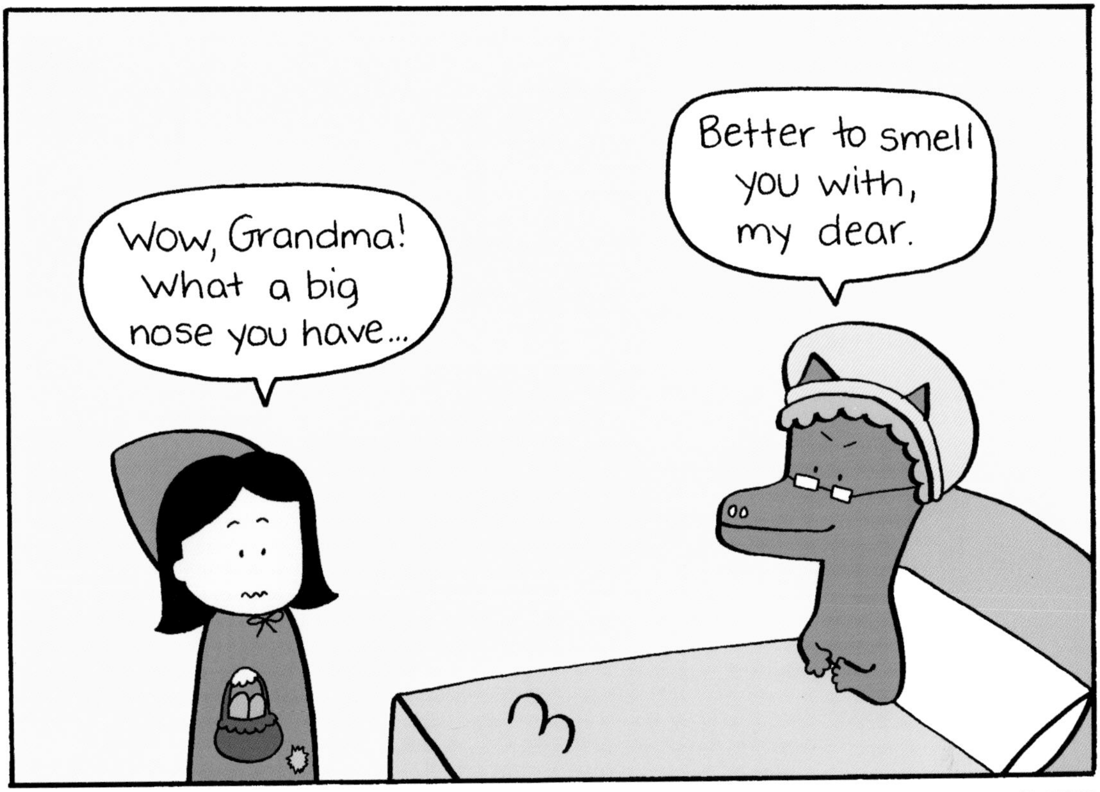
Wow, Grandma! What a big nose you have...
Better to smell you with, my dear.

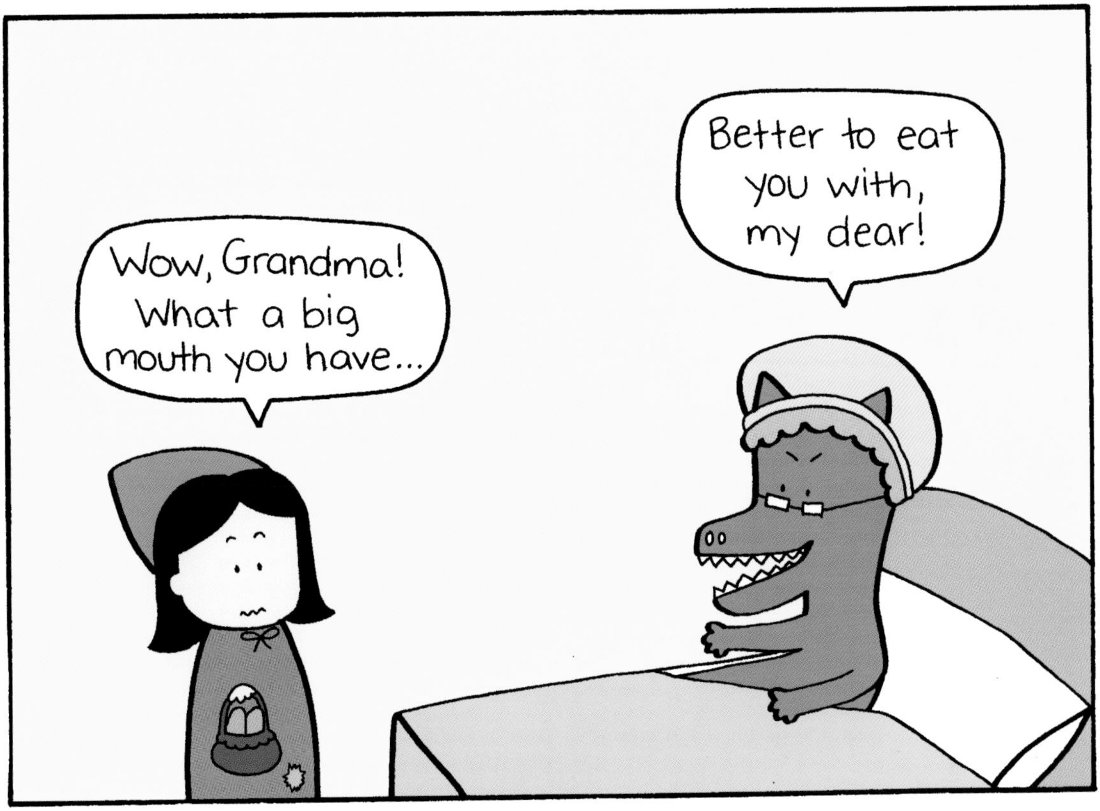
Wow, Grandma! What a big mouth you have...
Better to eat you with, my dear!

The wolf sprang out of bed to gobble up Little Miss Wears-a-Hood!

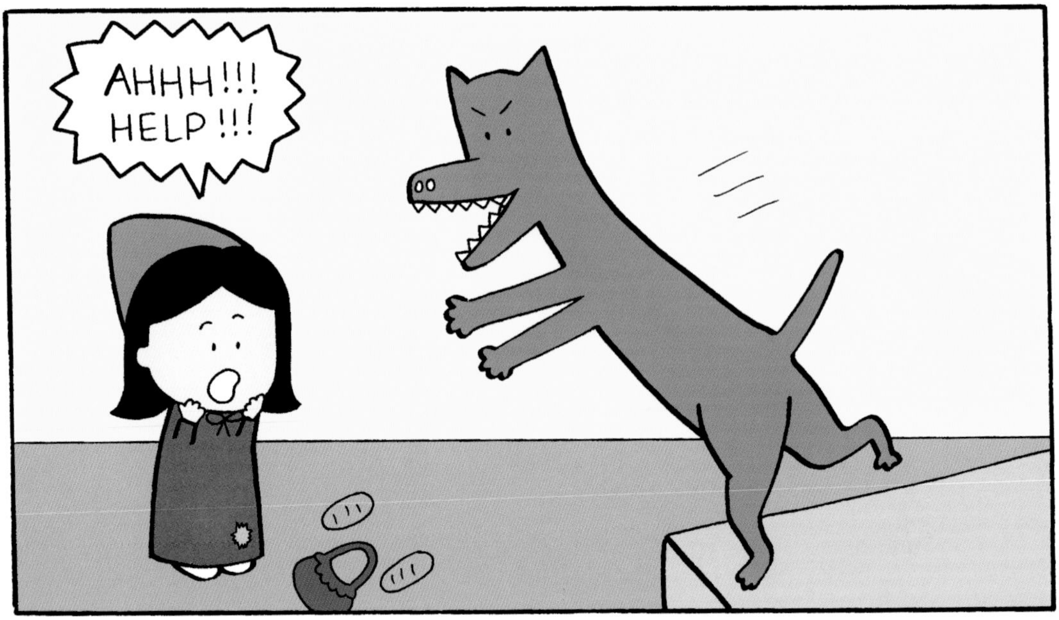
AHHH!!! HELP!!!

The woodsman heard her cry for help!

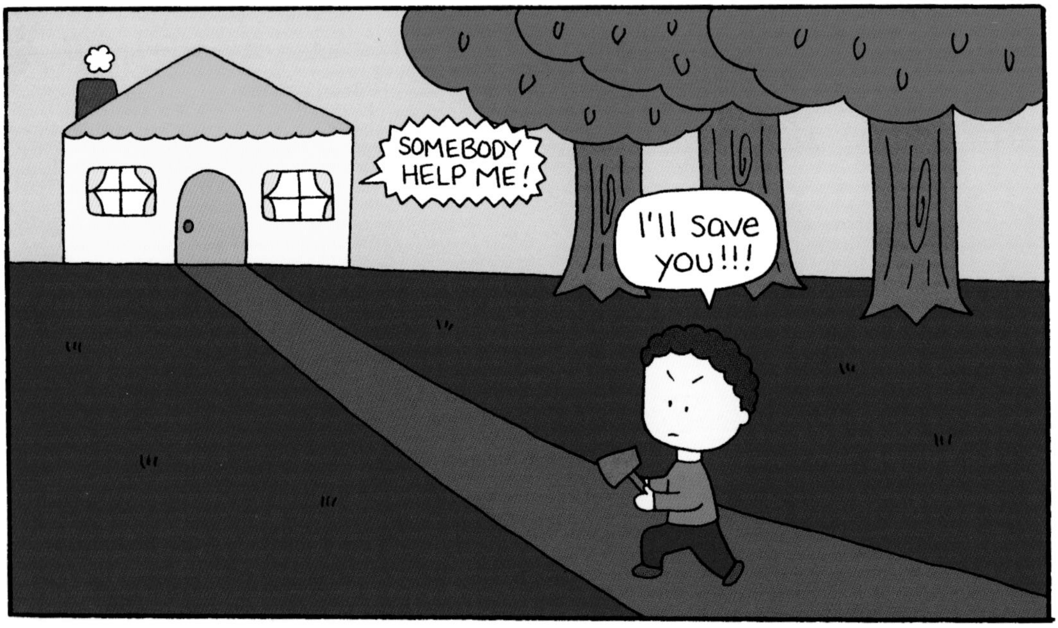
SOMEBODY HELP ME!
I'll save you!!!

The woodsman scared the wolf away.

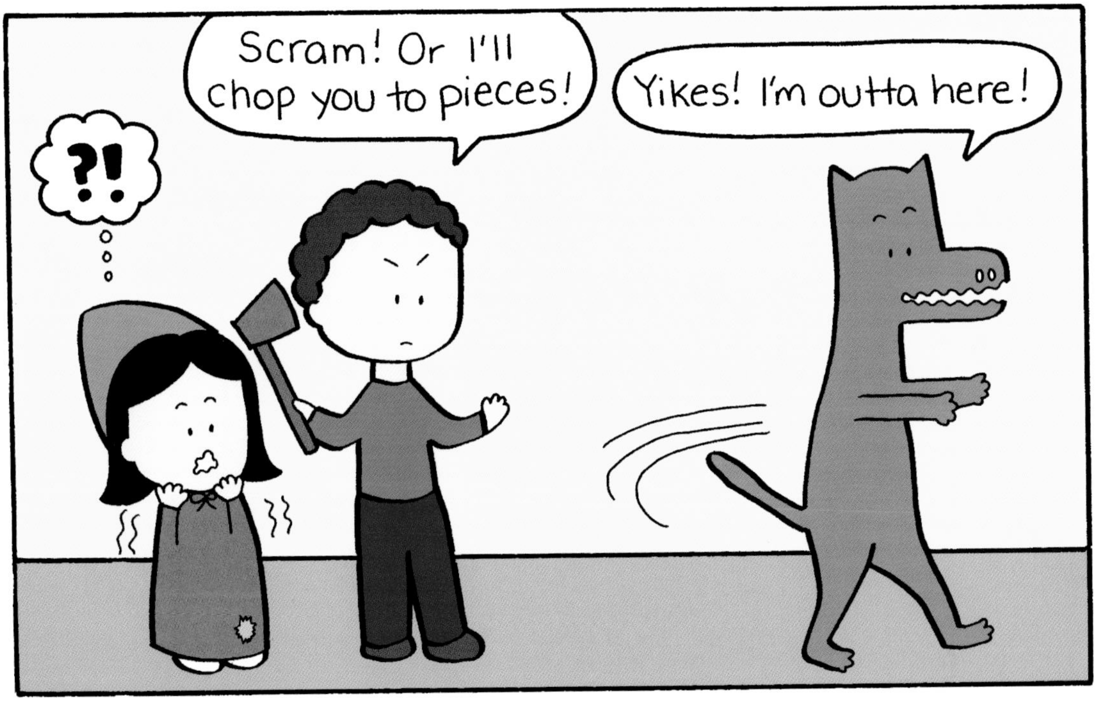
?!
Scram! Or I'll chop you to pieces!
Yikes! I'm outta here!

He saved Little Miss Wears-a-Hood!

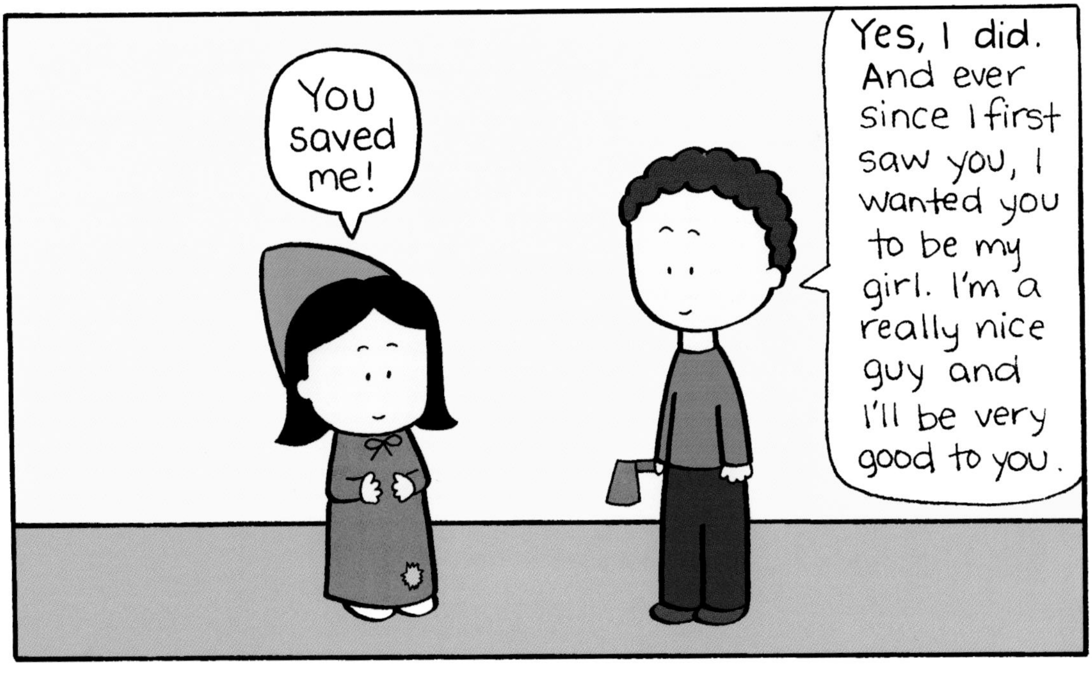
You saved me!
Yes, I did. And ever since I first saw you, I wanted you to be my girl. I'm a really nice guy and I'll be very good to you.

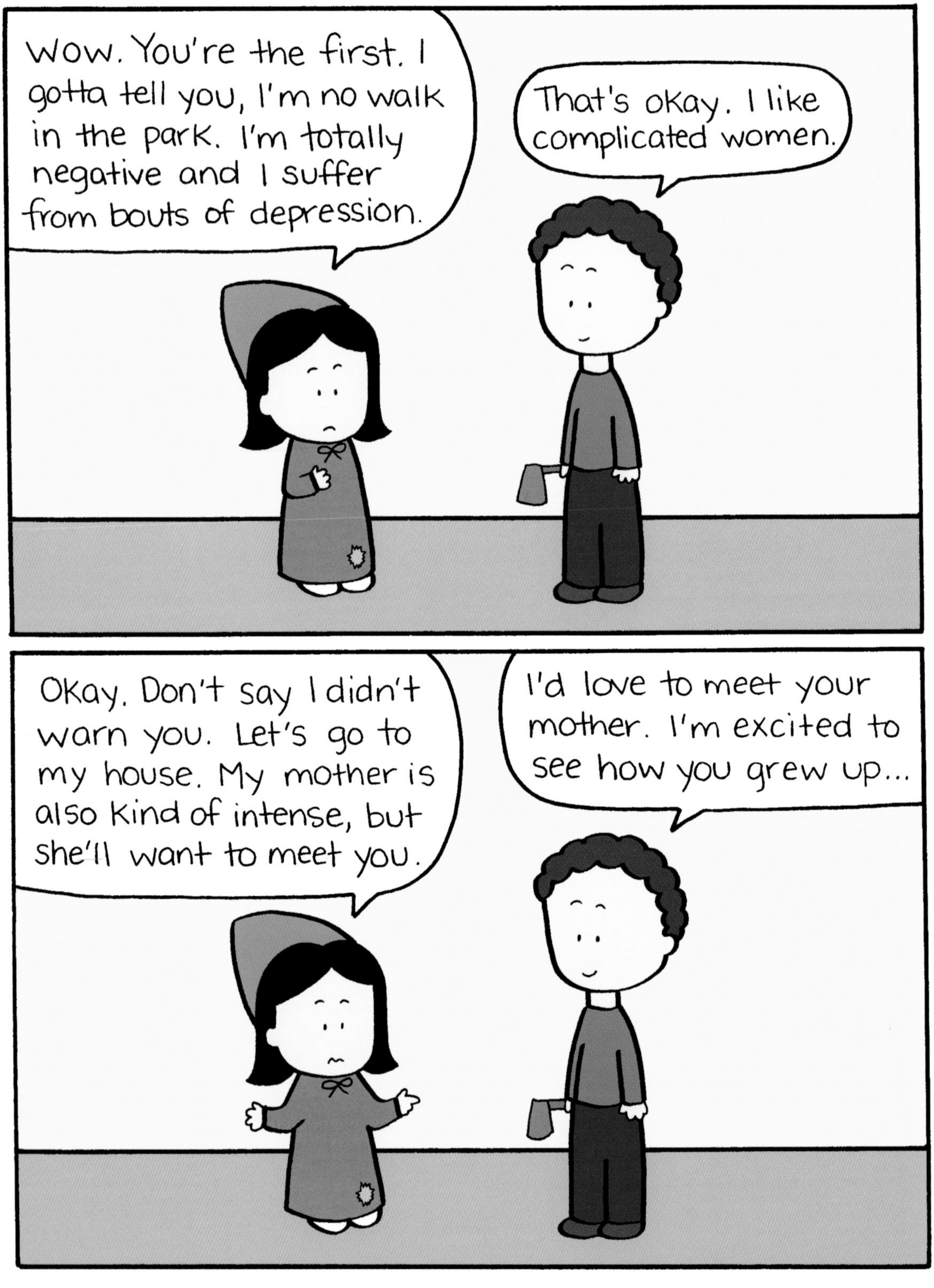
Wow. You're the first. I gotta tell you, I'm no walk in the park. I'm totally negative and I suffer from bouts of depression.
That's okay. I like complicated women.
Okay. Don't say I didn't warn you. Let's go to my house. My mother is also kind of intense, but she'll want to meet you.
I'd love to meet your mother. I'm excited to see how you grew up...

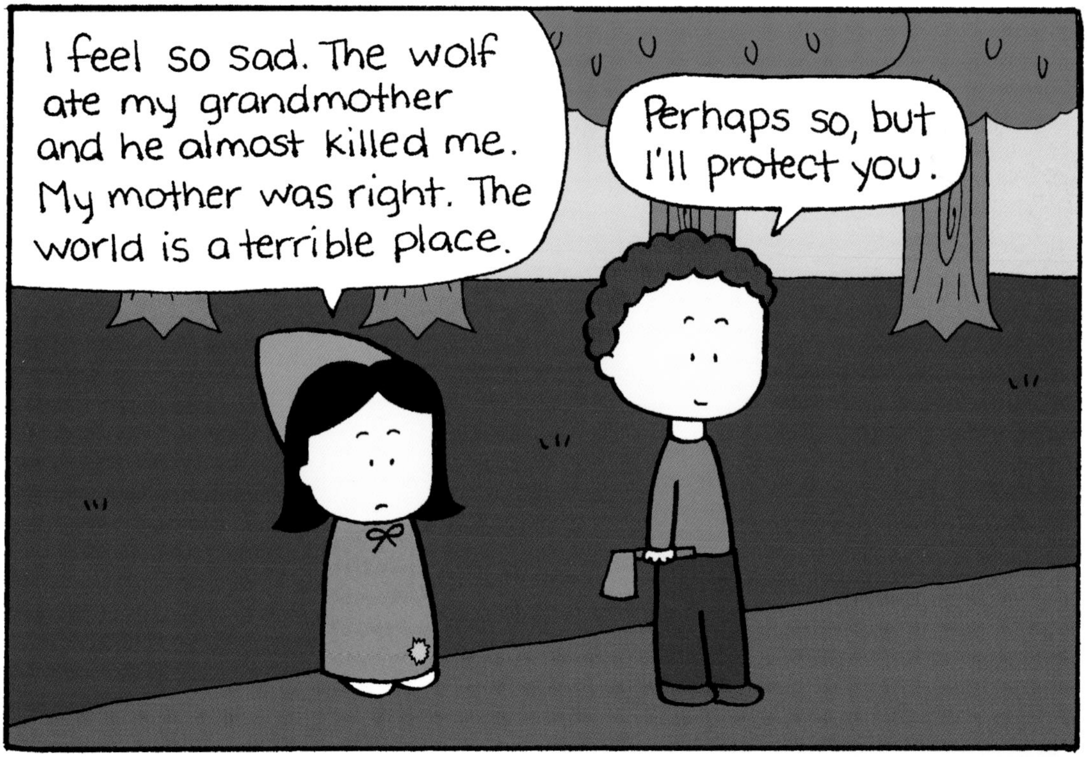
I feel so sad. The wolf ate my grandmother and he almost killed me. My mother was right. The world is a terrible place.
Perhaps so, but I'll protect you.

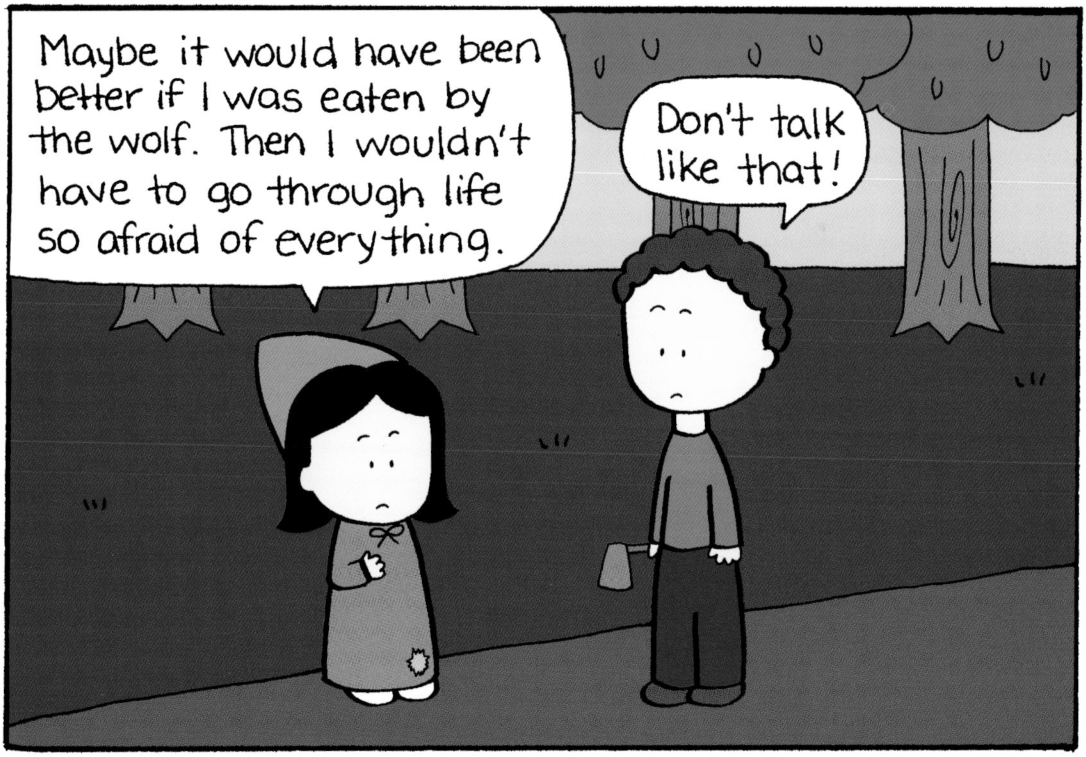
Maybe it would have been better if I was eaten by the wolf. Then I wouldn't have to go through life so afraid of everything.
Don't talk like that!

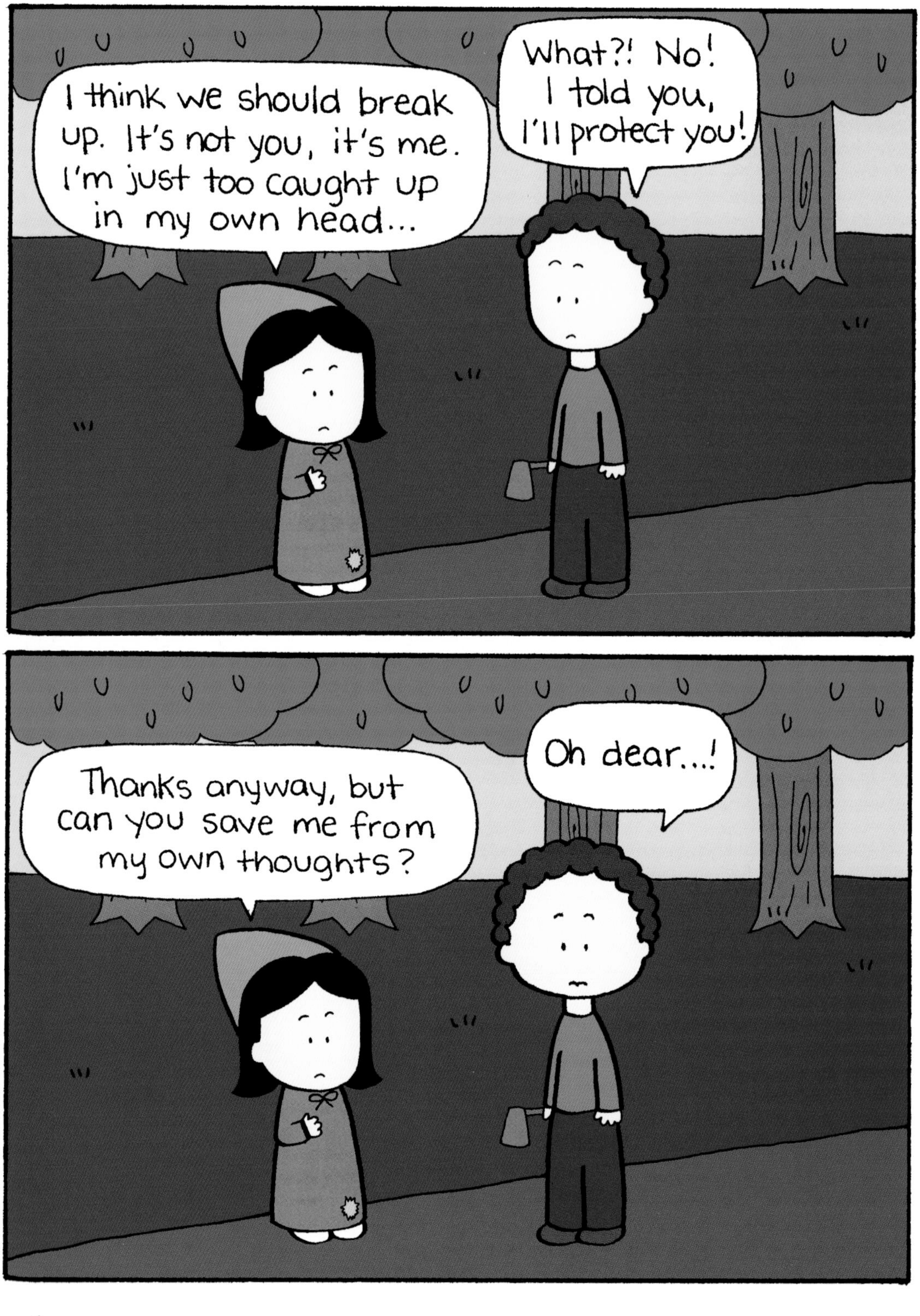
I think we should break up. It's not you, it's me. I'm just too caught up in my own head...
What?! No! I told you, I'll protect you!
Thanks anyway, but can you save me from my own thoughts?
Oh dear...!

And they lived happily ever after...

I drew these fairy tales back in 1999. Then five years later, the first Angry Little Girls book of comics was published, next was *Still Angry Little Girls* and then *Angry Little Girls in Love*. I kept asking my publisher when we could release these fairy tales that I am so proud of. Now, more than a decade later, the Angry Little Girls version of fairy tales is available for all the angry girls of the world.

I'd like to thank my mom for making me work at her dry cleaners. Without this forced servitude to my mother's store and the resulting boredom and frustration of being an over-educated counter girl, I would have never worked on these five special *Fairy Tales for Angry Little Girls.*

Enjoy!

Lela Lee